MAN, MYTH & MAGIC

VOLUME 10

Illu-Juda

MAN, MYTH & MAGIC

The Illustrated Encyclopedia of Mythology, Religion and the Unknown

Editor-in-Chief
Richard Cavendish

Editorial Board
C. A. Burland; Professor Glyn Daniel;
Professor E. R. Dodds; Professor Mircea Eliade;
William Sargant; John Symonds;
Professor R. J. Zwi Werblowsky;
Professor R. C. Zaehner.

New Edition edited and compiled by
Richard Cavendish and Brian Innes

MARSHALL CAVENDISH
NEW YORK, LONDON, TORONTO, SYDNEY

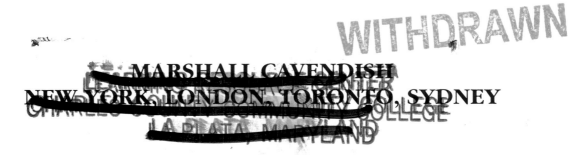

Frontispiece: In William Blake's *The Fall of Man*, God looks on as Adam and Eve are gently led from the Garden of Eden by Jesus: deprived of immortality, they are at the same time assured of it in the Redemption (Michael Holford)

Library of Congress Cataloging in Publication Data

Man, myth and magic: the illustrated encyclopedia of mythology, religion and the unknown / editor in chief, Richard Cavendish

Rev. ed. of Man, myth & magic.
Includes bibliographical references and index
ISBN 1-85435-731-X (set)
1. Occultism – Encyclopedias. 2. Mythology – Encyclopedias. 3. Religion – Encyclopedias.
I. Cavendish, Richard. II. Man, myth & magic.
BF 1407.M34   1994
133'.03 – dc20

94-10784
CIP

Published by Marshall Cavendish Corporation
2415 Jerusalem Avenue
North Bellmore, New York 11710

© Marshall Cavendish Corporation 1995
© Marshall Cavendish Ltd 1983, 1985
© B. P. C. Publishing Limited 1970

Printed and Bound in Italy by L.E.G.O. S.p.a. Vicenza.

CONTENTS Volume 10

ILLUMINATI

THE ORDER OF THE ILLUMINATI, which was founded in 1776, took its name from the Latin, meaning 'the enlightened ones'. Its aims were to combat ignorance, superstition and tyranny in various forms. It has been called a prototype secret society and accused of paving the way for the French Revolution, but nothing could be further from the truth. It never recruited adherents outside Germany and Austria. If we ignore its childish mystification, it was merely a society which attracted men of progressive rather than conservative views. The Order began as a protest against the old-fashioned Jesuit-run system of Bavarian education. It achieved little, mainly due to the strangeness of its founder, Adam Weishaupt.

Adam Weishaupt (1748-1830), who was Professor of Law at the Bavarian University of Ingolstadt, planned to use Jesuit methods to found a secret school of wisdom. He wished young men of intellectual promise to discover the new ideas banned in southern German universities – typically Voltaire's writings and the works of the French Encyclopedists such as Diderot. Secrecy was essential in order to avoid attacks from the Bavarian Jesuits. Weishaupt studied the history of secret societies such as the Pythagoreans, but without learning much. In 1774 he met a Protestant Freemason from Hanover who told him a little about that society, about which he had hitherto known very little. He considered,

but rejected, a union with Masonry because it was not an Order in the full Jesuit sense. Although anti-Jesuit, he proposed to fight them with their own supposed methods.

The Order of Illuminati was founded on 1 May 1776 with five members, all of whom took fanciful pseudonyms, Weishaupt being known as Spartacus. He expected that German Freemasons would flock to join his Order. But nothing happened; after two years the total number of Illuminati was only 20. Finally, in Munich, a few eminent citizens joined, on learning that they would be granted the impressive-sounding title of Areopagite. In 1779 Weishaupt created a real organization and a 'curriculum'. The Order now had three grades: Novice, Minerval and Illuminated Minerval.

Monthly Intelligence Reports

At the end of every month the Novice had to deliver to his proposer a sealed letter, with a report on every aspect of his relationship with his mentor, who sent it on unopened to Weishaupt. The proposer had to furnish similar information about the Novice. Weishaupt devised printed forms for these 'intelligence reports'. He wanted complete details about a man's character, family, friends, financial standing and so on. Every Novice had to undertake a course of prescribed reading, based on classical and modern authors, including those of the French Encyclopedists, and write regular essays. He could know only his proposer.

This situation changed when he was promoted to the Minerval grade after a solemn

initiation ceremony. The candidate was taken at night to a dimly lit room where he was interrogated by an unknown individual. If correct answers were given, a password and secret signs were then communicated.

As a Minerval, a member could know others of his grade, but the identities of those in the higher Illuminated Minerval degree were not disclosed. They met to discuss books they had recently read, like any learned society. The degree of Illuminated Minerval could be taken without much ceremony. But, by 1779, the Order had achieved little and Weishaupt realized that, far from its attracting Freemasons, members were leaving it to join Masonic Lodges.

He decided that the Illuminati must infiltrate Freemasonry. A charter for a new Masonic Lodge at Munich was obtained from the Berlin Grand Lodge. The Munich Lodge, which quickly recruited members, including some who were already Freemasons, then declared itself independent. Initially, most of those concerned had no real idea of Weishaupt's aims.

The most influential of these Masonic Illuminati was Baron Adolph Knigge (1752-96), who became the most important man in the Order. Knigge, who took the pseudonym Philo, soon put an end to the quarrels between Weishaupt and the senior members at Munich. Since he travelled very widely in Germany, he immediately brought in new recruits. To his dismay, however, he rapidly discovered that Weishaupt's plans for the Order were very vague. Knigge, who was a first-class organizer, gave it a new structure on more or less Masonic lines and there was a very rapid expansion. Among those who now joined were Duke Ferdinand of Brunswick, Duke Ernest of Gotha, and even the illustrious Goethe.

Hitherto the Order had been so obscure that it had attracted little attention. Now, however, it had a number of enemies, not least among the Freemasons, who realized that they had been duped. To add to the complications, Knigge quarrelled with Weishaupt. The Baron was in favour of a more democratic organization and wished to restrain his colleague's anti-clerical and, above all, anti-Jesuit policies on the grounds that they were politically and tactically unwise. Weishaupt was stubborn and Knigge left the Order.

Politically Suspect

So far the Order had not experienced any trouble with the Bavarian authorities. But its expansion coincided with a period when conservative and clerical forces were gaining ground in Bavaria. All manner of rumours, mostly untrue, about Weishaupt and the Order were now circulated. The Order became politically suspect, although there were few grounds for considering it as a dangerous revolutionary organization. Without naming the Order, the Elector of Bavaria sanctioned a decree forbidding all secret societies, including the Freemasons, on 22 June 1784.

Yet another decree, dated 2 March 1785, named both the Illuminati and the Freemasons and confirmed the ban on all further

activity. There were many arrests and Weishaupt was obliged to leave Bavarian territory. The Order collapsed in southern Germany and was soon moribund elsewhere.

The Order of the Illuminati was revived in Berlin in 1906 by Leopold Engel at the behest of Theodor Reuss, who had a hand in every conceivable variety of pseudo-Masonic activity. It then came under the spacious umbrella of Reuss's Order of Oriental Templars. Yet another revival of the Order has been attempted very recently at Frankfurt am Main.

ELLIC HOWE

FURTHER READING: Arkon Daraul, *Secret Societies* (Muller, 1961).

Michael Holford

The man who designed the great Step-Pyramid at Sakkara was transformed into a god some 2000 years later, and became the Egyptian god of healing

IMHOTEP

THE ANCIENT EGYPTIAN SAGE Imhotep has two claims to unique distinction. He provides the best documented instance of the deification of a man and he is the first individual of genius known to us. His reputation, moreover, was due to his wisdom and technological ability, not to success in war, too often the qualification for fame.

Imhotep was the vizier of the Pharaoh

Zoser of the 3rd Dynasty (c 2778–2723 BC). Among his titles were 'overseer of the king's records', 'chief of all the works of the king' and 'supervisor of that which heaven brings, the earth creates and the Nile brings'. His personal name Imhotep meant 'he who comes in peace'. His father was Kanofer, 'chief of the works of the south and of the north-land'; his mother's name was Khreduank. These facts are significant; for they show that Imhotep's human origins were well known and recorded.

One famous monument created by his genius still survives – the Step-Pyramid at Sakkara. This is the first-known stone building, and it was planned by Imhotep as a tomb for Zoser. Interesting evidence of the connection between king and architect has

The Step-Pyramid at Sakkara, tomb of the Pharaoh Zoser and first of the great Egyptian pyramids, bears witness to the technological genius of its architect, Imhotep, Zoser's vizier and 'chief of all the works of the king'; he was also renowned as a great healer

been provided by the finding, within the mortuary-temple complex of the Step-Pyramid, of a statue of Zoser bearing both his and Imhotep's names. The scientific and technological knowledge involved in the erection of the pyramid and its adjacent buildings at this early period impressively attests to the genius of Imhotep. But such an achievement does not explain how Imhotep came to be regarded as a god some 2000 years later, in about 525 BC, according to the

Imhotep, 'he who comes in peace': his wisdom became a legend in Egypt. This bronze statuette shows Imhotep wearing a skull cap, without any of the attributes of divinity which he later acquired

British Museum/Chris Barker

earliest available evidence of his deification.

From Egyptian sources, however, we learn that Imhotep had a reputation for other abilities than his skill as an architect. An inscription of the Ptolemaic period (330–30 BC), on the island of Sekel near Aswan, preserves an ancient legend about Imhotep. Egypt, during the reign of Zoser, was afflicted by a terrible famine owing to the failure of the Nile for seven successive years to reach the flood level necessary for the irrigation of the land. Zoser appealed to Imhotep to find the cause. After withdrawing to consult the sacred books, Imhotep revealed to the king 'the hidden wonders, the way to which had been shown to no king for unimaginable ages'. In the inscription Imhotep is described as 'the chief *Kheri-heb* priest ... the son of Ptah'. The description, in this context, is significant. The office of Kheri-heb involved the reading of magical texts during the performance of rituals believed to achieve supernatural results. Hence the holder of the office was associated with magical knowledge and ability. The legend indicates that Imhotep had a pre-eminent reputation in this connection. It also shows that he was regarded as the son of the great god of Memphis, Ptah (see EGYPT), although the name of his earthly father was also known.

An interesting reference to Imhotep occurs in the curious sceptical poem known as the *Song of the Harper,* which dates from the Middle Kingdom (c 2060–1788 BC), and was sometimes inscribed on the walls of tombs. It reads: 'I have heard the discourses of Imhotep and Hardedef, with whose words men speak everywhere — what are their habitations (now)?' The 'Harper' seems to imply that the wisdom of the great sages of old had not saved them from the ravages of time — Hardedef, incidentally, was the son of the Pharaoh Khufu (Cheops), builder of the Great Pyramid; but he never attained the posthumous fame enjoyed by Imhotep.

Healed in a Dream

In some way Imhotep also acquired great renown as a physician or healer of disease. A Greek papyrus found at Oxyrhynchus, an ancient city of the Nile valley, dating from the 2nd century AD but claiming to preserve an older Egyptian record, suggests that Imhotep's medical reputation was already well established by the reign of the Pharaoh Menkaure (c 2600 BC). The papyrus, which was written by a certain Nechautis, who sought appointment as priest in a temple of Imhotep, contains interesting evidence of the Egyptian practice of incubation – sleeping in a temple in the hope of divine healing. It relates how the mother of Nechautis, suffering from quartan ague, slept in the temple of Imhotep and was cured after dreaming that the god had visited and healed her by 'simple remedies'. After this miracle, Nechautis also became ill. He too slept in the temple, accompanied by his mother who remained awake. She suddenly saw 'someone whose height was

more than human, clothed in shining raiment and carrying in his left hand a book.' The presence intently regarded the sleeping Nechautis from head to foot and then vanished. Recovering herself, the mother found her son bathed in perspiration, but free of his fever. On awaking, he described a similar vision, and was conscious that Imhotep had cured him. When mother and son duly offered sacrifices of thanksgiving to Imhotep, they learned that the god wished Nechautis to fulfil a long-standing promise. This was to translate into Greek the ancient Egyptian book which the papyrus claims to embody, so that 'Every Greek tongue will tell thy story and every man will worship the son of Ptah, Imouthes (the Greek form of Imhotep).'

The story graphically illustrates the manner in which the ancient architect of the Step-Pyramid had been transformed, some 2000 years later, into a healing god. The Greeks identified Imhotep with their own divine physician, Asclepios.

The gradual deification of Imhotep seems to have been completed about 525 BC. It was paralleled by a change in his iconography. Previously he had been represented, in small bronze statuettes, as a man, generally seated, wearing a short waist-cloth and skull cap, and without any symbol of deity; he held an opened papyrus scroll on his lap. Later, particularly in mural representations, he was shown with all the customary attributes of divinity: the Puntite beard, a long narrow artificial beard worn after the fashion of the men of Punt (Abyssinia), the

uas-sceptre (see EMERALD) and the ankh, symbol of life. His divinity is clearly attested in the following inscription, adjacent to his picture in the small Ptolemaic temple at Kasr el-Agouz, near Luxor: 'Son of Ptah, beneficent god, begotten by the god of the south wall (Ptah), giver of life, who bestows gifts on those he loves, who listens (to those who call upon him), who provides remedies for all diseases.'

Imhotep's deification led, in turn, to the deification of his mother and his wife Renpet-nefert. His father did not share in this exaltation, for already Ptah had been credited with the siring of the divine physician. At Memphis Imhotep came to form a divine triad with Ptah and the goddess Sekhmet.

Three temples are known to have been dedicated to Imhotep in Egypt, the chief being at Memphis, which became a famous medical centre, and on the sacred island of Philae in Upper Egypt. Many temples contained special shrines for his worship; on the upper terrace of the temple of Hatshepsut at Deir-el-Bahari there was a sanatorium for those who sought his help. The centre of his cult was probably at his tomb at Sakkara, near the Step-Pyramid. Excavations are now in progress at Sakkara and there are hopes that the tomb of the man who became the Egyptian god of medicine will eventually be discovered.

(See also HEALING GODS.)

S. G. F. BRANDON

FURTHER READING: J. B. Hurry, *Imhotep* (Humphrey Milford, 1926).

Imitative Magic

The use of a doll, made of wax, clay, lead or other material, to kill, injure or seduce the person the doll represents, is known from all over the world, ancient and modern

The quickest way to murder someone by witch-craft is to 'make a Picture of clay, like unto the shape of the person . . . then take a Thorn or a Pin, and prick it in that part of the Picture you would so have to be ill'

MIMICRY for magical purposes is deeply embedded in human nature. One of the common reactions to danger, for instance, is to keep absolutely still and shut your eyes. What you are doing is to pretend you are not there, so that the danger cannot strike you. We all know that this is not a sensible way to avoid a car which is out of control, or the anger of someone who is offended, but we do it automatically.

At racetracks and athletics meetings you may find yourself tensing and straining, to imitate a surge of energy in a runner, in the magical hope of spurring him on. Another simple example is observable at bowling greens where, after releasing the bowl, a player gestures with his arms and curves his body to persuade the bowl to curve in the way he wishes. Another is the simple device employed by doctors to make an embarrassed patient urinate when a sample is needed. The doctor turns on a tap and very quickly the sound of trickling water produces the desired result. This is an interesting parallel to primitive rain-making magic in which water is poured out to make the gods urinate from on high.

A familiar piece of imitative magic is to look at yourself confidently in a mirror and say, 'Every day in every way I am getting better and better.' This depends on mimicking what your inner feelings and outward behaviour would be if you improved each day, with such conviction that you do improve. Though much mocked, it is often effective, and this type of playacting to yourself is

an ingredient in most ways of trying to change your character. In his book on *Magical Ritual Methods*, which contains many examples of imitative magic, W. G. Gray describes a method of banishing a bugbear by mentally imitating it looming up in the mind and then mentally shrinking it away to nothing.

Image Magic

The use of a doll, made of wax, clay, lead or other material, to kill, injure or seduce the person the doll represents, is known from Egypt and Mesopotamia, from India, Greece and Rome, and from all over the world, ancient and modern. The quickest way to murder someone by witchcraft, according to old Mother Demdike at the trial of the Lancashire witches in 1612 (see LANCASHIRE

WITCHES), is to 'make a Picture of clay, like unto the shape of the person whom they mean to kill, and dry it thoroughly: and when they would have them to be ill in any one place more than another; then take a Thorn or a Pin, and prick it in that part of the Picture you would so have to be ill: and when you would have any part of the body to consume away, then take that part of the Picture, and burn it. And when they would have the whole body to consume away, then take the remnant of the said Picture and burn it: and so thereupon by that means, the body shall die.'

The principle is not extinct in the modern West. In 1964 the figure of a naked woman, six inches long and made of modelling clay, with a sliver of hawthorn piercing its heart,

Left A painting of witches, by the English occultist and artist Austin Osman Spare. Their paraphernalia includes a figure with a pin stuck into it, and imitative magic of this type, meant either to kill or to seduce, is known from all over the world and all through history. It has its roots in the experiences of childhood, when a child believes that a doll is a real person and can be cosseted or hurt
Right This Brazilian Indian chieftain is being painted to resemble a jaguar, a piece of mimicry which is intended to give him the strength and hunting skill of the animal

Harald Schultz

was found near Sandringham in Norfolk. It may have been meant to kill its victim or to seduce her by piercing her heart with love. In 1939 it was reported from Cairo, Illinois, that 'a sure way to kill a man is to place his picture under the eaves at the corner of your house during rainy weather and let the water pour upon it.' Modern technology has allowed sorcerers and witches to use a photograph of the victim, pinned on to the doll to make identification certain, and the reluctance of some primitives to be photographed, because it puts them in the photographer's power, is well known.

In 1900 a figure of President McKinley, riddled with pins, was burned on the steps of the American Embassy in London. According to Lady Charlotte Campbell in her diary for 1814, Caroline of Brunswick, the unhappy wife of the Prince Regent (afterwards George IV), frequently made wax images of her husband with fell intent. One evening after dinner, she made one of these dolls and 'gave it an amiable addition of large horns; then took three pins out of her garment and stuck them through and through, and put the figure to roast and melt at the fire.'

The Killing Doll

In England in 1324 a magician named John of Nottingham was said to have made seven images of wax and canvas to represent King Edward II and other notables, in order to murder them. The seventh figure represented a courtier named Richard de Sowe who, as C. L'Estrange Ewen dryly remarked, 'somewhat inconsiderately was

included for experimental purposes'. To test the procedure, a 'curious pin wrought of sharp lead' was driven into the forehead of de Sowe's image, two inches deep. The next day one of the magician's accomplices went to Richard de Sowe's house and found him raving and shrieking. They left him in this condition for a month or so. Then they pulled out the pin and stuck it into the image's heart, and Richard de Sowe died.

Image magic was also used by medieval Jews, frequently to force a thief to restore stolen goods. A picture of the suspected thief would be drawn on a wall and nails would be driven into it, usually into the eyes. This would cause the thief such pain that he would give himself up. A man's name could also be used against him (see NAMES).

In 1649 John Palmer and Elizabeth Knott were executed at St Albans. They were said to have made a clay figure of a woman which they put on a fire. As the figure was slowly roasted, their victim writhed in agony and when it was completely consumed, she died. Not only human beings but inanimate objects could be harmed in this way. Margaret Barclay, an Ayrshire witch executed in 1618, had quarrelled with her brother-in-law, who afterwards went on a sea voyage. She was accused of making wax models of the ship and captain, with which she caused the ship to sink and her brother-in-law to be drowned.

The British tradition crossed the Atlantic. In the walls of the cellar of the house of Bridget Bishop, one of the witches of Salem (see SALEM), 'poppets' were discovered, made of rags and hog's bristles into which

Above **The soldier at bayonet practice is not far removed from the primitive warrior performing a war-dance; in both cases the actions and emotions of a real battle are vigorously and violently imitated**

headless pins were stuck. In Goody Glover's house were found small dolls made of rags and stuffed with goat's hair. She was prevailed on to admit that she tormented a victim by wetting her finger with spit and stroking one of the dolls.

Images have been used to provoke love, as well as to injure. A magical textbook called Picatrix (see PICATRIX) provides a method of making a girl fall in love with a man. Make an image of each of them, from pulverized stone mixed with gum, and put the two images, facing each other, into a vase with seven twigs. Bury the vase in the hearth, then light a fire in the hearth and put a piece of ice in the fire. When the ice has melted, dig up the vase and the spell is complete. The fire melting the ice, of course, is love melting the hearts of the man and the girl.

A Black Vitality

As an alternative to sticking an image with pins or burning it, it can be sunk in a running stream to be gradually worn away. Or it can be broken, twisted, mangled, buried, hanged on a tree, plunged in boiling water or suspended in a chimney.

It is significant that the images are so often called dolls, 'child's babies', poppets, puppets or mommets — names which point to the roots of image magic in the experience of

Axel Poignant

Above Australian aborigines performing a dance round a shark totem: they mime the taking of young sharks from the belly of the totem as a way of magically ensuring an ample supply of sharks

childhood. A child accepts that a doll is alive, is a person, and can be cosseted or hurt. For many sorcerers of the past, the fact that the doll represented the victim, and the mimic torments inflicted on it, would be enough by themselves to cause the victim harm.

In more sophisticated magical theory what harms the victim is the concentrated malice of the sorcerer, for which the image acts as a focus. In the making of the doll, in the gleeful torture of it, the magician arouses his own inner hatred, concentrates it and projects it at his enemy. If the image is accidentally damaged, the victim is not harmed. Only when the image is 'charged' with hatred and deliberately maltreated does the victim feel the effects. The rites of 'charging' are ways of concentrating the sorcerer's fury but, even so, the image takes on an evil vitality of its own. Bernard Bromage says (in *The Occult Arts of Ancient Egypt*): 'An image can be charged in a number of ways: inverted "prayer"; the burning of incense; actual blood sacrifice in its vicinity; the sheer impact of petrifying venom — all these can play their part in causing an image — especially one already associated with destruction — to spring into a black, abounding vitality which can burn itself into the conscious and sub-conscious, especially during sleep. . .'

It is essential that the image be linked

with the victim, so that the magician's hatred hits the right target. 'It is not enough to pretend that your wax image is the person you want to bewitch,' says a character in Aleister Crowley's novel *Moonchild*, 'you must make a real connexion. That is the whole art of magic, to be able to do that.' The image should look as much like the victim as possible, and it may be given his name. The witches of North Berwick (see NORTH BERWICK WITCHES) made a wax image of James VI (afterwards James I of England) which they intended to roast on a fire. But first ten of them met the Devil, their master, near Preston-pans and passed the doll from hand to hand, saying formally, 'This is King James the Sixth. . .' Other ways of linking the victim with the image are to mould into it his nail parings, a lock of his hair, a piece of his clothing, or anything else that has been in close touch with him.

That it is the venomous hatred focused on the image, and through it on the victim, which does the damage is not a new theory. In the 14th century Antonius de Monte Ulmi said that image magic may work in practice, especially if the maker of the image exerts 'strong volition, so as to affect his own body and multiply emanations from its pores'. He goes on to say that some people of strong personality can cure diseases by incantations, though the words themselves are idle.

In cases where image magic works, as it sometimes does, the simplest explanation is that if you believe in a magician's powers and you know that he is projecting a violent current of hate at you with a determined

resolution, this knowledge itself may bring about the harm which the magician intends. A curse or any other form of hostile magic can equally be damaging and even lethal when directed at a victim who believes in it. Cursing procedures themselves frequently involve imitative magic — the twisting of a piece of cord in the Azande ritual of blood-brotherhood, for example, which imitates the grip the blood will take on the vitals of a man who breaks the oath, or the tying of a piece of wire round a lead cursing tablet to make the spell 'binding' (see CURSE).

Leaping for Increase

In *The Golden Bough* Frazer regarded the principle of mimicry, 'that like produces like, or that an effect resembles its cause', as one of the two basic principles of magical thought. The other he called 'the law of contact or contagion', which is 'that things which have once been in contact with each other continue to act on each other at a distance after the physical contact has been severed.' In practice, as he noted, the two are often combined (as in the case of adding the victim's nail parings to a wax image) and he gave the two principles together the label of Sympathetic Magic, the belief 'that things act on each other at a distance through a secret sympathy.'

Certainly, the principle of imitation is fundamental to magic and to many religious rituals as well. Ritual gesture, for instance, often involves mimicry. Fingers are crossed for luck, to bar the path of evil influences, or in a gesture of blessing two fingers are closed

Banishing a Bugbear

A good way to begin is to take some problem or other which is a matter of personal worry, annoyance, or to which there is a definite and constant reaction. Evoke and conjure it up in the consciousness until reaction sets in, then deliberately banish and neutralise it into Nil, the principle being that what is called up on purpose can also be dismissed on purpose. The diminishing effort is but a continued and inversed energy-flow of the original invocation. The purpose of all this is to bring the power of consciousness under control of the will and intention.

To ritualise all this is quite simple. It needs associating with appropriate circuits of consciousness through components of adaptation such as gestures, words of command, visual vehicles, and so forth. Suppose we try putting this in practice.

First the Time-Space-Event field is rapidly built up. Then a simple invocatory gesture and command is made while the subject of invocation is brought to mind as strongly as possible. Elaborate pentagrams and wordy pieces of prose are a complete waste of time and effort. A neat and effective gesture is opening a double door, which is that of bringing both hands forward together, then back towards the body and out to both sides. At the same time the plain command; 'Come in' is given either aloud or mentally, while the concept invoked is considered as advancing through the open doors upon the invocant. A positive reaction must be made appropriately. If the concept is enjoyable, then pleasure must be felt, or if otherwise, then whatever is called for in the way of aversion. We have now 'called up' or 'raised' a definite formation of consciousness and recognised it reactively, which gives it reality in mental dimensions.

Now we must expel the concept from our world. This is done by mentally pushing it through the open portal, making the closing gesture of bringing the hands together and forward again as if pressing the door shut, and saying clearly: 'Go out'.

W. G. Gray *Magical Ritual Methods*

---

so that the open thumb and two fingers are left to represent the Trinity (see GESTURE). In magic a symbol does not merely stand for something else, it *is* the something else, hence the Egyptian reluctance to put a complete hieroglyph of an animal inside a tomb in case the animal came alive (see ALPHABET), or the simple belief that an image of the victim is the victim. In religious ceremonies, especially at the popular level of belief, there is always a tendency to confuse the mimicry or the symbol with what is imitated or symbolized, hence the widespread belief in the magical powers of the consecrated host, and the theological debate over whether the elements of the Eucharist are really the body and blood of Christ or only represent them, whether the ceremony, in imitating the Last Supper, re-enacts it or only commemorates it.

Striking modern examples of imitative magic are found in the cargo cults of the Pacific (see CARGO CULTS), where air strips are built and model planes set up in shrines in the hope that real planes will arrive, full of desirable goods. At the other end of human history, it has long been thought that some prehistoric cave paintings are examples of imitative hunting magic — an animal is shown wounded so that the hunters will wound it in reality (see CAVE ART).

Games in which children ceremoniously jump up and down have been connected with imitative magic, in the form of leaping to make the crops grow tall, as in the old hymn of the Curetes: 'To us also leap for full jars, and leap for fleecy flocks, and leap for fields of fruit. . .' European customs in which girls rise high into the air on swings or people are lifted up in the air seem to have had the same magical purpose, and became connected with Easter through another imitative link, that of rising in the air with Christ rising from the grave (see CHILDREN'S GAMES; EASTER).

The Horse Sacrifice

Imitative magic ranges all the way from minor spells and superstitions, like the use of words which shrink away to nothing to reduce fever (see ABRACADABRA) or the belief that if a dying man's bed is set across the floorboards, instead of parallel with them, he will 'die hard' (see HOUSE), to major magico-religious rituals like the mock death and burial of an Ibo king, which is followed by his restoration to life on a new, divine plane (see IBO).

Other examples are those rituals which depend on the principle that sexual intercourse magically promotes the growth of crops and the fertility of cattle. One of these, described by Benjamin Walker in *Hindu World*, is the *asvamedha* or horse sacrifice offered by kings centuries ago in India. A young male horse, preferably white, was chosen and sacrificed, after elaborate preliminary rites. Once the animal was dead, the king's four wives walked nine times round its corpse, fanning it with their robes. The horse was identified with the god Prajapati and it was necessary for the chief queen to be 'impregnated' by him. The sacrificial pit was covered with a sheet, under which the queen went through a mimic copulation with the dead horse. After this the chief queen, the other queens and the four officiating priests exchanged obscene remarks, and it is possible that the queens had intercourse with the priests. 'The whole ceremony is believed to be part of a long-forgotten fertility rite for bringing prosperity to the realm.' An asvamedha was offered by a ruler of Jaipur as late as the mid-18th century.

Dance and drama are largely rooted in imitative magic, in the principle that by mimicking an animal, a person or a supernatural being you can be carried out of yourself and become that being, momentarily at least, share in its innermost nature and sanctity and control its actions (see DRAMA). In ceremonial magic, the 'assumption of god-forms' depends on the same principle, the imitation of a supernatural

In magic, to imitate or act out an event with sufficient vividness and concentration is to make the event occur in reality, a principle also found at the roots of dance, drama and many religious rituals *Below left* A doll may be pierced and mangled to inflict the same injuries on the real victim *Below centre* Two 'bones' strung with human hair, used by Australian aborigines for 'pointing the bone', in which the medicine-man jabs the bone in the direction of his victim with fierce thrusts and twists, acting out the harm he means to inflict *Below right* Sheep's heart riddled with pins and nails to neutralize a spell put on sheep and cattle *Right* The Inca offers a libation to the sun and since he is an incarnation of the sun god, he acts out the drinking of the offering himself: from a 17th century Peruvian manuscript

Chris Barker/Prodnose studio

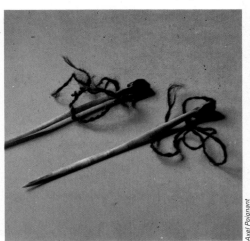

Axel Poignant

Horniman Museum/Michael Holford

EL TERZERO CAPITAN
CVCVNAVICHIRE

hasta tanbo ynga

Imitative Magic

Chinese illustration of the curious child-birth custom of couvade, known in many parts of the world. The father takes to his bed and behaves as if he, not his wife, is having the child. Sometimes he roars and rocks about in agony, evidently with the intention of magically transferring the birth pangs from his wife to himself by imitating them. The origin and underlying significance of the custom is uncertain. It may have kept the father quiet so that no evil influences could harm the baby through him

being or force, through which the magician attempts to become it and control it.

A love of playacting is another human characteristic which comes out strongly and spontaneously in children, but the point of it is not a mere liking for dressing up and strutting the boards but a longing to escape from yourself and, by imitation, to become someone or something else. We require a willing 'suspension of disbelief' by both actors and audience, a temporary agreement to accept that an actor *is* what he impersonates. Long ago, and in societies less affected by Western rationalism, 'suspending disbelief' was more easily achieved. In the totem-lodges of Australian aborigines, for example, where the actors imitate the actions of the hero-ancestors of the Dreamtime: 'the chanting goes on and on; the decorated actors appear; but they are no longer the men of a few hours earlier. They are now the heroes of the Dreaming' (see AUSTRALIA).

RICHARD CAVENDISH

FURTHER READING: R. Cavendish, *The Black Arts* (Capricorn, 1968); C. L'Estrange Ewen, *Witchcraft and Demonianism* (Muller, 1970 reprint); J. G. Frazer, *The Golden Bough* (St. Martin's Press, 1980); G. L. Kittredge, *Witchcraft in Old and New England* (Atheneum Pubs., 1972); R. H. Robbins, *Encyclopaedia of Witchcraft and Demonology* (Spring Books, 1959); J. Trachtenberg, *Jewish Magic and Superstition* (Atheneum Pubs., 1970). See also W. G. Gray, *Magical Ritual Methods* (Helios Books, 1969).

Immaculate Conception

Virgin birth; in theology, the Roman Catholic dogma asserting the sinlessness of the Virgin Mary who, alone among humanity, was conceived free from sin and preserved from all taint throughout her life; this long-held Catholic belief was made an article of faith by a papal bull in 1854; the Feast of the Immaculate Conception is celebrated on 8 December.
See MARY; VIRGIN BIRTHS.

Immanent

Indwelling, inherent; term applied in theology to God, to express the idea that God pervades the universe, existing within and throughout the created world; the opposite of 'transcendent', which suggests God's existence above and apart from his creation, and not subject to its limitations.

If man survives in some form into the future, may he not also have had an existence in the past? Plato's proposition, one of the greatest puzzles concerning immortality, was echoed by the poet Wordsworth, who said that 'the soul that rises with us . . . cometh from afar'

IMMORTALITY

THE BURIAL CUSTOMS of primitive man cannot be cited in proof of his belief in human survival of death and continuance into endless life. The fact that many of the skeletons found at Mount Carmel and other prehistoric sites had the legs tucked up behind the pelvis could be taken to mean that the living were afraid that the dead might 'walk' and were seeking to immobilize them. It could just as well mean that they thought of death as a return to the womb from which life came and that they were preparing the dead body accordingly, in the posture of an unborn child; or it might mean that they thought that the dead body had to be bundled up small so as to gain access to a new world, to which the sun retired each day through a tiny hole in the western sky. Finally, given the limitations of primitive tools, the real reason might be that the living did not want to have to make a very large hole to serve as a grave. Not until written records became available along with burials (see BOOK OF THE DEAD) is it possible to infer anything about the beliefs of the people concerned.

The great value of Herodotus, that observant Greek historian of the 5th century BC, is that he went about taking notes in the manner of the modern anthropologist. His reports of the burial customs of the Scythians in South Russia agree remarkably with what has been found there in modern times; royal *kurgan* graves have yielded up skeletons of horses (as many as 50 at a time), cup-bearers, attendants and concubines, just as Herodotus describes. These practices, which ensured that the dead prince would be provided with a retinue, point to a belief in immortality of a sort, even though it might have been a selective immortality that was to be enjoyed by princes only.

Mesopotamian literature tells of the descent of the goddess Ishtar (or Inanna) to the underworld through its seven gates; there she is sprinkled with the water of life and then ascends through the seven gates to rejoin the world of men. The *Epic of Gilgamesh* includes an episode where the hero brings up a wonderful plant from the sea bed, the virtue of which is to restore life and youth. Where such tales were told, the belief in survival cannot have been weak.

An Egyptian papyrus dated as early as 2000 BC contains a sophisticated dialogue between a man and his own soul. At the end his soul advises: 'Desire to reach the West (the abode of the dead) when thy body goes into the earth, that I may alight after thou hast grown weary.' The papyrus describes 'those who are yonder'. They are shown as 'men of knowledge; they punish sinners and 'stand in the barque of the sun, giving choice gifts to the temples'. This is a remarkable description, far removed from what Hebrew thought had achieved by the same epoch.

The sojourn of the Jews in Egypt did not affect their beliefs about the fate of the dead. Jacob grieved for his lost son, Joseph, saying: 'I shall go down to Sheol to my son, mourning' (Genesis, 37.35). Sheol was the darkling abode of the dead, where personal survival was at a very low ebb. Those in Sheol could not praise God but were condemned to a state of weakness and dullness. Saul might visit the witch of Endor and call up the spirit of Samuel from Sheol, but the rest of the dead had to bear an existence that was a pale shadow of life upon earth.

Escape from Sheol

Gradually, towards the end of the Hebrew Scriptures, there appears the idea of a general rising from the dead, an escape from Sheol to a life that is once more enriched with bodily sensation. The just, in the words of the Wisdom of Solomon (in the Apocrypha), are to receive the kingdom of glory and the diadem of beauty from the hand of God. They will confront their persecutors, who will then become objects of ignominy suffering remorse. A similar picture is given by the prophet Daniel.

The Greek philosophers, according to their habit, looked at the problem in rational fashion. A distinction between body and soul, and the destiny of each, was current in Greece in the time of Herodotus, for the war memorial to the Athenians killed at the siege of Potidaea (in Macedonia) speaks of their bodies committed to the ground and their souls flying upward. Over a generation later Plato (in the dialogue *Phaedo*) draws a portrait of Socrates discoursing on immortality during the last hours that his disciples were allowed to spend with him in the condemned cell. The setting of the dialogue implies that it was in the main a true report of what was said. The argument runs from the existence of eternal objects of knowledge which are not liable to change (such as the idea of beauty) to the eternity of the knowing subject. The whole Greek theory of knowledge rested on the proposition that like is known by like. Plato was at pains to show Socrates refuting the Pythagorean idea that the human soul was a harmony, for a harmony could be dissolved. Since death and life are contraries, the onset of death forces the soul either to withdraw or be annihilated; it cannot be annihilated, and so it withdraws from the function of animating the body.

Existence Before Birth

In an earlier dialogue, the *Gorgias*, Socrates is shown by Plato propounding a purified version of the Greek myth that there was a judgement after death and that souls passed either to the Islands of the Blest or else to prison and torture. In the *Meno* he presents the case for the pre-existence of the soul, based on the phenomena of memory and of the spontaneous understanding of mathematical problems by the young; this can be made to look like a memory of what was understood in a previous phase of existence. With this conclusion Plato formulated what has proved to be one of the great puzzles about immortality: if it is good for the future, why not for the past also? If the soul is to exist in the future, may it not also have existed in the past?

Plato never quite made up his mind about the individuality of the human soul. If it was strictly of the same nature as the eternal objects of knowledge (from which its existence was deduced) it ought to be looked on as a universal idea. Aristotle accepted this conclusion readily; for him there was a world-intellect which performed in each man the higher functions of understanding and which withdrew from man at death. In life a man should 'play the immortal as far as he can', but there would be no future for him when he had done.

Transmigration of a human soul from one body to another lent it a bogus universality, and it was to this solution that Plato himself inclined. The charm of his work won for Plato many Christian admirers. In 380 Gregory, the Bishop of Nyssa, wrote a dialogue *On the Soul and the Resurrection* after the death of his brother, Basil, and his sister, Macrina; it is a close imitation of the *Phaedo* in style but its argument reaches out beyond Plato.

Christian thinkers from the 2nd century

The Egyptians believed that the dead might be brought to life, provided the funerary rites were correctly carried out. The process was often illustrated by a god holding an ankh, symbol of life, to the nostrils of the corpse to restore the breath of life. In this relief from the temple of Abydos in Upper Egypt the Pharaoh Seti I holds to his nose the sa ankh, a symbol which combined life-giving properties with those of protection

onwards speak of themselves as a third race, neither Jew nor Greek, and thus one may look for some attempt by them to combine the Jewish idea of a risen and restored body in the hereafter with the Greek idea of immortality for the soul alone. It is not surprising that some of the early Christian thinkers found it difficult to combine Jewish ideas from the Old Testament with the Greek philosophy they had learned as young men. Thus in the writings of Theophilus of Antioch in the 2nd century AD, one finds a notion that God did not make man mortal or immortal by nature, but indifferent; if he lived a good life, he would be immortal but otherwise he would be condemned to mortality. St Paul had left no doubt about his own beliefs; he spoke of the resurrection of the body for the just and unjust alike, as he acknowledged to the Roman governor Felix (Acts 24.15). The Athenians to whom St Paul was preaching, seem to have thought that he was advocating the worship of two gods, Jesus and Resurrection, so much had he to say about the latter (Acts, chapter 17).

Left Brazilian Indians cover a dead boy with red ochre so that he may be reborn; the face and genitals are left uncovered so that he may have the choice of being born either as a boy or a girl. The practice of painting dead bodies red in order to endow them with life is common to other primitive peoples
Below A similar ceremony will be performed by a Nepalese fakir on his dead assistant *Below right* During the proceedings the body is covered with a cloth

Purpose of the Soul

Athenagoras, a Christian Platonist of the late 2nd century, wrote a lengthy treatise on the resurrection of the body, since it was this feature in Christian teaching which most scandalized the Greeks. Why say that the body would be reconstituted, when Plato and so many others had argued that immortality came through getting rid of the body? The Christians claimed that their ideas about the future life had come to them from Christ but the human mind could grasp them, when once they were set out, and could find reasons to make them plausible. It was these reasons that Athenagoras undertook to give. He dropped the threefold view of human nature, which divided it into body, soul and spirit, though Plato, the Stoics and the Jews all accepted it; instead, Athenagoras used a twofold division, body and soul, and this afterwards became generally accepted. His main argument for immortality was based on the purpose of the creation of the soul. God did not make the soul idly, nor yet for any need of his own, nor again for the service of any other creature, since no creature with reason and judgement has been created for any other's sake. The only purpose that will answer is that man was created for society with God who is eternal.

The theologian Origen (c 185–254 AD) was so taken with this argument that he developed from it the conclusion that, since society with God was the goal for man, there would be a general amnesty for all men at the end of the world, whatever their sins might have been. The Church rejected this on the evidence of the New Testament but also on the rational ground that human free will, if once it becomes immobilized in enmity to God, is enough to exclude a man from society with God for ever. The other line of thought developed by Origen was a renewal of the Platonic theory of the pre-existence of the human soul. He held that the fact of some men being born with active minds and others with minds wholly obtuse and incapable of instruction pointed to their having existed in another world, where some had sinned and drawn upon themselves a punishment in the next round of life. Other Christian Platonists, such as Gregory of Nyssa, brushed aside the transmigration theory: a soul at death was left incomplete, but this did not mean that it must seek another body and another life. It would be completed by the resurrection.

Immortality before and after life on earth was still a difficulty for St Jerome (340–420 AD), who in a famous letter sets out the possibilities of the case. He rejected the idea of the emanation of the soul from God, and envisaged three alternatives: all human souls could have been created at one time and then kept in reserve until wanted for life in the world; or they could be created each time there was a human conception; or else they might be passed on from the parents. Jerome himself adhered to the second alternative.

Love Eternal

St Thomas Aquinas (c 1225–74), theologian and philosopher, held that the eternal truths which the human mind can contemplate must be anchored in a supreme truth, and that this is the goal desired by the human mind as it

contemplates. He also held strongly that it was good and natural for the soul to be in a body; if all souls had been created at one time, then most of them would have suffered violence and been under restraint until they received their bodies, and of this there was no sign. In 1513 the fifth Lateran Council defined that it was heretical to say that the soul was mortal, but it did not elaborate the grounds for immortality. Luther accepted this definition.

Gradually in modern times interest in proving immortality has centred upon the value of the person and of that most personal of relationships, love. The unique quality of love lends more force than ever to the traditional argument that man is meant for society with God, once it can be entertained that love of God is a possibility. The British philosopher McTaggart (1866–1925), who was professedly an atheist, held a firm conviction of human immortality which was based upon the unique and timeless quality of love.

One of McTaggart's difficulties about

The Ascension of Christ; the gospel account of how the resurrected Christ was taken up from the sight of the disciples and ascended into heaven, as pictured by a 15th century Italian miniaturist. St Paul took the resurrection of Christ, 'the first fruits of those who have fallen asleep', as proof of a general resurrection; generations of theologians after him hotly debated the questions raised by the Christian doctrine of the immortality of the soul

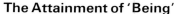

G. Tomsich, Rome

immortality was that 'even the best men, when they die, are not in such a condition of intellectual and moral perfection as would fit them to enter heaven immediately.' As if in answer to this, Karl Rahner has recently been advocating the idea that death is not simply a passive condition of being snuffed out but a personal deed, a final affirmation of what one's life has been, since death must be considered to affect both body and soul. A certain amount of experimental evidence has been gathered from those who have come very close to death through some accident and then been restored to life; the trend of this evidence is to support the idea that at the moment when death was nearest they passed in review the events of their whole life. Thomas de Quincey (1785–1859) noticed this fact, a kinswoman of his having reported that she had seen the whole of her life arrayed before her when she had fallen into a river, not successively but simultaneously, 'and she had a faculty developed as suddenly for comprehending the whole and every part.'

The Attainment of 'Being'

Investigation into the phenomena of telepathy and other branches of psychical research in the present century have greatly increased the interest in the problems of immortality. The French philosopher Gabriel Marcel, in the Myers Memorial lecture of 1955, recounts that it was these factors that quickened his own interest. He has elaborated a distinction between 'being' and 'having': fears and desires belong to the realm of 'having', while a loving collaboration with the liberty of another helps both to attain 'being'. Thus a basis is provided for justifying the unique and timeless quality of love. Thought transference without any physical link, where it can be verified, offers the prospect of an activity of the human mind that does not depend upon the body. The phenomena of Spiritualism are of more doubtful quality, for whatever their causation they do require a physical basis.

The value of the human person may thus be seen as the main prop of all arguments for immortality. Stunted or split personalities, or other psychological wreckage, make no difference to the argument, which takes 'person' in the metaphysical sense of an intelligent being who is an end in himself. When Aristotle said that slaves were animated tools, cogs in the social machine, he was repudiating the notion of person as he had repudiated immortality.

(See also BURIAL CUSTOMS; CULT OF THE DEAD; HELL; PARADISE; PURGATORY; REINCARNATION.)

J. H. CREHAN

FURTHER READING: J. Burnet, *The Socratic Doctrine of the Soul* (Oxford Univ. Press, 1916); F. Copleston, *History of Philosophy* (Burns & Oates, 1944–66); E. O. James, *Prehistoric Religion* (Thames & Hudson, 1957); G. Marcel, *The Mystery of Being* (Regnery-Gateway, 1960); C. Morgan, *Liberties of the Mind* (Century, 1979); E. F. Sutcliffe, *The Old Testament and the Future Life* (Burns & Oates, 1946); G. N. M. Tyrrell, *The Personality of Man* (Penguin, 1946).

IMP

AN IMP is a small demon, usually malignant, though at least one magician in London will provide an invisible but allegedly helpful imp that lives in an empty wine bottle. The bottle is corked and sealed with red sealing-wax. Around it is a piece of paper bearing magical signs and numbers in pencil and green crayon. The imp's chief duty is to prevent papers from going astray.

Paracelsus was supposed to keep a small demon shut up in the crystal pommel of his sword but the most indefatigable demon-bottler of history was a Frenchman named Alexis Vincent Charles Berbiguier, who died in 1851. For the first nine years of his life he was crippled and he early decided that demons were persecuting him. His room was full of ox-hearts stuck with pins and the aroma of anti-demonic soups, and his clothes and bed were riddled with pins, each of which transfixed the body of a wriggling imp. He stupefied the imps with tobacco and shut them up in bottles, 'where they would later awaken to grin and gibber at their conqueror.'

An 18th century French grimoire, *Secret des Secrets,* has a formula for conjuring a demon into a bottle. It is summoned by God, by Jesus, by the Holy Trinity, by the virginity of the Holy Virgin, by the four

An imp with a broomstick at *The Witches Banquet*: detail, 16th century Flemish painting

sacred words spoken to Moses by God (Io, Zati, Zata, Abata) and by the nine heavens, to appear 'visibly and without delay in a fair human form, not terrifying, without or within this phial, which holds water prepared to receive thee.'

The small familiar spirits of British witches were commonly called imps. In Suffolk in 1645, for example, Mary Scrutten of Framlingham confessed that she had three familiar imps which she suckled at night. She told her husband they were mice but he was not convinced.
(See also FAMILIARS.)

FURTHER READING: for Berbiguier see E. J. Dingwall, *Some Human Oddities* (Home & Van Thal, 1947).

Museo de Bilbao

Language is one of the great weapons of sorcery, and the magical use of words can be seen not only in the incantations of the grimoires but in many prayers

INCANTATION

WORDS ARE WEAPONS of power in magic because they are weapons of power in ordinary life. We use them to influence each other. Gestures and facial expressions help, and are also used in magic, but to state your wishes with commanding clarity or persuasive charm you usually resort to speech. The magical theory is that just as someone of powerful personality can use forceful words to dominate other people, so the magician armed with the lightning of concentrated will-power and the thunder of overwhelming language can dominate anything in the universe, natural or supernatural. 'In magic,' according to the French magician Eliphas Levi, 'to have said is to have done', and again, 'to affirm and will what ought to be is to create; to affirm and will what ought not to be is to destroy.'

In other words, to assert that something is so makes it so − at least under certain conditions. One condition is that the assertion must be made with sufficient strength of will. Another is that the words used must be the right words. They may be 'right' because they are tested by experiment and found effective by the magician who uses them or because they are hallowed by time and tradition, which means that they have seemed effective in the past. The Lord's Prayer, for example, has often been turned to magical uses. In the 13th century Arnald of Villanova said that a priest cured him of over 100 warts in 10 days. The priest touched each wart, made the sign of the cross and repeated the Lord's Prayer, but substituting for 'deliver us from evil' the words 'deliver Master Arnald from the wens and warts on his hands'. Then he took three stalks from a plant and put them in the ground in a damp and secluded place. When the stalks began to wither, the warts began to go.

Evidently the priest believed that the words of the prayer contained power which could be used for wart-charming, and Arnald believed it too and it worked. In some societies, among the Maori in New Zealand, for instance, or some of the Pueblo tribes in North America, the words of an incantation or a prayer must never be changed. In others, as in Europe, the magician may experiment with words and phrases until he hits on those which seem to work best for him, though considerable respect is still paid to traditional formulas. This respect is not confined to magicians. In 1963 the Ecumenical Council voted to authorize the saying of Mass in languages other than Latin, provided that Latin was retained for 'the precise verbal formula which is essential to the sacrament', the words spoken by the priest, assuming the person of Christ and using the same ceremonies used by Christ at the Last Supper, which transform the bread and wine into the Body and Blood.

Perhaps long ago, as language developed, the use of words had natural elements of awe and magic in it, a feeling that words gave man a grasp of reality which he had previously lacked. This is suggested by the old and persistent belief that everything has a 'real' name, a name which enshrines the essence of the thing, which *is* the thing. To know and pronounce the real name of a god, a man or an animal is to exercise power over it.

Lord of the Gods

For magicians in Europe the great example of the magical use of language was the creation of the world as described in Genesis. 'God said, Let there be light; and there was light.' It was assumed that God brought his creations into existence by pronouncing their names.

Besides knowing the name, knowing and reciting the qualities of a thing gives a man magical power over it. The Semang people of Malaya have a song about a particular species of monkey, which describes its behaviour. It tells how the monkey stamps his feet, drags along, climbs up and away, swarms up the bamboo, hangs down, seizes fruit, bends the bough for a leap, lets the bough fly upwards. This song is not just an expression of delight in Nature (though it is that in part) but a hunting spell. The vivid description of the animal, the clear picture of it in the hunter's mind, gives him power over it, and the moment at the end of the song, when the monkey is about to jump, is the moment when the hunter means to kill it. Similarly, early Greek hymns to a god begin with a recital of the god's names and attributes, which was probably intended to catch the god in the net of his own nature, and to concentrate the worshipper's mind on him, so as to give some measure of control over the god.

In the same way, in a magical ritual devised by Aleister Crowley and called *Liber Samekh*, the magician recites the names and characteristics of a supremely powerful 'spirit', who created the heavens and the earth, night and day, darkness and light. 'This is the Lord of the Gods: this is the Lord of the Universe: this is He whom the winds fear.' He commands this

William MacQuitty

In the same way as the poet or orator depends on the power of words to convey impressive ideas and to sway his audience, so the magician with his incantations and sometimes the suppliant with his prayers, although fulfilling different needs, make deliberate use of compelling language, both engaging in sound and clear in meaning *Left* Wall painting on the tomb of Senedjem at Luxor near the ancient Egyptian city of Thebes, showing Senedjem and his wife chanting prayers to the sun *Right* Imaginative picture from *The Astrologer of the 19th Century*: by means of magical incantations the sorcerer commands a spirit to appear and orders it to do his bidding *Far right* This Buddhist pilgrim to a temple in Katmandu, Nepal, although silent, makes pious avowals of faith by repeatedly turning a prayer wheel

spirit, 'Come thou forth and follow me: and make all spirits subject unto Me so that every Spirit of the Firmament, and of the Ether, upon the Earth or under the Earth: on dry Land, or in the Water: of Whirling Air or of rushing Fire, and every Spell and Scourge of God, may be obedient unto me.'

The spirit is the divine being who is the magician's own inner self, and he announces his identity with it at the climax of the ritual by repeatedly proclaiming, 'I am He'. By describing the spirit, by vividly imagining it, the magician summons it up and controls it. He commands it to come forth and with every ounce of energy in his being he asserts that he and it are one. Finally the command 'Come thou forth' is repeated again but as if by the spirit itself, which has now taken possession of the magician.

Sound and Fury

This ritual was adapted from a Graeco-Egyptian magical text, itself descended from ancient Egyptian spells and incantations, like those in the Book of the Dead which identify the dead man as Osiris, or protect him from dangers in the afterlife, or give him power over his enemies. Here again, the belief that saying a thing is so makes it so is fundamental. The dead man's identification with Osiris depends heavily on the solemn assertion that he is, as in the spell identifying the dead Pharaoh Unas with Osiris (see BOOK OF THE DEAD).

Crowley's *Liber Samekh* also illustrates another essential principle of incantation, the use of sonorous, rhythmical, rhetorical language which is not spoken flatly but chanted, with steadily rising intensity as the ritual proceeds. This contributes to a rising state of intense excitement and self-intoxication, in which the magician convinces himself that the words he utters are charged with invincible power and are actually taking effect.

Because the chanting is an aid to self-intoxication, a magical operation of high importance and difficulty is likely to involve repeating several incantations several times over. A short spell or charm is usually applied only to comparatively minor and simple acts of magic. This is not always the case: a grimoire called *The Black Pullet* says that you can open any lock at a touch by reciting the words Saritap Pernisox Ottarim, but you can equally call up all the powers of heaven and hell by chanting the magic words Siras Etar Besanar. But it is doubtful whether many magicians would take this seriously.

The words 'incantation' and 'enchant' are both derived from Latin *cantare*, 'to sing' (and 'charm' is from Latin *carmen*, 'song'). The element of singing or chanting is magically important because it means that the words are put together deliberately — not in the slapdash hurry of most everyday speech — and are rhythmical. Not only do they build up the magician's own excitement but their impressive sound and beat influence the supernatural forces which he attempts to control. These forces are believed to be swayed by compelling sound in the same way

that human beings are moved by poetry, oratory, preaching or honeyed words of love — all of which depend for their effectiveness on their combination of meaning and sound.

In *The Anatomy of Puck*, Katharine Briggs quotes an incantation in which the magician appeals to the judge of hell to discipline an obstinate demon. Part of it runs:

> O thou most puissant prince Rhadamanthus, which dost punish in thy prison of perpetual perplexity the disobedient devils of hell, and also the grisly ghosts of men dying in dreadful despair, I conjure, bind and charge thee by Lucifer, Belsabub, Sathanas, Jauconill and by their power, and by the homage thou owest unto them, and also I charge thee by the triple crown of Cerberus his head, by Stix and Phlegiton, by your fellow and private devil Baranter, that you do torment and punish this disobedient N. (naming him) until you make him come corporally to my sight and obey my will and commandments in whatsoever I shall charge or command him to do. Fiat, fiat, fiat. Amen.

This incantation uses language which is impressive in sound, evocative and atmospheric, and clear in meaning, a combination which, with all his own inner powers concentrated on his object, the magician believes will exert an irresistible force on the lords of hell.

There is an obvious basic difference between a magical incantation and a prayer.

John Webb

William MacQuitty

The essence of incantation is command and the magician orders supernatural forces to do his bidding. A prayer is not a command but a request: the worshipper begs for help (though prayer can be turned to many other purposes, including thanksgiving, praise, confession of sin, and repentance). The prayer of Jesus in the garden of Gethsemane, in horror of his approaching torment, makes the difference clear: 'Abba, Father, all things are possible to thee: remove this cup from me; yet not what I will, but what thou wilt' (Mark 14.36).

Apology to an Elephant

But though this distinction is clear in theory, and often in practice, human beings do not always keep their attitudes to the supernatural in separate compartments. Many of the incantations in the European grimoires mingle prayers, perfectly sincere petitions that God will come to the magician's aid, with monomaniac declarations of supreme power. On the other hand, prayers are not always free of a magical use of language, an underlying belief that the right form of words, the right tone and delivery, will themselves compel the desired effect. The prayers of primitive peoples tend to run the gamut from respectful petition to reproaches, orders and even threats. Among the Pueblo tribes, a farmer puts down prayer-feathers in his field and says commandingly, 'My field, you will be good all the time.' Part of a song found among the Pygmies, apologizing to a slaughtered elephant, nicely blends orders and cajolery.

> Do not make us feel your wrath.
> Henceforward your life will be better,
> You go to the country of spirits.
> Our fathers go with you to renew the alliance.
> Henceforward your life will be better,
> You go to the country of spirits.

This verse, with two significant lines repeated, may also be intended magically to send the elephant to the spirit country and make him happy there.

In the account of Elijah's great contest with the prophets of Baal (1 Kings, chapter 18) there seems no essential difference in the methods used by both sides, and Elijah's address to the Almighty is distinctly peremptory in tone. There is an inextricable mixture of the magical and religious frames of mind in the vengeful prayer of the priest Chryses to Apollo in the *Iliad* (book 1): 'Hear me, god of the Silver Bow, Protector of Chryse and holy Cilla, and Lord Supreme of Tenedos. Smintheus, if ever I built you a shrine that delighted you, if ever I burnt you the fat thighs of a bull or a goat, grant me this wish. Let the Danaans pay with your arrows for my tears.'

Some prayers employ a magical 'as . . . so' formula, based on the underlying belief that if an appropriate past event is cited, a parallel future event will occur. St Hildegard of Bingen (12th century) mentions a cure for bewitchment. You take a wheaten loaf and cut a cross on it. Draw a jacinth through one arm of the cross and say, 'May God who cast away all the preciousness of gems from the Devil when he transgressed his precept (the reference is to Ezekiel, chapter 28), remove from you, so-and-so, all phantoms and magic words and free you from the ill of this madness.' Then draw the jacinth through the other arm of the cross, saying, 'As the splendour which the Devil once possessed departed from him because of his transgression, so may this madness which harasses so-and-so by varied fantasies and magic arts be removed from you and depart from you.' Then the patient should eat the bread around the cross.

When prayers have fixed formulas, or are accompanied by prescribed postures and gestures, or are associated with sacrifice, an element of magic, if not always present, may at least be in the offing. Humanity's sense of the magic of language is so strong that its use creeps even into sincerely religious prayers and ceremonies.

(See also ALPHABET; MANTRA; NAMES; POETS; RITUAL MAGIC; SONG.)

RICHARD CAVENDISH

FURTHER READING: C. M. Bowra, *Primitive Song* (Weidenfeld, 1962); R. Cavendish, *The Black Arts* (Routledge, 1967); A. Crowley, *Magick in Theory and Practice* (Castle Books, N.Y. reprint); Idries Shah, *The Secret Lore of Magic* (Citadel Press, 1970); A. E. Waite, *The Book of Ceremonial Magic* (University Books, N.Y. reprint). See also K. M. Briggs, *The Anatomy of Puck* (Arno, 1977).

INCARNATION

A FUNDAMENTAL TENET of Christianity is the incarnation of the Second Person of the Trinity as the historical Jesus of Nazareth. The term devised to express this derives from the Latin: *in carne,* meaning 'in flesh'; *incarnare,* 'to make flesh'. In this context flesh is understood to mean the physical being of a human person, including the mental and psychical constituents of personality. Although it has only been strictly defined and formulated as a doctrine in Christianity, the idea is both ancient and widespread.

The ancient Egyptians believed that the pharaoh was the incarnate son of the sun god Re, the chief state deity. How the acts of divine generation and birth were accomplished is graphically depicted in a series of sculptured scenes in the temple of Amun at Luxor. The scenes portray the divine birth of the Pharaoh Amunhotep III (1402–1364 BC): at this period Amun was identified with Re. Amun is shown with Queen Mutemuya as she conceives the future king. The goddesses Selqet and Neith, beneath the bridal couch, assist the conception. Another scene represents the consequence of the divine act of generation. The god Khnum fashions on a potter's wheel the infant king and his *ka* or soul, while the goddess Hathor animates them with the *ankh,* the symbol of life. In other scenes the actual birth, and the presentation of the infant Amunhotep to Amun-Re, his divine father, are depicted. According to Egyptian belief, the pharaoh acted on earth as the viceregent of his heavenly father, and at death he was reunited with him. The idea of the pharaoh as an incarnate deity was long-established and effective in Egypt (see EGYPT); but its metaphysical implications were never discussed.

Belief in divine incarnation *(avatara)* is a basic tenet also of Hinduism. It finds its most notable expression in the cult of the great popular deity Vishnu, who, as Narayana, is conceived as the Supreme God and upholder of the cosmic and moral order of the universe. In the *Bhagavad Gita,* Vishnu declares: 'For the rescue of the pious and for the destruction of the evil-doers, for the establishment of the Law I am born in every age.' Ten incarnations of Vishnu are popularly recognized. Some are of an obviously mythical kind, for instance, as Fish, Tortoise and Boar; some have an apparent historical character; such as in the form of the heroes Rama and Krishna, and as the Buddha.

In Buddhist thought the Bodhisattva is really thought of as a divine saviour who becomes incarnate periodically to save mankind. Buddhist metaphysics, however, made the idea of incarnation by way of sexual intercourse unacceptable, and other modes of entry into the world were devised: Maya, the mother of Gautama, conceived the future Buddha through a vision of a white elephant (see GAUTAMA BUDDHA).

The story of the Virgin Birth of Jesus served a similar purpose in Christian theology. The deification of Jesus of Nazareth, which the apostle Paul initiated, inevitably entailed a number of theological and metaphysical problems, among them that of the nature and mode of the Incarnation. For Christian thinkers had to explain and reconcile two obviously incompatible beliefs: that Jesus was essentially God, and that he had become truly a man. After much bitter controversy about metaphysical niceties concerning human nature and divine nature, the orthodox position was authoritatively established at the Council of Chalcedon in 451 AD. The declaration was there made that Jesus Christ was 'the same perfect in Godhead, the same perfect in manhood, very God and very man, the same consisting of a reasonable soul and a body, of one substance with the Father as touching the Godhead, the same of one substance with us as touching the manhood, like us in all things, sin except . . . born of the Virgin Mary, the Mother of God . . .' But the definition of the orthodox view of the Incarnation did not justify it intellectually, and it remains an abiding problem of Christian theology. In one respect, the idea of Christ's Incarnation differs from other conceptions: it is regarded as a permanent state of being, and not a temporary aspect. Christ is believed to have ascended into heaven in his human state.

(See also JESUS.)

FURTHER READING: J. Dunn, *Christology in the Making* (Westminster, 1980); A. Grillmeier, *Christ in Christian Tradition* (John Knox Press, 1975).

The Hindu god Vishnu assumes a different physical form in every age in order to succour the pious and destroy evil-doers: Indian drawing of Vishnu's second incarnation as the turtle

INCAS

CHILDREN OF THE SUN

The Incas were invincible in their faith that the ruler of their powerful empire was a direct descendant of the sun; but when the throne was usurped the theocracy with its glittering temples of gold fell to the invading Spaniards

WITHIN FOUR CENTURIES the Inca family expanded from rulers of part of a small town to a semi-divine tribe of which the head, the Sapa Inca, ruled an immense empire which they termed *Tahuantinsuyu*, the Four Quarters, to imply that their father the sun god destined them to rule the entire known earth. In the mid-11th century, about the time of the Norman Conquest of Britain, a family of American Indians came from the East and ascended the mountains into a civilized country which had broken up into warring tribal troups. Their legend tells us that they were commanded to find the very centre, the navel or *Cuzco*, of the earth. To ascertain this they carried a wedge of gold, symbol of a sun ray, and at each stopping place they placed the wedge upon the ground to see if it would sink into the earth and disappear. This at last happened when Inca Manco and his sister Mama Occlo, who were the only survivors of the family, came to a little mountain town near the headwaters of the Apurimac river. They were allowed to rule half of the town which they now named The Cuzco, and although they were respected because of the mystery of their origin, it was not until the reign of their great-grandson that the Incas ruled the whole of the town. This must have been in the first half of the 12th century of our era.

At the time of the Inca arrival Peru was divided. The mountain peoples were heirs to three previous empires. The earliest originated around Chavin de Huantar well before 1000 BC and its characteristic art styles enable archeologists to show how it dominated much of the northern part of

the Peruvian Andes. It has a close artistic relationship with the peoples of the more southerly part of the Peruvian Coast around the Paracas Peninsula, where there was a typically Peruvian cult of the dead, important people being sun dried after death, and then wrapped in great quantities of elaborately embroidered cloths. The strange art of these peoples was obsessed by the forms of serpents, pumas and condors, sacred animals representing earth, mountains and sky. A slightly later development of this religious art centred around Nasca on the southern half of the Peruvian Coast and was expressed in the creation of beautifully painted pottery, which in the early centuries AD included the first near realist figures of human beings in Peru.

Further to the north, again in the early centuries AD, another culture had arisen. These Mochica people lived in city states, were apparently often at war with each other, and built temples on great pyramidal mounds of brick. Their pottery is well modelled and painted simply with terracotta colours on cream, and here also arose true portrait modelling. Presumably this was part of the cult of the dead for the best vases are all found in the pits in the coastal sands where the mummified bodies of people were buried with their household treasures bundled in fine tapestries and woven cloths.

The people of the highlands seem to have developed separately and by the 6th century AD formed into two rather similar groups around the northern city of Huari and the

Left Lost city of the Incas; the remains of the city of Machu Pichu, first discovered by explorers in 1911, is sited on an almost inaccessible ridge of the Andes. The advanced culture of the Inca sun kingdom declined rapidly with the arrival of the Spaniards in the early 16th century *Right* Modern Peruvian witch-doctors, like their earlier Inca counterparts, are thought to be able 'to converse with the spirits of the air, and the creatures of the earth'

Right Many Christian festivals among the Sierra Indians of Peru contain practices which are relics of forgotten Inca beliefs. At the feast of Corpus Christi, dancers wear masks bearing both the cross and the ancient Inca symbol of the sun *Centre* Headhunting was prevalent in Peru before the advent of the Spanish; it was believed that the possession of another man's head increased the new owner's spiritual powers: llama wool fabric depicting warriors grasping shrunken heads *Far right* In honour of their great father the sun, the Incas celebrated elaborate festivals of feasting and rejoicing: wooden beaker showing a ceremonial procession

Camera Press London

famous southern one of Tiahuanaco near Lake Titicaca. In the 8th century or perhaps a little later, the Tiahuanaco people defeated the tribes around Nasca and imposed their culture upon them. But the conquest did not last, and eventually Tiahuanaco itself fell in some catastrophe beyond our knowledge. Similarly the Huari power broke up. In the 10th and 11th centuries central and southern Peru and all the highland regions fell into a chaos of small conflicting tribal states. Only on the northern half of the coast was there much development. The Mochica towns were taken over by a warrior group who came on balsa rafts from the north, led by a great king known as the Great Chimu.

Chimu culture prospered exceedingly and from the 12th to the 15th centuries the kingdom was centred around the great city of Chan Chan. On that rainless coast it was built of mud brick covered with brilliantly painted plaster. The artisans worked in gold, silver, turquoise and crystal. Women created beauty in workshops, weaving quantities of clothing for the townspeople. Irrigation of the narrow river valleys passing through the arid coastlands made the plantations of maize, beans, pumpkins, melons and chilli peppers fruitful and rich. These people worshipped the stars and forces of Nature, but above all they adored the moon god, Si, who spared them from the fierce heat of the sun and guided their fishing boats over the calm seas on moonlit nights. From all the evidence they were a rich comfortable people, loving colour and jewellery. Their fertility festivals were gay and often enough thoroughly and happily pornographic, to the shocked indignation of their highland neighbours, the Incas, who were becoming a powerful force to be reckoned with by the late 14th century.

Merciful Masters

The Inca city of Cuzco had been slowly growing in importance, and the Inca family claiming descent from the sun god actively worked to spread their rule. The Inca was so holy that he could not be born from normal human parents. He was always the firstborn son of the divine marriage of the previous Sapa Inca with his sister (some say first cousin) the Ccoya, who was of equally pure lineage from the sun. In the male line there was only one breakdown – the Prince Yahuarhuaccac, He Who Weeps Blood. It seems that the growth of Inca power in the Cuzco Valley roused the

jealousy of a group of Highland tribes known as the Chanca confederation. The young Inca was terrified of the power of the confederated armies and he lost a battle. His own family had him killed and appointed his brother to rule. The new ruler dared first to state the gravity of their plight by taking the name of Viracocha, the Creator. Only under that protection could they hope to win. In a series of outflanking raids and unexpected attacks the Inca forces destroyed the Chanca confederacy and Inca Viracocha found himself in command of all the mountain tribes around Cuzco. In another generation the Incas spread their rule over the whole Peruvian part of the Andes, including the sacred though ruined ancient city of Tiahuanaco.

Eventually the clash with the Chimu kingdom developed. The ruling Inca was becoming elderly but he sent his son Prince Tupac to conduct the campaign. After some fighting the Chimu capitulated. The Inca made their burden light, taking all the gold in the country for the glory of the sun god, but allowing the Chimu to retain silver ornaments. The Chimu were permitted to worship their own gods, but every temple had to support an oratory to the sun which made it quite clear that his children, the Incas, were the real rulers of the country. The Chimu crown prince was taken to Cuzco to learn Inca ways. He was treated well and married to an Inca Princess, which made sure that his children would also be of proper Inca descent.

The capture of the Chimu kingdom made the Incas masters of all the civilized areas of Peru. Under the great Tupac Yupanqui

when he became Sapa Inca, the Inca armies faced a movement of tribes from Argentina, so he decided to spread the Empire down to Chile. His son Huayna Ccapac turned northwards and captured the Cara kingdom of southern Ecuador and took the Cara princess as one of his hundreds of junior wives. He was so in love with her that he decreed that on his death Huascar, his son by his sister, should be Supreme Inca in Peru, but that his son by the princess, Atahuallpa, should rule the northern section of the Empire. As things turned out, on the death of Huayna Ccapac, the two princes engaged in a terrible civil war. The true heir, Huascar, was taken prisoner and shut up in a cell in Cuzco and the false Atahuallpa called himself the Supreme Inca. Peru was paralysed because the people realized that this was no true child of the sun. Just at this time the Spaniards arrived. In a short campaign they captured Atahuallpa, and murdered him; but not before he had had Huascar, the true heir, killed. Thus in 1533 fell the divine sun kingdom of the Incas.

Golden Temple of the Sun

In their years of power the Incas achieved a great deal. Believing themselves to be directly descended from the sun god they felt it to be their duty to spread the benefits of divine rule throughout the lands which they controlled. They improved the road systems and arranged for storehouses of food and clothing in all parts of Peru so that in times of catastrophe there was always a reserve for the people. They greatly extended the

Michael Holford

use of the coloured knotted cords by which they transmitted messages instead of writing. Most important of all from their point of view was the establishment of a sun temple in every town of their dominions.

In Cuzco the great sun temple was surrounded by smaller buildings which held the lesser gods of all the peoples of the empire, as if they were servants waiting to obey their master. There was only One more powerful than the sun. Inside the sun temple was a wall covered with gold. Upon it there were figures of the sun, moon, thunder, and rainbow. The first humans were there and the first Inca. Then there were the constellations of stars and in their midst an open blank space, which astronomers now know as the 'coal sack' because of its comparative blackness in the Milky Way. This centrepiece of the golden wall was always empty. It represented the mystery of the Creator, Viracocha, the Breath of Life who was everywhere unseen but eternally giving life, even to father sun. The temple was so placed that once a year the rays of the rising sun shone through the doorway and lit up the golden wall with living burning light. On that occasion the Sapa Inca was alone in the temple. He was without his crown and barefoot, having meditated all night and prayed that the sun, which was now at its furthest point away from his kingdom, should return to spread light and life again. Outside, the people of the city had spent a night of penitence without fire and food, weeping for their past evil-doings. The priests had worked magic over a black llama so that it would take the sins of the peoples on its back before being driven away into the mountains.

Then when the returning sun had shone upon the golden wall the Inca put on his diadem and his golden sandals. After he had sacrificed a pure white llama the people burst into songs of rejoicing and the city was filled with processions, singing and dancing. On that occasion strangers kept outside the city for fear. From the royal storehouses food was distributed and every individual was given a vase holding about half a gallon of maize beer. After the day of rejoicing was over the streets of the city were lined with people in a quiet, happy stupor, for the drunken Peruvian preferred sleeping to fighting. They were happy that once again the sun was returning through

There is nothing else in history to compare truly with Inca Peru; it is an example of divine kingship taken to the ultimate extreme

the skies, every day shining higher and higher, until the day came when he sat on his stone throne in every town and cast no shadow because he was right overhead, showering blessings on the four quarters of the earth ruled so wisely by his son, the Sapa Inca.

In addition to the great powers of Nature the Peruvians found magic in all manner of things which they thought were lucky charms. They collected strangely-shaped stones, reverenced unusual animals, and found an aura of power in the dried bodies of the dead. Wise men knew how to interpret the language of animals and predict the future from the flight of birds. On occasions of great disasters they might offer a few human sacrifices, but normally they made little presents of food and small animals and birds to their gods. They well understood that sometimes the powers of Nature were terrible, but they accepted that the Nature gods took their own human victims as they pleased. Famine might be sent by the gods but the storehouses of the sun and the Inca existed to return the divine bounty to help the afflicted people.

Society and Custom

Under the Incas social organization was thorough. Every event in a village was recorded on the knotted string *quipus*, or cords, and sent to the town for the archives. Abstracts of these reports were knotted up and sent to the supreme administration in Cuzco. The Inca was in his massive stone palace for all great festivals, but he also travelled widely inspecting towns, ordering the construction of roads, bridges and storehouses, and impressing his people that all were interdependent in the kingdom of the sun. The taxes for the Inca and the sun god, each taking a third of the harvest of every field, were largely returned in the paternalistic welfare service. Only his direct servants, the High Priest and his closest relatives might look closely on his face. Others threw themselves down and turned their faces to the earth as the divine king passed close to them.

It appears that people discussed the Inca as an individual, and on a very few occasions protested against new regulations, but on the whole they regarded him as a natural phenomenon, a divine sun child sent to guide them in the pleasanter paths of life.

In such a society marriage was important because good family organization was the basis of the state. Once a year in every district there was a great ceremony in which young couples were married. They had only a very small choice of partners, but there seems to be little record of domestic unhappiness. They accepted the chosen partner whom they had almost certainly known from childhood, reared their families, looked after the flocks, cultivated the fields, and made pots and wove cloth for the home. For the family of the Inca himself, however, arrangements were different. Each Sapa Inca was married to his sister who was the sacred queen, the Ccoya. In addition he was expected to take many more wives. The daughters of defeated chiefs were often

Gold funerary mask of the Chimu people, who were conquered by the Incas: they worshipped the stars and the forces of Nature, but especially the moon god who guided their fishing boats 'over the calm seas on moonlit nights'

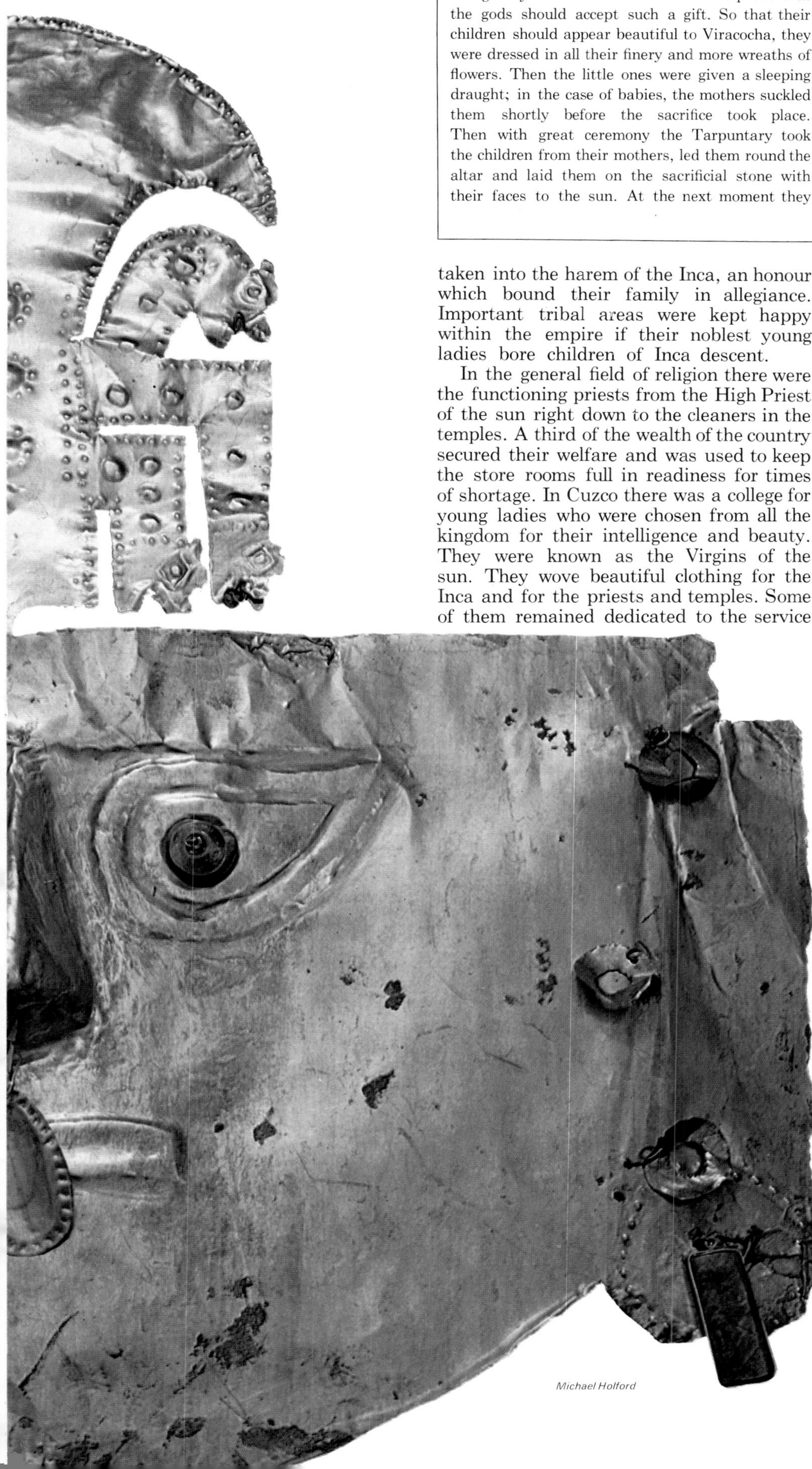

Infant Sacrifice

The children destined for the sacrifice were brought by their own mothers who were proud that the gods should accept such a gift. So that their children should appear beautiful to Viracocha, they were dressed in all their finery and more wreaths of flowers. Then the little ones were given a sleeping draught; in the case of babies, the mothers suckled them shortly before the sacrifice took place. Then with great ceremony the Tarpuntary took the children from their mothers, led them round the altar and laid them on the sacrificial stone with their faces to the sun. At the next moment they were killed in the particular manner prescribed by the ritual — strangled, garotted or their breasts torn open with a sharp obsidian knife. With their blood the ceremony of 'Vilacha' or 'Pipano' was performed; this consisted in the smearing of the sacrificer or certain privileged persons with red stripes from ear to ear. The same blood was allowed to dye sacrificial utensils and finally these and the children were lowered into a common grave.

Siegfried Huber *The Realm of the Incas* trans M. Savill.

taken into the harem of the Inca, an honour which bound their family in allegiance. Important tribal areas were kept happy within the empire if their noblest young ladies bore children of Inca descent.

In the general field of religion there were the functioning priests from the High Priest of the sun right down to the cleaners in the temples. A third of the wealth of the country secured their welfare and was used to keep the store rooms full in readiness for times of shortage. In Cuzco there was a college for young ladies who were chosen from all the kingdom for their intelligence and beauty. They were known as the Virgins of the sun. They wove beautiful clothing for the Inca and for the priests and temples. Some of them remained dedicated to the service of religion all their lives; but most were married off to nobles and visiting rulers. They became the gifts of the Inca to those whom he delighted to honour.

The position of women in Inca Peru was of equality with men, but within the sphere of women's work. They were not warriors and roadmakers, but no men made pottery or wove cloth. Everywhere in the empire the woman and mother was treated with respect and honour, and the Ccoya was queen of women's employment just as the Inca was king over the male side of life. Some women became professional healers. They had a deep and scientific knowledge of herbal medicine, and knew the value of massage and of bone-setting. There were also many women as well as some men who were inspired by spirits and who gave advice when in a state of trance. They were supposed to be able to converse with the spirits of the air, and the creatures of earth.

There is nothing else in history to compare truly with Inca Peru. It is an example of a divine kingship taken to the ultimate extreme. By good fortune the individual Incas seem to have been men of very high character with a real care for the welfare of their kingdom. They used the thousands of cousins in the Inca family as a disciplined and closely knit civil service. The organization of every facet of life made administration easy, but it was also scientific. There was not much freedom, yet very few revolts. Progress was not great because there was enough food, clothing and entertainment for everybody and no one wished to introduce innovations into a contented, divinely-inspired civilization. On the whole the gods and mankind had found a *modus vivendi*, a way of living that was mutually acceptable, for a few generations. But at the beginning of the 16th century came the strange end, with the Divine Inca deposed and murdered by his more earthly brother; and then a total change when the bronze age theocracy was taken over by the feudal iron-using Spanish invaders from over the great oceans.

C.A. BURLAND

FURTHER READING: C.A. Burland, *Peru Under the Incas* (Evans Brothers, 1967); B. Cobo, *History of the Inca Empire* (University of Texas Press, 1979); *The Incredible Incas and their Timeless Land* (National Geographic, 1975); E. Hyams/G. Ordish, *The Last of the Incas* (Simon & Schuster).

Michael Holford

INCENSE

THE BURNING of sweet-smelling substances in religious ceremonies, both public and private, is of great antiquity and common to many peoples. Pleasing odours have been thought to delight the gods and to be offensive to evil spirits. Smoke from glowing aromatic substances has been taken to symbolize the ascent of prayer to heaven, and in death rooms and at funerals it is believed to bear the souls of the departed to their eternal rest. Sweet fragrances have been used to ameliorate the stench of blood and burnt offerings and as purifications to clear the air of nasty material smells and, by implication and extension, of foul immaterial presences.

Many different combustibles have been used for ritual purposes, particularly aromatic woods, barks, resins and herbs. North American Indians offered the smoke of tobacco to their gods and the Aztecs and Mayas that of copal, a kind of resin. Some substances used in pre-Columbian Mexico gave off narcotic fumes that drugged the senses of human sacrificial victims. The ancient Egyptians worshipped the sun god Re with the burning of resin as he rose in the morning, of myrrh as he stood at the zenith at noon and of *kuphi* as he sank westwards in the evening. Kuphi, an elaborate compound of 16 ingredients including honey, wine and bitumen, was mixed by the priests according to a secret ritual, to the accompaniment of the chanting of sacred texts. It had a mystical significance of order and harmony, since the number of ingredients, four times four, represented the squaring of a square and brought calm and quiet to those who breathed it.

Such burnt aromas are commonly spoken of as 'incense' but true incense is what is properly called frankincense, the gum resin of trees of the *Boswellia* family growing chiefly in the hinterland of the Somali coast of East Africa. Frankincense was one of the 16 ingredients of kuphi and the Egyptians valued it highly. They organized expeditions to the 'land of Punt', as this area was known to them, to acquire it. The Greek traveller and historian Herodotus mentions this trade in the 5th century BC and says that the trees were guarded by winged serpents. The more prosaic historian Pliny (c 23–79 AD) records that the trees were tended by 3000 families which had a hereditary right to them. When the trees were being pruned or tapped, the men were forbidden intercourse with their women or the sight of a corpse.

The use of incense seems to have spread south-east and west from the Semitic lands. From early beginnings in Egypt and Babylonia, it was taken up by the Greeks (probably in the 8th century BC) and later by the Romans. It was often included in the aromatic substances with which burnt offerings were stuffed and was much used in processions and ceremonials. Grains of incense were customarily burned privately by the Romans before the images of the *lares,* the household gods, and publicly before those of the emperor. Incense has never been used in Moslem religious rites, as such, but may be burned at the shrines of holy men and during funerals. It was also used for magical purposes in Islamic countries, to ward off the Evil Eye and in a curious ritual of incantation. Different perfumes were associated with letters of the alphabet and the initial letter of the name of the person on whose behalf the incantation was made determined the choice of the aromatic used.

Frequent references to incense in the Old Testament have given rise to the mistaken view that its use goes back to very early times among the Jews. In fact, the Authorized

Aaron, brother of Moses, burning incense during a religious ceremony: detail from a 16th century fresco in Bressanone Cathedral

A. Tomsich

Version often uses the word to refer to the aroma of burnt offerings and the ancient Hebrews may indeed have regarded the use of incense, so popular with the Babylonians, as a mere trapping of idolatry. Scholars are now agreed that the burning of incense was not introduced into Judaic ritual until the 7th century BC but that, once adopted, it became more and more important in the acts of worship. The incense used was compounded of few ingredients – stacte, onycha, galbanum and pure frankincense – and its mixture by the priests was regarded with much the same reverence as was given to the making of kuphi by the Egyptians. It was burned with meat offerings and with the first fruits and, on its own, at morning or evening on a special altar; and also once a year on the Day of Atonement, in the inner sanctum of the temples.

Christianity was also slow to adopt incense into its rites. The services of the early Church were very simple, and incense, save as a practical purification, was eschewed as something Jewish or pagan. Indeed, during the Roman persecutions the burning of grains of incense before the statue of the emperor was a test of an individual's loyalty to the state, and hence to the state religion, and also a symbolic act of apostasy. From the 5th century onwards, however, incense was gradually but increasingly used in church services. By the 14th century it had become part of the established ritual of High Mass and other services such as Vespers, at the consecration of churches and in processions and funerals. Although usage varied from place to place, incense, along with other external rituals, was driven from the churches by the Reformation. In the second half of the 19th century its use by the High Anglican movement to enrich church ceremonial became a highly controversial issue.

The passions aroused by the 'incense question' in the English church may now strike many people as somewhat ridiculous. But incense is curious stuff and may be if not physiologically at least psychologically addictive. It is a matter of personal temperament but, for many people, the sweet smell and the swirling patterns of the smoke, in a candle-lit church filled with solemn music, have a strange power.
(See also PERFUME.)

CHARLES DE HOGHTON

INCEST

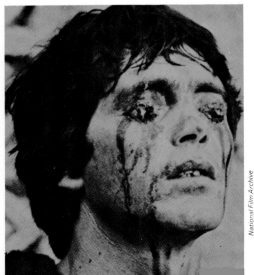

National Film Archive

AN ESKIMO MYTH relates that the sun and the moon were once sister and brother. They lay down together and made love in a house where there was no light. When the sister discovered that her lover was her own brother, she tore off her breasts in her shame, and threw them to her brother with the cry, 'Since my body pleases thee, taste these too!' Then the sister took a torch and fled, pursued by her brother,

Freud suggested that 'the beginnings of religion, ethics, society and art, meet in the Oedipus complex'; scene from Pasolini's film *Oedipus Rex*

who was also carrying a torch. As the sister rose in the sky, her torch burned bright, and she became the sun. The brother's torch spluttered out, as he ascended after his sister, and he became the moon.

Almost all human societies prohibit marriage and punish or disapprove strongly of even casual sexual intercourse between persons of certain specified degrees of relatedness. Modern investigators set themselves the task of distinguishing clearly the problem of incest, which has to do with sexual relations, from the institution of exogamy, the rule which forbids marriage within a group. This distinction is not always made however, in the older anthropological literature, and it is by no means certain that it is absolute in the minds of all the

Nichte

Neue

John Webb

16th century woodcut by Gerard de Jode of an incestuous relationship; incest myths of great antiquity often make a brother and sister the first pair of all mankind

to explain how both these crimes were committed in complete ignorance. Oedipus's reaction on the discovery of his true relationship to Jocasta is also one of extreme horror and shame, and he, too, punishes himself through mutilation, putting out his eyes (the source of light in ancient Greek belief).

Freud was not the first to sense the universality of the Oedipus myth. As early as 1855, Burckhardt wrote that there was 'an Oedipus chord in every Greek that longed to be directly touched and to vibrate after its own fashion.' For every Greek, Freud substituted every man, and made the Oedipus complex, as he called it, the pivot of his psychoanalytical theory. In the book he devoted to the twin problem of incest and totemism, Freud wrote: 'the beginnings of religion, ethics, society and art meet in the Oedipus complex. This is in entire accord with the findings of psychoanalysis, namely that the nucleus of all neuroses as far as our present knowledge of them goes is the Oedipus complex.'

According to Claude Lévi-Strauss, however, social constraints such as incest taboos, cannot be explained as the effects of emotions which crop up again and again in different parts of the world at different periods in time. It is, rather, the taboos and rituals which give rise to the emotions. But both Freud and Lévi-Strauss would agree in putting the incest taboo at the very basis of the human condition. For Freud, the incest prohibition blocks the infantile longing for the mother, and forces the libido along the path of life's biological purpose. For Lévi-Strauss, the 'universal presence of the incest taboo means that in human society a man must obtain a woman from another man, who gives him a daughter or a sister.'

Awareness of incest as a practice to be hedged about with prohibitions goes back to a very early stage in man's development. The earliest known incest myths agree in imputing the practice to the first-born among gods and men: in Greek mythology, Rhea is the sister-spouse of Cronus, and Hera of Zeus. In Hawaii, Kii (or Tiki) is the ancestor of all men by incestuous union with his mother, and myths which make a brother and sister the first pair of all mankind are found over the face of the earth. The myths also show that incest has an ambivalent power of attraction and repulsion to the majority of mankind. It is not without reason that the *Oedipus Tyrannus* of Sophocles is the one surviving ancient Greek tragedy that retains an undiminished hold over modern audiences.

DAVID PHILLIPS

FURTHER READING: Robin Fox, *The Red Lamp of Incest* (University of Notre Dame Press, 1983) and *Kinship and Marriage* (Penguin, 1967); J.G. Frazer, *Totemism and Exogamy* (Macmillan, 1910); Sigmund Freud, *Totem and Taboo* (Routledge, 1950).

members of the societies which have been most intensively studied in this respect. An important point is that the group on which the exogamy rule is based need not be a family in the sense that the word would normally be understood in contemporary civilized society. In many societies, the group is identified with a specific plant or animal which constitutes its totem (see TOTEM), and though totemism is found without exogamy and exogamy without totemism, the two are so frequently associated that some writers have treated them as inseparable.

The complex of incest — exogamy — totemism crop up in unrelated societies all over the world, and the near universality of taboos on incest does invite the formation of an all-embracing theory. In the Eskimo

myth already quoted there are several features which have striking parallels in incest myths from other parts of the world, and other periods in history. Thus the offending pair act in ignorance, accounted for here by the naïve device of their lying together in darkness. The sister's reaction on discovering her sin is to mutilate herself out of horror and shame.

The Story of Oedipus

Several of these details find an echo in the most famous incest myth of all, the story of the Greek king Oedipus. Oedipus obeyed the inexorable rule of his own destiny in murdering his father Laius and marrying his mother Jocasta. The Greek myth incorporates an imaginative episode

INCUBUS
& SUCCUBUS

Incubus and Succubus

The theme of the demon lover occurs repeatedly in Romantic poetry. The antecedents of this nocturnal visitor are far older, however, and reach back to the incubus, one of Satan's legions sent to torment mankind in terms of sex

THE INCUBUS was a devil who was thought to visit his lust upon women, while the demonic succubus attended to men. Most Christian demonologists of the Middle Ages, and later, agreed that unbridled sexuality (which they apparently defined as anything this side of joyless procreation) offered one of the most slippery paths to hell. And if human seducers did not present threat enough to the potentially virginal, these lecherous demons – and in rare cases even the Devil himself – would happily perform the same function.

Usually the incubus or succubus was believed to assume human form for its purposes and, naturally, a sexually attractive form. The theologians insisted, however, that demons were spirits: hence the human form they put on had to be an animated corpse, or a fleshly fabrication endowed with movement and artificial life; the notion that devils can create life was and is a heresy. Frequently the demon lovers appeared to their partners, or victims, in the semblance of a human husband, wife or lover. Sometimes, too, they appeared in equally familiar but less welcome shapes – as in the case of a medieval nun who claimed to have been sexually attacked by one Bishop Silvanus, though the Bishop insisted that it was an incubus who had assumed his form.

But certain signs could reveal the true demonic nature of the incubus in human form. When a woman willingly admitted it to her bed, it had the ability to put others in the house into a deep sleep – and could even render a husband so soundly asleep that it could enjoy his wife in the bed beside him. At times, the demons gave away their evil origins by the unpleasurable sensations they caused. But this aspect of their love-making did not gain wide credence until the time of the great witch persecutions. The witch-hunters believed on the one hand that initiate witches had to have sexual relations with their Satanic master, and on the other hand that they never enjoyed it. Victimized witches claimed at their trials (or rather, were made to claim, usually by torture) that Satan's sexual organ was cold as ice, or painfully large, or made of iron, or all of these. Some even described it as two-pronged. Occasionally, too, men would confirm the unpleasurable nature of this supernatural intercourse.

Demon Lovers

It was a common belief in the Middle Ages that the Devil himself could easily assume female form, to tempt some male saint such as the beleaguered St Anthony. It was a short step, therefore, for the incubus and succubus to be seen as the same devil, putting on a male body one night to visit a woman, a woman's body the next night to tempt a man. Out of this idea came the belief that devils, spirits or not, could impregnate humans. Some demonologists

said that they saved up the semen of corpses; but most theorists preferred to assert that the incubus ejaculated semen which it had gathered, earlier, when in the guise of a succubus. In spite of the fact that this demonic form of artificial insemination used human sperm, the children of such unions were generally expected to be monstrous – physically deformed, or more subtly odd. Even twins were viewed with suspicion, as likely products of an incubus's attentions. The magician Merlin was in some tales reputed to have had one demonic parent. Because devils were not humans, sexual intercourse with incubi or succubi was considered to be bestiality – and some writers threw in sodomy as well – so any humans suspected of willingly taking a demon to bed would be punished not only for diabolism but also for sexual perversion.

And of course the demonologists and their hysteric inheritors the witch-hunters were by nature suspicious people; their victims were guilty until proved innocent. These people believed that witches were given incubi as lovers and familiars in return for entering the service of Satan. Necromancers, black magicians and the like also received demonic mistresses from their master, rather in the way that Mephistopheles conjured up Helen of Troy and other delights for Faust. Such people, when caught, and when 'confessions' had been wrung from them by torture, were invariably punished for their general heresy – of which sexual relations with devils played only a minor part. But ordinary people who were accused of sleeping with devils, were tried entirely for sexual sins. They might defend themselves by saying that they were seduced – even raped, for the incubus took by force what it could not get by blandishment and temptation. And then the line of innocence or guilt had to be drawn too finely for the judges in the days of the witch-hunting frenzy. Seduction by an incubus was as punishable as succumbing to temptation in other sinful directions; besides, the witch-hunters said, a girl who 'falls' sexually (to a devil or not) is more easily drawn into total corruption.

Nevertheless, many young women (including, during the Middle Ages, quite a few nuns) claimed rape by an incubus when the loss of their virginity became evident. So the belief became a convenient

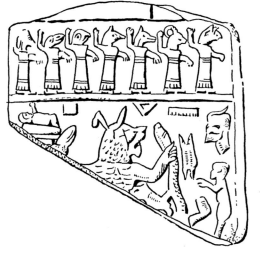

excuse for unmarried mothers, adulterous wives, women ashamed of a deformed child, and so on. Men found it a handy escape from accusations of paternity of an illegitimate child, and also an easy road out of marriage; evidence, however spurious, that their wives were sleeping with devils usually brought a quick annulment. In a famous 17th century case a noblewoman gave birth to a child in spite of the fact that her husband had been away from home for four years; she claimed that her husband had come to her in a dream, and had impregnated her. Learned theologians wrangled over whether the dream lover had really been the husband (in which case the child would be an heir to the estate) or an incubus in her husband's semblance. No one seems to have doubted for a moment the lady's honour – not, at any rate, in public. The husband's opinion is not recorded.

This extreme of credulity on the part of demonologists, whose gullibility reached astonishing proportions and complexity, indicates some crucial thinking about the incubus and its origins. In the legend of this demon it appears in one instance as a night visitor in the flesh (whatever flesh), but in another as a spirit visitor arriving in the form of an erotic dream. Naturally, it was assumed that any lewd thoughts entering the sleeping mind of a devout and celibate churchman, or a maritally devoted churchgoer, must have been sent by a devil. No one conceived of the idea that such dreams might erupt because the lid was clamped too firmly on a normal sexual drive. So the devil as incubus or succubus came to be seen as interchangeable with the nightmare, a word then in use both for horrifying dreams and for the devils who were thought to give rise to them.

The Latin word for nightmare, *incubo*, comes from *incubare*, meaning 'to lie upon'; the nightmare's content was described as uniquely terrifying, usually erotic, and conveying a feeling of a great weight pressing on the chest. Clearly, to the celibate clergy and other 'pure' minds, any erotic dream was horrifying; but of course the erotic content might often have been symbolic rather than explicit. Havelock Ellis, in company with other modern sexologists, sees erotic dreams and fantasies as the main impulse behind 'those conceptions of *incubi* and *succubi* which played so important a part in the demonology of the Middle Ages.' He adds the comment: 'Such erotic dreams of the hysterical are by no means always, or even usually, of a pleasurable character.' So the chaste and devout medieval Christian, fearing and abhorring his or her own

Previous page Nightmares with their sensation of horror and eroticism, were long considered the work of incubi and succubi, demons who could assume either male or female form: in Fuseli's *Nightmare,* the young girl is tormented by an incubus *Left* The Hebrew demon Lilith, queen and mother of succubi, was the successor of sexually insatiable Babylonian demonesses: amulet of the lion-headed Lemashtu and her seven demons *Right* Female devils assailed St Anthony, to tempt him from the path of righteousness

sexuality, was denied any enjoyment even in the dreams that the unconscious mind put up to try to correct the dangerous imbalance.

Bachelors' Invisible Wives

The belief in incubi and succubi did not spring entirely from the murky depths of medieval hysteria and repression. It had its antecedents in more permissive times and places. Many ancient civilizations had their forms of the nightmare or incubus demon and also saw it as operating either in the flesh or in dreams. The early Assyrian *lili* was a sexually insatiable female demon who roamed the night looking for a mortal men to lie with; and she became, in ancient Hebrew myth, the monster Lilith (referred to in the book of Isaiah as the 'night hag'), the very queen and mother of succubi (see LILITH). The Graeco-Roman world had its equally sexually rapacious wood nymphs and the like, who led men to their doom. Their male counterparts, the satyrs and fauns, are pre-Christian incubi; just as the woodland god Pan, with his horns and cloven hooves, antedates Satan and influenced early Christian conceptions of the Lord of Evil.

The Teutonic Lorelei and the Greek Sirens were succubus figures, leading men to disaster through sexual desire. The Arab *jinn* were spirits who tended to kill their human lovers by means of excessive sexual demands — in exactly the way that an early Christian hermit, seduced by a succubus,

was said to have died within a month trying to satisfy her. Such relations were not always fatal, however: in Arab tales of the jinn the female version was believed to serve as the invisible wife of any unmarried man — and many men who in legend had such wives were exceedingly unwilling to exchange them for mortal women.

The Celtic *dusii* and the Hindu *bhut* are further examples of the demon lover. A great many of the fairies, elves and other creatures of British legend operated sexually in this way until their stories were prettified and bowdlerized for children's consumption. Along with these slightly more distant relatives of the incubus can be included the vampire, who visits its victims at night while they sleep; the werewolf belongs here too, with its definite overtones of perverted sexuality, as do those shaggy and virile wild men of the woods of folk legend, variations on the satyr. The gorillas in the 'penny dreadfuls' of the 19th century, who spent most of their time carrying off beautiful white women, may also be numbered among this company.

So it seems that to some extent man's mistrust of his own sexuality has at all times caused him to depict it as a demonic figure. Medieval Christian man, however, took this depiction to new and obsessive extremes. He even saw the incubus as powerful enough, in its obtrusion into our most rational or spiritual lives, to resist exorcism: many stories exist of the sexual devil ignoring the exorcist, laughing at him,

even attacking him personally. Demonologists ascribed the ability of the incubus to withstand exorcism to the fact that it was of the lowest order of demons, and so more thick-skinned and stupid. Similarly, remarkably few magical cures exist in folklore for people plagued by incubi. One or two writers allude to certain herbs that can protect innocent beds, including St John's wort, vervain, dill, and garlic, which is also reputed to hold off vampires. Otherwise, the early Christian fathers apparently relied solely on the hope that their usual prescription of prayer, mortification of the flesh and so on would keep their chastity intact.

If these tactics failed, the medieval Church and the later witch-hunters resorted inevitably to driving out the incubus through punishment of the victim. The revolting tortures that followed were obviously aimed, by the vicious hysterical minds that devised them, at the normal sexual urges of men and women. It is clear that the Church believed that no innocence could escape tainting, once exposed to the devil of lust in dream or otherwise. That belief, and the cruelties perpetrated in its name, reveals the scale of the sexual repression that existed in those centuries of the Church's dominance. The myth of the incubus remains one of the most ugly manifestations in all history of man's frequent attempts to cripple and pervert his own sexuality in the name of religion. (See also EVIL.)

DOUGLAS HILL

Unlike the lords of Olympus, the deities of prehistoric India cannot be arranged in a neat family tree; brought together from a variety of sources, they imparted a breadth and tolerance to later Hindu thought

INDIA

THE HISTORY OF INDIA, in any modern sense of the term, begins to take a personal and coherent shape in the 6th century BC. Then great moral philosophies, which still between them influence millions of people in the East, combined with a spreading literacy and a complex but increasingly codified religion to introduce historical elements into the Indian record. There remained large gaps and uncertainties in that record, but the year 500 BC may be taken as the approximate divide between prehistoric and historic India.

The prehistoric period is not an entirely uncharted landscape. India was a land where oral tradition flourished with an astonishing persistence and exactitude. Thus when we speak of the hymns of the *Rig-Veda* as the oldest literature, not merely in India but in any Aryan language, and ascribe them to the second millennium BC, we are thinking of hymns transmitted then by word of mouth and not written down (as the word literature implies) until unknown centuries later. Nevertheless those ancient hymns convey to us with something of the precision of literature the

ideas and belief of the Aryan invaders who entered north-western India perhaps between 1700 and 1200 BC and helped to shape the cultures of the northern half of the subcontinent down to modern times.

These Aryan invaders were a rough, mobile folk with no cities and few material possessions of a durable kind but with a close-knit tribal organization eventually systematized in four classes: priests *(Brahmins)*, warriors *(ksatriyas)*, peasants *(vaisyas)* and serfs *(sudras)*. The tribal chieftain

The most accomplished products of the prehistoric Indus civilization to survive are steatite seals: pectoral from Mohenjo-daro of an ox-like beast shown with a single horn, nicknamed a 'unicorn'

Josephine Powell

was the *raja* who led his tribe into battle but did not interfere with religious ritual, though he and his peers were partial to an inebriating drink, *soma*, sanctified and used at sacrifices. This *soma* or nectar, has been identified tentatively as a drug derived from hemp or, in a more recent theory, from the fungus fly agaric (see DRUGS).

The Aryan religion was based upon sky worship, and the early gods were *devas* or 'the shining ones', the father god being known as Dyaus, equivalent to the Greek Zeus and the Latin Jupiter. But when the Aryans reached India this remote Almighty had faded into the background and survived principally as the parent of a more real and active brood. Of these the most prominent was Indra, god of war and the weather, who destroyed his foes with a thunderbolt, drank soma immoderately and bragged freely of his prowess. Typically, in one of the hymns of the *Rig-Veda* he proclaims, 'Like wild winds the draughts have raised me up. Have I been drinking soma? As a carpenter bends the seat of a chariot I bend this frenzy round my heart. In my glory I have passed beyond the sky and the great earth. Have I been drinking soma?' Across the sky with him rode into battle the charioted spirits of the storm, singing wild and warlike songs as they sped. Amongst his achievements was that of dragon-slayer. In one way and another he links up with religious ideas of Mesopotamia and as far afield as Germanic Europe. He was pre-eminently the warriors' god, violent and jovial in an age of heroic barbarism.

But though foremost, Indra was not the only Aryan god whose special zone was the sky. There was, for example, Surya or the sun god who drove across the heavens in a flaming chariot, like the Greek Helios or Apollo. The twin husbands of Surya's daughter, the Asvins, also used the sky and are comparable with the twin Dioscuri of the Greeks, but were specially concerned with shipwrecked mariners and generally with warding off the ills that beset mankind. Vishnu, who was later to become one of the two great gods of the Hindu world, was another frequenter of the Vedic skies. So too was Pusan, though, like the Asvins, occupied with peaceful missions such as protector of herds and herdsmen.

Next in esteem to the boisterous Indra was the somewhat mysterious and complex god or presence, Varuna, who reigned as a heavenly king in a celestial palace and was surrounded by a godly court. Upon Varuna rested responsibility for the order of the universe, for ensuring that day and night and the seasons followed one another in proper succession. Varuna's great quality was that of knowledge. He was present at all human interchange, and he abhorred sin, including the drinking and gambling which characterized Aryan society. He punished wrong-doing and was approached with awe and penitential humility.

In this he was quite unlike Rudra who had no moral sense but was a stormy archer god whose arrows brought disease; grim, though like so many of the ancient gods, capable of occasional beneficence.

Ritual Slaughter

A significant feature of the Indo-Aryan system, in distinction from that of the classical theocracy of the West, was its lack of close corporate inter-relationship. The Olympian complex can be expressed genetically in the form of a family tree. Not so that of the Vedic Aryans. These were content with a loose assemblage of divine skills and characters, brought together no doubt from a great variety of sources and confronted on arrival in India with a further multitude of regional deities and powers, which they lacked at first the political cohesion to co-ordinate into any very closely knit unity. In large measure this heterogeneous quality remained a characteristic of the developing religions of the subcontinent.

The ritual focus of the Aryan cult was animal sacrifice. In the *Rig-Veda* mention is made of great sacrifices in which numbers of animals were slaughtered for the pleasure of the gods and doubtless also for that of the worshippers, with whom the gods shared the sacrificial feast. The more mystical and elevating aspects of the occasion were no doubt encouraged by the soma which accompanied the banquet. Later records speak of smaller sacrifices at the domestic hearth, and the basic principle of the cult, on whatever scale, would appear to be the widespread reverence for the hearth as a centre of life and comfort, of dreaming and of utterance, which the *Rig-Veda* combines in the mystical word *Brahman*. The possessor of this supernatural quality was *Brahmana,* the priestly magician of the Vedic tribe (see BRAHMAN). In a special sense the Brahmana was the priest of the fire god Agni (equivalent to the Latin *ignis*) who was the spirit of hearth and home and dwelt in the timbers of the sacrificial fire itself as a sort of intermediary between gods and men. The sacrificial priest alone had full knowledge of the divine mystery and of the exact meaning of the words and formulae which themselves had a magic value and so were preserved with an astonishing fidelity.

Sacred Horse of the Sun

Of individual sacrifices the greatest fame attaches to the *ashvamedha* or horse sacrifice, which was the prerogative of kings. It is not known to the *Rig-Veda* but appears in the later Vedic period, approximately 1000–500 BC, when the centres of Aryan dominance had moved from the north-west frontier to the jungles and rivers of the northern plains. In this region and period the old tribal assemblies were being replaced by a defined monarchical system, comprising the king with his relatives and court officials; a system which, in however shadowy a form, continued in many parts of India until modern times. An obvious weakness of this regime arose when a ruler's advancing age and decreasing powers encouraged the ever-ready intrigues of an entourage chosen perhaps on grounds other than ability. It was important therefore to preserve or increase the king's vitality, from middle age onwards, by every heavenly device. The most potent medium was that of the horse sacrifice. The procedure was to release a specially consecrated horse so that it ran wild for a year. It was followed by a band of selected warriors, who saw that the rules were strictly observed: namely, that any king on whose territory the horse chose to wander must either do homage or fight. The thinking behind this strange ceremony is, as usual in such cases, hard to discern. It may be observed, however, that the horse had specific associations with the nomadic and warlike Aryans; that it was associated with the sun, one of the major powers of life; and that the ceremony included a quasi-coupling with the queen, thus representing the fecundity of nature. In other words, it symbolized an Aryan life-source (see also IMITATIVE MAGIC).

In one way and another, the act of sacrifice, however difficult of interpretation and probably in part because of its incomprehensibility, became the central mystery of the Brahman doctrine. This meant that by the late Vedic period (middle and latter part of the first millennium BC) — that of the *Upanishads* — the individual characters and qualities of many of the gods of the *Rig-Veda* had become obscured, or had merged into new complexes: a process which may be ascribed partly to the fusion of Aryan with non-Aryan elements and partly to inevitable changes wrought by time and changing environment. A notable example of this was the gradual exaltation of the fierce Rudra of the *Rig-Veda* into the mighty Shiva of classical Hinduism. *Shiva* meant 'propitious', and was in origin the placatory epithet of Rudra but eventually assumed a separate and independent status as one of

Seals from Mohenjo-daro showing cult scenes *Top to Bottom* A 'unicorn' seal: the animal is by an incense burner. A horned ithyphallic god squats in a yoga position, bangles along his arms: possibly an early form of Shiva. The three-headed animal on the next seal may be Shiva in the character of Pasupati, Lord of Beasts. Seal depicting a rhinoceros. Horned goddess in a fig tree with priestesses or sacred dancers. Horned animal

the two great cosmic deities of the Hindu world, the other being Vishnu. In character, Shiva was an irreconcilable mingling of the hopes and fears and questionings of his worshippers. He is the destroyer; he haunts battlefields and burning-grounds; he is himself both time and death; he wears a garland of skulls and is surrounded by demons. At the same time he is the creator and is ithyphallic (represented with an erect phallus). Again, on Mount Kailasa in the Himalayas he sits upon a tiger skin in deep meditation. But also he is Lord of the Dance. He wields the trident, and is constantly accompanied by his gracious wife Parvati and his 'vehicle', the Nandi bull. He rules menacingly over his adherents, with whom he nevertheless shares the Hindu urge towards reflection and yogi. He brings together in one stern but ineluctible Being many of the principal strands of Indian religious thought and sensation.

Antecedents of a God

Archeology suggests that, in spite of links with the Aryan Rudra, Shiva owes much in his complicated character to native Indian, non-Aryan, prototypes. Although difficulties, often insurmountable, obstruct the interpretation of undocumented material relics in terms of religious or metaphysical thought, it is permissible to recognize elements of a worship approximating to that of Shiva in the great prehistoric Indus civilization of north-western India. This civilization extended from the foot of the Himalayas at Rupar to the Arabian Sea west of Karachi at an approximate period of 2500 to 1700 BC, and there can be little doubt that its walled citadels such as those of Mohenjo-daro, Harappa and Kulibangan, represent the fortified sites proclaimed in the *Rig-Veda* to have been destroyed by the invading Aryans sometime within that millennium. At least there are no known rival claimants. Now amongst the steatite (soapstone) seals which are the most accomplished products of that civilization are three from Mohenjo-daro in Sind bearing the figure of a Shiva-like deity squatting on the ground or a low stool. One of these is particularly notable: it shows a somewhat sinister three-faced and horned god squatting in an attitude of yoga on a low throne; he is apparently ithyphallic, and his arms are covered with bangles. On either side of the god are four animals — elephant, tiger, rhinoceros and buffalo — and beneath the throne are two deer. It is generally accepted that the representation is that of Shiva, or a proto-Shiva, in the character of Pasupati, Lord of Beasts. And, since it is equally accepted that the Indus civilization is rooted in pre-Aryan India, it would appear necessary in this instance to reconcile this pre-Aryan 'Shiva' with the Aryan Rudra. The answer may well lie in the probability that the so-called 'Aryan invasion' was a fairly protracted penetration and that there was some sharing of ideas and beliefs.

Other seals from Mohenjo-daro show cult scenes, including suggestions of some sort of tree worship such as has survived into modern Hinduism. One seal shows a horned goddess sitting in a peepul, or sacred fig tree.

Josephine Powell

Stone bust of a priest-king or deity from Mohenjo-daro: the many gods of the Vedic Aryans bequeathed to later Hinduism a liberalness and tolerance which tend to be lacking from more sternly monotheistic faiths

Another seal shows a god or hero grappling with two tigers, a scene recalling the familiar representation of the Sumerian hero Gilgamesh between two lions.

In one way and another it is evident that the main outlines of Hindu belief took shape in the second millennium BC, and represent a fusion of Aryan, non-Aryan and perhaps Sumerian sources, with an appreciable admixture of more local elements. As time went by, and more settled social and economic conditions supervened, there was an increasing trend towards meditation and introspection, culminating in the great moral philosophies of Buddhism and Jainism during and after the 5th century BC (see BUDDHISM; JAINS). But alongside these philosophies, and rarely in active opposition to them, the traditional religious beliefs and practices continued as they continue today to provide the religious beliefs and usages which still form the broad basis of Indian life. (See also HINDUISM; SHIVA; VISHNU.)

MORTIMER WHEELER

FURTHER READING: G.W. Cox, *Mythology of the Aryan Nations*, 2 vols. (Kennikat, 1969, c1870); S. Tilcomb, *Aryan Sun Myths* (Longwood, 1979, c1889); Sir Mortimer Wheeler, *Early India and Pakistan* (Thames and Hudson, 1968 reprint).

INITIATION

The youth in a primitive society who submits to being severely stung by hornets, and the Western apprentice who accepts the bullying and ragging of his workmates are both activated by the same principle: the acceptance of an ordeal which must be undergone and surmounted before initiation into a new status

IN EVERY INITIATION ceremony there is some idea of a new birth as part of the process of assuming full status in the group. 'Except a man be born again' is the Christian phrasing for a process which in many ceremonies involves acting out a return to a symbolic womb. Part of the ritual of the Kunapipi, an Australian aboriginal group, involves the initiates being brought into the sacred ground 'to enter the Mother; they go into her uterus, the ring place, as happened in the beginning.' In acting out the ritual they are covered over with bark and hung from a pole. 'They are', as Mircea Eliade shows, 'in the womb, and they will emerge reborn — "their spirit comes out new".'

The theme of rebirth is paralleled by the equally important recurring theme of death. Both are closely linked structurally in the whole process of initiation. The new life cannot start until the old has been disposed of. Ritual death to the old life, the former sinful, corrupt condition, is expressed in the elaborate mythology surrounding most puberty rites. In the Congo on the Loango coast boys between ten and twelve years old have a ritual death in the village when they are given a potion to make them unconscious as a prelude. Now 'dead', they are taken into the jungle, circumcised, buried in the fetish house and painted white, a sign that they are ghosts of their former existence.

Rebirth may be similarly expressed by the infantile behaviour of the initiates when they return. They may appear helpless, like babies. The stay in the bush serves the important function of signifying the death of the previous relationship between a son and his mother. Initiation ceremonies serve several functions in relation to the social

Puberty rites, frequently involving circumcision of boys and artificially induced vaginal bleeding in girls, are an initiation into adulthood, connected with the religious and magical qualities associated with sex: puberty rites among Brazilian Indians

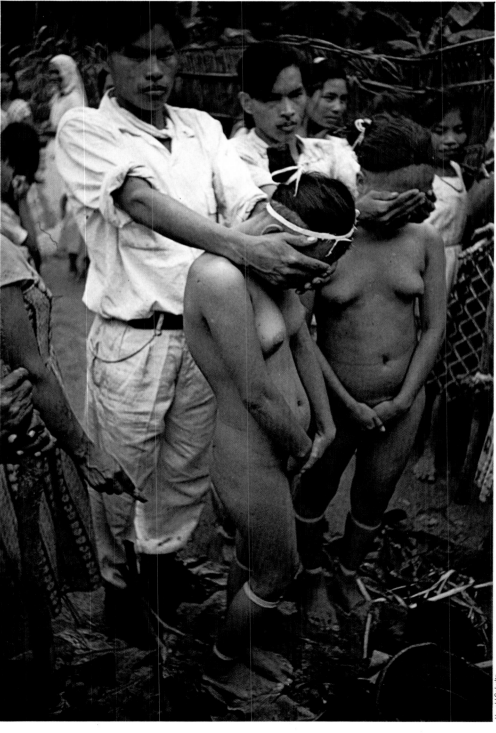

Harald Schultz

Trials of strength and endurance as tests of fitness to share the sacred membership with the ancestors or folk heroes, are common to all initiations

Camera Press

structure but they also emphasize the deeper belief system. The newly initiated have a special status because they have learned the mysteries, survived the ordeals, having escaped the belly of whale or serpent or whatever other experience may be central to the creation myth of the group.

Initiation into secret societies, shamanic or other groups of priests, witches or warriors, follows a similar pattern but with a more elaborate and distinctive indoctrination of the individual. In these ceremonies the demonstration of some magical, divine or shamanic power by the initiate is looked for as a sign that he has attained the appropriate characteristics of a god, animal or spirit. A transcendent existence, and the powers that go with it, replace the mere human

condition. In most hero legends the young warrior characteristically undergoes an experience of a sacred, mystical kind which gives him superhuman powers or magical elements which he can use in his ordeal. The tasks which are set to those who hope to win the hand of the beautiful princess in the classical fairy tales depend on more than normal attributes in the performer. The hero becomes seized with power, he becomes heated, baptized with fire. Eliade describes how in Germanic secret societies the young man became a berserker in a frenzy of fury. 'He became "heated" to an extreme degree, flooded by a mysterious, non-human and irresistible force.' The initiation of the Kwakiutl Indian warrior in British Columbia involves a similar frenzy of possession

Initiation marks a change of status, a break with the old life *Above* Africans perform their last warrior dances before becoming junior elders *Right* Apache maiden during initiation: she is coated with yellow pollen to ensure that she will be fertile

and heating and the same thing is recorded in the Irish hero legends of Cu Chulainn or the Greek and Indo-European initiations of cultural hero figures.

Rebirth Through Pain

Trials of strength and endurance, as tests of fitness to share the sacred membership with the ancestors or folk heroes, are common to all initiations. Formal learning and preparation for the new status in the

During the recent initiation of a new garage hand, he allowed himself to be tied up and petrol was sprinkled round him and set alight

'initiation school' is only part of the experience which is bound up with a complex of fear, awe and dread in face of the mysteries. The adult must be brave in the face of danger and must be steadfast in the face of pain. Consequently the novice is subjected to the fearful noise of the Melanesian bull-roarer – a wooden instrument which makes a booming sound – or to the beating with stinging nettles and the dropping of hornets on to their backs which the Naudi adolescents in East Africa experience.

The common experience of fear and pain provides an important social bond between the novices who have survived the experience. They are incorporated into a group distinguished sharply from outsiders who have not shared in the ordeal. By having passed through the sacred experience they have attained a new status prescribed by tradition. Their circumcision, the decoration of their skin by cuts, their ordeals in the initiation school, their skill as warriors, show that they are boys no longer but men ready to take a full part in the life of the community.

One Melanesian experience described by R. M. Berndt includes a progressive series of nose bleedings caused by slivers of bamboo which are covered with salt and then twirled in the nostrils. The tongue is also cut and the penis rubbed with rough, abrasive leaves. By the time he is 18 or 20 years old the young man is introduced to penis bleeding caused by progressively larger objects pushed into the urethra and twirled. Some of the puberty rites for girls include similar insertions into the vagina to cause bleeding. These rites demonstrate strength (if a man's penis is strong his arrows will be also) while blood has importance both as a symbolic representation of menstruation and of the religious and magical qualities associated with sexual elements.

Ritual Rapes and Panty Raids

The ritual rapes of Kikuyu warrior bands following circumcision have attracted a certain amount of notoriety, particularly when English women living in the Kenya highlands were the victims. The explanation for the ceremonial rape lies in the need of the young men to purify themselves after the initiation rites. This could be achieved by passing on the 'contagion' to a woman through intercourse before they could

return to the group to claim a wife of their own. Often a band of young men wandered the countryside far away from their homes until they found a woman who was of married status and a stranger to them.

Something very similar is to be found in some of the ceremonies and 'dares' demanded of newcomers to the armed forces and in particular those aspiring to membership of male fraternities in American colleges and universities. These may range from the 'panty raid' on the women students' residence (ritual rapes) to tasks requiring the initiates to collect some prized possession which signify their manliness and daring – bringing back G-strings from night clubs or placing chamber pots on Oxford spires. Various forms of the 'chicken' game, especially when played with cars or motor-cycles, are of the same order. Such activities may be part of the official conditions of membership of the group but often they represent an unofficial response by the existing members to the newcomer. Apart from tests of skill and daring, initiates are often subjected to debasing ceremonies of an equivalent kind. Initiates of one fraternity must wear an iron ball and chain padlocked to their ankles for a week, others must wear women's or children's clothing or have their hair cut in a special way. Another quite common practice involved an initiate being taken to a deserted spot often at a considerable distance and there left without clothing or money (or with a minimum of each) to see if he could get back.

Similar, less formal initiation rites are conducted in most social groupings to emphasize the common and shared trials through which members have passed and on which their solidarity is based. A typical newspaper report (*Daily Telegraph*), from the 1970s, describes the bullying of a 16-year-old garage hand on his first day at work. After a certain amount of general ragging of the 'new boy' he was tied up and petrol was sprinkled round him and set alight. In this case he was badly burned but it was noted in the court hearing that he had submitted willingly – recognizing that this kind of initiation ritual was a condition of his acceptance by his workmates.

Tests of endurance, strength, ridicule and fear are used in the more elaborate initiation 'schools' as a means of emphasizing and disciplining the novice as he learns the

cultic knowledge and mysteries of the group. An important feature of many initiation ceremonies, especially in the secret preparation period or 'school', involves the use of figurines symbolizing traditional magical or religious characters, ancestors, or elements in the total knowledge and moral structure of the society. These figurines are often carefully guarded by the members of a particular group and are not allowed to be seen by those who have not been initiated. They have spiritual significance and consequently are carefully guarded from enemies. The special rituals appropriate to each are similarly reserved for fear that the sacred objects might be angered or polluted by those who had no right to see them, or did not know 'how to behave' in their presence. The sacraments are similarly reserved in the Christian Church for those who have become full members.

Lessons in Sex

Initiation figurines are either kept as part of a store of sacred objects or are fashioned anew for each group of novices. Examples from East Africa include instructive, cautionary and punitive figures. They are all associated with songs, proverbs or riddles which the novice must learn. One example of a simple and obvious kind is the model of a hare used by the Sambaa as part of the rites for boys. The teaching that is depicted is that it is foolish to be quarrelsome and the associated words state that the hare is cleverer than most animals but he is never anxious to start a fight. A large majority of the figurines are used to convey lessons about sexual behaviour or morality and here again proverbs are taught to the initiates to define correct behaviour. A good example of such a riddle is shown in the female figurine used by the Zigua with a riddle which runs: 'There is only one person who laughs when she should mourn and who rejoices in her loss', to which the answer is 'A girl on her wedding night'. As well as being used in puberty ceremonies, these figurines are used in the entry rites to secret societies and associations. Clay or wooden figures are handled ritually and associated with a fixed form of words sung or recited. Again the objects depict familiar social roles, or common objects as well as highly stylized art with a very complex symbolism. The figures and the form of words are treated as sacred and are kept

The transition from youth to adulthood, acceptance into an order or into a trade, are important turning points in a person's life and are marked with appropriate ceremony *Right* Barmitzvah cakes are presented to Jewish children as part of the celebrations marking their coming-of-age *Centre* The candidate for admission to the Order of Freemasons undergoes an initiation ordeal *Below* A cooper apprentice is initiated by being rolled in a tar barrel

secret from those who are not initiated.

The initiation schools and the lengthy process of disciplined teaching of the lessons associated with the puberty rituals in tribal societies have inevitably been affected by social change. Often lack of time and the constraints of formal education or occupation have meant that both the ceremonies and the training period of the initiation must be curtailed. Where figurines are used the number may be limited or the verses only will be learned. These effects of social change only serve to emphasize the important and complex function served by the initiation of adolescents in tribal society. They ensured that each individual was fully educated in the central belief system, moral codes and normative standards of the society and was intellectually as well as emotionally prepared for an adult role in the community.

One particular set of initiation ceremonies involves the installation of new incumbents into various offices. Kings, chiefs, presidents, professors are all expected to observe formal ritual procedures and take part in ceremonies connected with their assumption of the prerogatives of office. Coronation ceremonies are an elaborate example of the combination of rituals designed to acknowledge formally and acclaim publicly and anoint the one chosen for the office. Part of the ceremony usually involves admission to a ritually appointed place or locus of office. The professor has no actual 'chair' but a bishop has a cathedral throne and knights of orders of chivalry are ceremonially led to their stalls in the chapel of their orders. Similarly with a mayor or president the office holder is sanctified with the symbolic elements of authority: orb and sceptre, crown and sword, seal or gavel. These objects signify that the incumbent has been properly chosen, indoctrinated and acquainted with the mysteries that surround the office. The laying on of hands, the anointment, represents the conferring of divine or magical power which alone sets the initiated incumbent of office 'apart'. Where the succession to office is hereditary, or where the successor is selected in childhood (as in the case of the Dalai Lama before the Chinese invasion of Tibet), the whole process of growing up forms an overall initiation which points toward the eventual attainment of office.

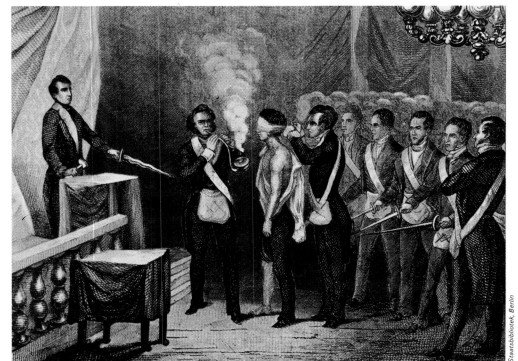

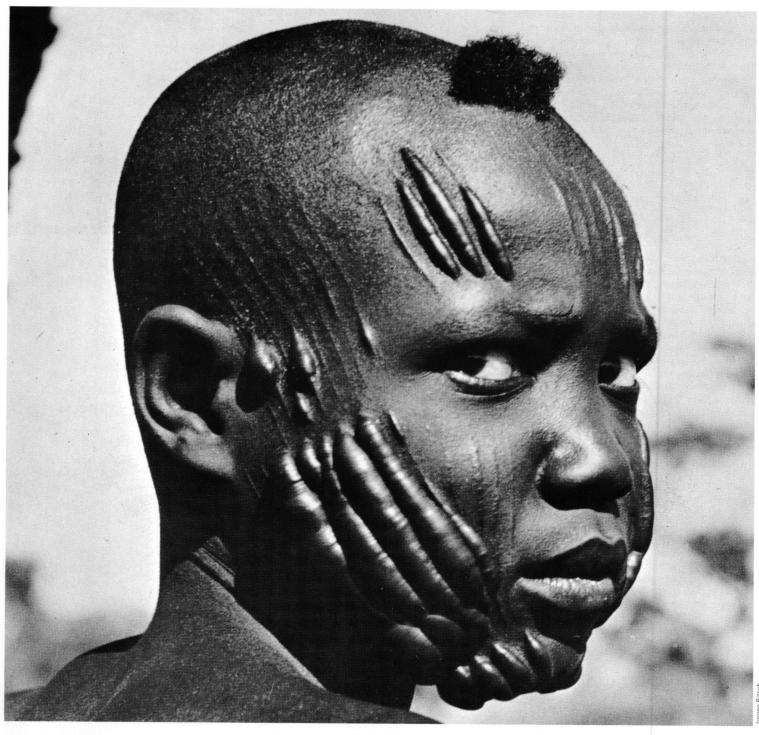

Jørgen Bitsch

Humiliation and Abuse

Much of the ritual surrounding the initiation of new holders of office shares the characteristics that have been noted in the rites surrounding puberty. The symbolic death of the old and rebirth to the new condition and status is represented in the divesting of original clothing, and the profane objects of life. The new ruler, as in the coronation ceremony of the British monarch, assumes a new royal robe as well as other symbols of office: orb or sceptre, crown and sword.

Some of the ceremonies are dignified and formal, enshrined with pomp and circumstance, but it is significant that even the most solemn occasions also have a festive and irreverent side in which 'the gods are mocked'.

The chancellors of Scottish universities, elected by the students, however honoured and dignified, endure a bombardment of flour, missiles and abuse as part of their inaugural ceremony, and it is customary for the professors at some American universities to be subjected to similar horseplay. These examples show clearly the conflicting and complementary elements of debasement and honouring that characterize the initiation process. Just as we have seen with puberty rites, the candidate must be 'cut down to size' and divested of his former status before he can assume the new. The experience of the army recruit is no different once he joins up. The admonition 'Get your hair cut — you're in the Army now' demonstrates the removal of the civilian status and

The common experience of fear and pain promotes a social bond, distinguishing the initiated from the outsiders: in Chad, cicatrization or the decoration of the skin by painful cuts, indicates the fully fledged member of the community

the assumption of the new status of 'soldier' with uniform, dress, style, regulations and equipment just as clearly.

Modern examples of initiation rituals abound and demonstrate many of the features already noted. In some cases the ceremonies are merely vestigial remnants of earlier, more elaborate and public rituals, involving the whole community. Infant baptism 'casts out the devil' and 'makes new' and the baptismal water is an

All religious groups, cults and societies develop a conscious boundary between those who have membership and those who do not

indication of the washing away of sin. Adult initiations in some churches often involve baptisms by total immersion and 'speaking in tongues', spiritual trance and 'possession' in the new member. The transcendental religious or magical recognition of the new member both fortifies the faith of the group and signifies that the initiation procedure was correctly performed.

The organization of fraternities and sororities probably has been most fully elaborated in the Western world in bodies such as the Masonic Order, Guilds, Knights, and more recently formed bodies, most of which claim ancient lineage such as the Orange Lodges, the Lions, Elks and many others. Freemasonry is defined in the ritual of symbolism associated with great religious orders and categories of progressive initiations in Ancient Egyptian, Hindu and Buddhist traditions. Similarities have been pointed out between the Eighteenth Degree of the Freemasons, 'Knight of the Pelican and Eagle and Sovereign Prince Rose Croix of Heredom' to which any Master Mason of one year's standing is eligible and the initiation rites of the Australian Bora aborigines. The symbolic teaching of this degree describes the passage of man through the valley of the shadow of death, accompanied by the Masonic virtues of Faith, Hope and Charity and his final acceptance into the abode of light, life and immortality.

Symbolic Social Statement

Just as in the initiation ceremonies of secret societies, in simpler societies membership represents a distinct and far-reaching social statement about the individual. Being adult or being a Mason or being a Baptist or a witch represent far more than the mere labels. They are involved statements about the whole society and the place and significance of different groups within the society; statements which have significance in all those aspects of the social structure in which particular kinds of belonging can be a means of articulating social relations. The questions of whom you may marry, where you can live or whom you may work with are not idle when belonging to the Roman Catholic Church or the Loyal Orange Order become the prime defining characteristics of life in Northern Ireland; or being a Jew or an Arab define sharply the

possible relationships in a situation of conflict in the Middle East. Where 'belonging' in this sense is open to the individual the significance of the transition from one condition to another is very apparent. Those who have 'passed' from Negro culture to white in the United States or those who have succeeded in the world of espionage, are acutely conscious of the dimensions and social significance of the new roles they have chosen to adopt. But even in these rather mundane examples the questions are not simply social in the sense of setting out rules of behaviour. They are symbolic, as all social statements are inevitably symbolic, because they are statements about man, the world, the cosmos and the possibilities of human existence, as well as statements about life and death. It is precisely in those areas where the maintenance of distinct boundaries is most important to the people in a particular society that one finds a particular emphasis on their maintenance and on the proper observation of the boundary-crossing rituals of initiation.

In some societies age distinctions may be pivotal, in most societies sex differences, and in many societies differences of race or ethnic origin or language may serve to demarcate structurally the bounds of social relationships. In many societies the division between male and female is sharply observed in territorial definitions of space in the settlement or living quarters. Male and female areas for eating, washing and defecation are reserved and this latter distinction can be seen also in contemporary Western societies. A good example is the division by sex of public lavatories and the recognition that for very small children the rigid differences generally observed are considered unimportant. In the Southern United States the problem was multiplied in some areas by the belief that it is necessary to provide facilities for white and coloured as well as for male and female: four separate spaces to fulfil one natural function. The point of importance is that these particular divisions are pivotal for the world view of these particular societies. It is not surprising that one finds fraternities of men or sororities of woman's groups of one kind or another which as distinct sex groups serve the important function of emphasizing and symbolizing these distinctions which their own initiation into the particular group

both recognizes and supports.

In her interesting book *Purity and Danger* Mary Douglas shows how important is the act of separation between sacred things, places and persons from the profane or polluting world. All religious groups, cults and societies develop a conscious boundary between those who have membership and those who do not. Fear of malevolent or benevolent spirits or beings often characterizes the concern with which it is felt necessary to observe the proper 'passage' ceremonies which connect these two states. Quite apart from the examples of initiation that we have already discussed, birth and death are surrounded by similar ritual observations designed to placate various forces which may have an influence on the destiny of the child or the dead person. Even in tribal societies no necessary claim will be made for these rites as essential and empirical measures which will bring the desired result. But man is not only a practical being and even in contemporary societies initiation ceremonies convey the mixture of beliefs at a variety of levels − mystical, magical, metaphysical and religious, as well as scientific − which can co-exist without difficulty in the same individual and group.

Initiation rituals surrounding death are often elaborate, both at the level of preparation and in the way in which the dead are treated. There are numerous examples in the rites of burial of the placing of money in the hand or mouth to secure the passage of the dead across the Styx which illustrate that the characteristics of initiation are found here as well. Burial in the foetal position also symbolizes the recognition of rebirth following death.

Death and rebirth indeed characterize the features of all initiation rites. We have seen this illustrated in boys' puberty initiation schools and it is found equally in the often less developed puberty rites for girls. Girls' ceremonies tend to involve a less intentional process than those of boys which represent a more deliberate introduction to a world of spirit and culture. For girls, as Eliade points out 'initiation involves a series of revelations concerning the secret meaning of a phenomenon that is apparently natural − the visible sign of their sexual maturity.'

This does not preclude considerable emphasis being given to some female puberty rites in certain societies. The Dyaks

Journeys through the Dark

The soul (at the point of death) has the same experience as those who are being initiated into great mysteries . . . At first one wanders and wearily hurries to and fro, and journeys with suspicion through the dark as one uninitiated: then come all the terrors before the final initiation, shuddering, trembling, sweating, amazement: then one is struck with a marvellous light, one is received into pure regions and meadows, with voices and dances and the majesty of holy sounds and shapes: among these he who has fulfilled initiation wanders free, and released and bearing his crown joins in the divine communion, and consorts with pure and holy men, beholding those who live here uninitiated, an uncleansed horde, trodden under foot of him and huddled together in mud and fog, abiding their miseries through fear of death and mistrust of the blessings there.

Attributed to Plutarch
(trans George E. Mylonas)

Initiation into the mysteries of Isis:
. . . I will record as much as I may lawfully record for the uninitiated, but only on condition that you believe it. I approached the very gates of death and set one foot on Proserpine's threshold, yet was permitted to return, rapt through all the elements. At midnight I saw the sun shining as if it were noon: I entered the presence of the gods of the underworld and the gods of the upper-world, stood near and worshipped them.

Well, now you have heard what happened but I fear you are still none the wiser.

Apuleius *The Golden Ass*
(trans Robert Graves)

exemplify this in the separation and isolation of girls for a whole year in a white cabin, dressed in white and only eating white foods. This separation — the wilderness experience — recognizes the fact that during this period the initiate is 'nothing', neither man nor woman, asexual. Together with other separations — Christ's 'forty days in the wilderness' — it is a condition of the attainment of spirituality. The emerging initiate is reborn in a symbolic and spiritual way. The return announces that the mystery of rebirth has been accomplished. Eliade gives the example of the Kavirondo Bantu to illustrate a characteristic imagery found also in Brahmanic initiation in India and the recognition of the double character of birth in the egg from which the chick emerges when the shell is broken. It is said of the Kavirondo initiates when they complete their ritual: 'The white chick is now creeping out of the egg, we are like newly fired pots.'

One final example will serve to illustrate something of the elaborate character of initiation mythology. An ascetic period of isolation is characteristic of many North American Indian initiations. The novice leaves the community in order to obtain those dreams and visions which will identify for him a particular spirit with which he will then continue to be associated. He will fast and exhaust himself until the spirit appears to him, usually in animal form. Once he has achieved this personal sacred experience he can return to the tribe, having died to be reborn with his guiding spirit.

The Dancing Societies of the Kwakiutl

A squire keeps an all-night vigil in church to dedicate himself before receiving his arms and being initiated into knighthood

Tate Gallery

Indians studied by F. Boas show a more elaborate version of the same isolating and sacralizing experience. The ritual commences with the initiate falling into a trance to signify his death to the profane world. He is then carried off to be initiated by the spirits. He may be taken to a cave or to a special hut in which the spirit lives. An extreme example is that of the Cannibal Society where as part of the initiation the candidate is served by a woman while he is secluded in the forest. He is identified with the god and demonstrates this by swallowing strips of a corpse which she prepares for him. His cannibalism is a reversal of the horror of the Kwakiutl for human flesh. To overcome this revulsion he must indeed be divine and the similar acts of frenzy in which he engages on his return serve also to demonstrate this possession by the god.

In the final ceremony he acts like a beast of prey attacking all he can reach, biting their arms. He is almost impossible to restrain but finally is subdued after the woman who served him in the wilderness dances naked before him with a corpse in her arms. His frenzy is finally subdued by repeated immersions in salt water and his new personality and identity is achieved.

J. A. JACKSON

FURTHER READING: M. Eliade, *Rites and Symbols of Initiation* (Peter Smith); J. Henderson, *Thresholds of Initiation* (Wesleyan Univ. Press, 1967); G. Herdt, ed., *Rituals of Manhood* (University of California Press, 1982); A. van Gennep, *Rites of Passage* (University of Chicago Press).

Inquisition

Or Holy Office, Roman Catholic tribunal instituted by Pope Gregory IX in 1233 to suppress heresy; in 1320 the Inquisition was ordered to deal with witchcraft, if connected with heresy; the Spanish Inquisition, which was particularly notorious, was established in 1479 by Ferdinand and Isabella with papal consent the Inquisition's cruelties made it the object of violent Protestant hatred, though Protestants themselves were not backward in persecuting witches and heretics.
See HERESY.

Until the 17th century it was generally believed insects were spontaneously generated; beetles, for example, were said to arise from putrefying flesh and from dung. In some parts of the world, butterflies were believed to be the wandering souls of men, and they have also been regarded as disease-carrying spirits; fire-flies were said to be the eyes of gods who had been killed in battle

INSECTS

THE INSECT WORLD comprises an enormous group of organisms, many with very different characteristics. There are, for example, over 250,000 species of beetle, some of which are microscopic, while others are bigger than the smallest birds; their coloration varies from dull and inconspicuous to brilliantly iridescent. The characteristics of insects have become associated with mythology and folklore and have given rise to remarkable beliefs and superstitions.

Humanity has been interested in insects not just out of curiosity, but because some have forced their attentions unpleasantly upon it as parasites, pests and destroyers of crops. The locust, the tsetse fly, the plague-disseminating flea and the mosquito have profoundly affected human history and economy. Only the bee and the silkworm have become 'domesticated'. The mythology of insects has been mainly concerned with their origins, transmigrations, oracular significance, explaining their characteristics, devices for expelling noxious species and the use of insects in magic and medicine.

From ancient times ants have been mentioned in proverbs and fables as paragons of industry. In Thessaly their digging activities caused them to be associated with agriculture through the myth of the nymph Myrmex, who falsely claimed to have invented the plough. Athene, who had actually done so, transformed her into an ant. There was also an ancient belief that the ants of Ethiopia and India dug for gold. An ancient German belief was that they could be driven away by ringing bells. In England it was said to be a sign of rain when ants were seen carrying their pupae, but in Germany this was interpreted as indicating fine weather. In ancient and medieval times, treatment in various ways with ants was believed to have medical value, especially for people suffering from fever.

Thunder Chrysalis

It was a common belief, mentioned by Aristotle and persisting well into the 17th century, that insects were spontaneously generated. Beetles were said to arise from putrefying flesh and from dung, where they were often seen to gather. The ancient Egyptian belief in the scarab (see SCARAB) as a symbol of life beyond the grave appears to have arisen from observations of beetles emerging from the ball of dung in which some beetles place their eggs. The ladybird is called by names which associate the insect with Our Lady, such as *Marienkäfer* (Mary beetle) in Germany. It is still the custom in Britain for children to place a ladybird on a finger and say to it:

Ladybird, ladybird, fly away home,
Your house is on fire and your children
   are gone.

In some areas it was thought that the direction in which a ladybird flew indicated where a girl's 'true love' could be expected; in Sussex, when a ladybird alighted on someone, its spots were counted to ascertain how many happy months to expect. In the Hebrides its five spots are said to represent the wounds of Christ, although the number of spots varies with different species.

Beliefs concerning the cockchafer have some similarities to ladybird beliefs and seem transferrable from one to the other. The cockchafer is regarded with favour in France and Germany; in Bavaria it was considered a good omen if a beetle settled on a person's hand; in France it was often carried in processions. Like the ladybird, it appears to have been anciently associated with spring and fertility.

The stag-beetle was connected with thunder and in Germany was called *Donner-puppe* (thunder chrysalis), perhaps

Below left A dragon-fly with its prey. Perhaps unsurprisingly, considering their great size and dramatic colouring, dragon-flies had an alarming reputation, being said to sew up the mouths of cursing men and scolding women *Below* Butterflies have enjoyed a rather ambivalent fame; at times they have been regarded as the souls of the dead, and so worthy of respect; at other times, they were thought to be witches or the souls of witches

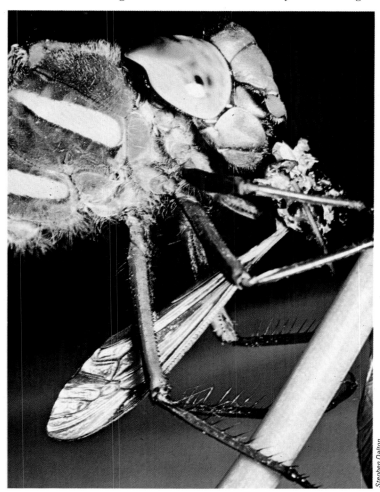

Stephen Dalton

W. Zepf, Bregenz

through its association with the oak tree, the tree most often struck in a thunderstorm. In Scotland blindfolded boys struck at it, probably on the assumption that a black-horned creature must be devilish. According to a Hebridean legend, the burying-beetle betrayed Christ during the Flight of the Holy Family into Egypt by telling his pursuers that he passed by the previous evening, but the dung-beetle contradicted it, saying that he went by a year ago. So boys kill the burying-beetle but merely turn the dung-beetle on its back, because it lied in a good cause.

The Irish traditionally say that the devil's coach-horse beetle is putting a curse on you when it raises its tail, and there are still people in Britain who are said to be upset by the ominous tapping of the death-watch beetle – and not just because such beetles devour wood with an appalling speed.

In Africa, Baronga women threw noxious beetles into a lake, screeching the obscenities which were characteristic of rain-making ceremonies. Arabs used to employ sympathetic magic to recall a runaway slave, tethering a beetle of the sex of the fugitive by a thread to a nail, in the belief that, as it crawled in diminishing circles,

Below Stag beetle: because these creatures appeared to have black horns they were sometimes thought to be connected with the Devil *Below right* The dung-beetle or scarab was a symbol of life to the ancient Egyptians, probably because it was seen to emerge from dung: beetle in a ball of dung

the slave would be drawn back. In East Anglia at the end of the 19th century a beetle was suspended by a thread round a child's neck to cure whooping cough, on the assumption that, as it decayed, the ailment would disappear.

It has been widely believed that butterflies, being ethereal creatures, were the actual souls of individuals. A myth of the Pima Indians of North America relates that the Creator flew around as a butterfly to find a place for man. On Greek vases the soul was at first represented as a tiny winged human being; later artists depicted it as a butterfly. Among some tribesmen of north-eastern Asia, it was thought that the soul-substance could leave the body during life, so causing illness or unconsciousness. A grey butterfly or moth was tied in a cloth round a patient's neck to restore him.

There was a Gaelic (Scots-Irish) tradition that a butterfly flitting over a corpse was its soul; in Ireland such an event indicated its everlasting bliss. In 1810 an Irish girl was reprimanded for chasing a butterfly because it might be the spirit of her grandmother. According to a Gaelic folktale, a soul in the guise of a butterfly went wandering and was about to enter a sleeping man when it was killed. In Calabria in southern Italy, a white butterfly fluttering around a cradle was called the baby's spirit, while in East Anglia to see a white butterfly signified that a baby had died.

According to an Australian tale, an aborigine who left his starving son in a shelter of bark and branches while he hunted for

food was reassured on finding the larva of a case moth (a species which surrounds itself with a case of bark) clinging to a tree. The boy had evidently been changed into this insect. In the Solomon Islands a man could choose the creature of his reincarnation and often selected a butterfly. In China and Japan this insect has propitious symbolism. One Japanese *Noh* play concerns a human soul transformed into a butterfly.

Perhaps the widespread association of butterflies with the disembodied soul has given them a sinister reputation in some areas and in particular circumstances. From Scotland to the Balkans, they were sometimes thought of as witches or as the souls of witches. Rumanians said that naughty children became butterflies and that these should therefore be killed. Butterflies have also been believed to be disease-carrying spirits. In some English counties it was the custom to kill the first butterfly seen and in Westphalia children knocked at doors on St Peter's Day, 22 February, bidding the butterflies go away. The householders themselves might go through the rooms to expel the insects by this sort of ritual which, if omitted, could entail misfortune such as the multiplication of vermin or outbreaks of cattle disease.

According to their numbers or their hue, butterflies could have different significance. In Cambridgeshire to see three butterflies was lucky, while in other counties this could mean misfortune. In the North of England red butterflies were often killed. A dark butterfly forecast illness in Bulgaria, a white

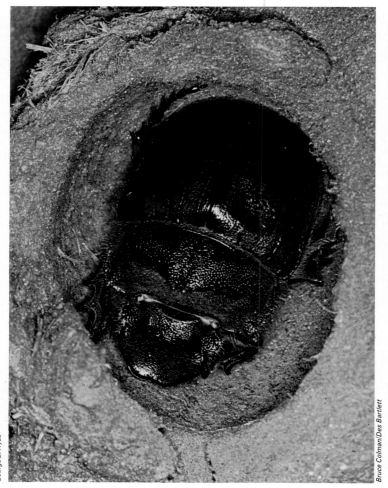

George E. Hyde

Bruce Colman/Des Bartlett

one in Ruthenia in the Russian Ukraine. The death's-head hawk moth, because of the similarity of its thorax markings to a skull and its ability to squeak, was also regarded as sinister.

The wormlike appearance of the caterpillar, the larva of the butterfly or moth, is probably the reason for the widespread superstition that it was made by the Devil, or by witches with the help of the Devil. In Switzerland there is a belief that tree spirits are responsible for caterpillars, and that they send them to creep into a man's brain and drive him mad. In Rumania they are said to have originated in the Devil's tears, and the Bantu of South Africa believe that the souls of the dead take the form of caterpillars.

The insect has some virtues in folk medicine; according to English lore carrying a caterpillar around will ward off fevers, and in ancient times the bite of a poisonous snake was rubbed with a mixture made from a cabbage caterpillar and oil.

The Devil's Darning Needle

Cicadas and crickets early attracted special attention because of their chirping or stridulating calls. Alike in ancient Greece and in Shantung in China they were believed to live on wind and dew. According to Plato's account of the story told by Socrates the Muses live again in these insect songsters. Early Chinese authors wrote enthusiastically about them and the Chinese still keep them in small cages. Aesop's fable of the Ant and the Cicada (or Grasshopper) is very ancient. In Japan the cricket is regarded as giving warning of the approach of winter.

In Europe if crickets forsake a house it may be regarded as an evil omen but occasionally one of these insects chirping in a house where they have not been heard before is considered to be an omen of death. These are instances of the tendency for some unusual occurrence to be considered to foretell a calamity.

Magical ceremonies were widely conducted with the aim of destroying or expelling locusts and grasshoppers. An Arab writer mentions a golden locust set up to guard a town from infestation and it is reported that Naples was rid of grasshoppers by means of bronze or copper images of them. In Japan straw images of larvae of a certain species of insect which was damaging the rice fields were paraded around the infested area by villagers bearing torches, ringing bells and beating drums. The images were then thrown into the river or burned. In the Argentine tin cans were beaten to frighten away grasshoppers, as in Europe beekeepers made a similar din to encourage swarming bees to settle.

When locusts or beetles were destroying the crops in Albania the women would go in funeral procession to a stream and drown a few in the hope of eliminating them all. In Mirzapur, India, an insect was caught, its head marked with a red spot and dismissed with a *salaam* on the assumption that it would lead its fellows away. Among the Wajagga in Africa a locust's legs were tied together and it was let fly in the belief that the horde would accompany it beyond the boundaries of the tribe. In 1590 a plague of locusts in Ethiopia was excommunicated and confidence in the effectiveness of the procedure was reinforced by the outbreak of a storm which destroyed them.

The long, slender bodies of dragon-flies have given rise to their being called 'Devil's darning needles'. They have been viewed with suspicion partly because their claspers at the end of the abdomen have been supposed to be stings. It was said that they would sew up the mouths of scolding women and cursing men. In Cambridgeshire an elderly man said recently that it was lucky to see a dragon-fly skimming over a pool. He would then cross his fingers and wish, as he had been told to do during his boyhood. In Japan, where the dragon-fly is an emblem of summer it is regarded as a lucky talisman. It symbolizes courage and the return of the dead to their homes on earth. On the South China coast when dragon-flies appear in numbers they are believed to presage a typhoon.

Fleas were said to be generated from dust, filth or horse urine, whereas lice were believed to appear spontaneously from greasy cloth or 'from the very flesh of man'. In East Anglia infestations of lice were attributed to the malevolence of witches. The remedy was to stick pins into a piece of flannel which had been next to the patient's skin and then burn it at midnight. In Ireland it was thought that strewing foxgloves around would cause fleas to leave and in England until the end of the last century a housewife would rise early on 1 March to brush around the lintel and hinges of the door; it was assumed that the fleas would know better than to enter or to remain where the lady of the house was so diligent.

It was also believed that one could rid one's person of fleas by leaping across the Midsummer bonfire. The 1st century writer Pliny advised those who would banish fleas to scrape up earth from beneath the right foot when the cuckoo was first heard. The ancient Egyptians smeared a slave with asses' milk to attract the insects to him and American farmers brought a sheep or goat into the house for the same purpose. The story of the fox which rids itself of its fleas by wading deep into a pond carrying moss in its mouth, until all the fleas retreat into the moss, and then lets it float away, is generally held to be a fable.

Children's Night-Lights

Luminous insects, such as the fire-fly and glow-worm, are so unusual that myths were devised to explain their origin. Among the tribespeople of Orissa in India a number of such myths are current. It is said that after a battle among the gods many were killed but their eyes remained and became fireflies. Another story relates that sparks from a fire kindled to drive off mosquitoes were transformed magically into these insects. Among these tribes, bats were reputed to carry fire-flies to their homes because their children could not endure any other light.

In the island of Nias in Indonesia the sorcerer treated a sick person as if his soul had escaped and had become, or taken refuge in, a lantern-fly, so he would catch one in a cloth and place it on the patient's forehead. In parts of China a luminous insect whose larvae live in decaying vegetable matter appears in swarms in hot weather about the time when the summer festival of the dead was celebrated. At such times illness tends to be commoner than usual and the insects were held responsible. The 'vital spirits' of corpses were believed to give rise to these flies which were said to have appeared as five girls in embroidered garments representing north, south, east and west and the centre of the universe. If these insects entered a house some calamity might be expected. Burning incense was used to expel them.

In England it was said that glow-worms were born of putrefaction. Possibly this belief was encouraged by observations of luminous fungi. During the Second World War the

---

Ants on the March

The 'vagrant' calls the ants to arms:
To arms! To arms! The road between the blades of grass
Is threatened. Do you hear? The cranny from blade to blade,
A span of earth from grass to grass, your sacred rights,
The greatest interests of the state, the greatest problem in the world,
All is at stake. Ants, to arms!
How could you live, if another possessed
The world between two husks. If another carried
Ant-baggage into a strange ant-heap.
A hundred thousand lives for these two blades of grass

Are too few. I was in the war, oh,
That's a handiwork for insects, indeed. Dig trenches,
Root yourself in clay, hurrah, an attack in extended order,
At the double over stacks of corpses, fix bayonets,
Fifty thousand dead, to capture
Twenty yards of latrines. Hurrah, to arms!
The interest of the whole is concerned, the heritage of your history is concerned,
Nay more, the freedom of your native land, nay more, world-power,
Nay more, two blades of grass. Such a mighty cause
Can be settled only by the dead. To arms! To arms!

CHRYSALIS   The whole earth is quivering
Something mighty it is delivering,
I am being born.

To the beating of a drum the troops of the ants advance with rifles, bayonets, and machine-guns, with metal helmets on their heads, and line up in ranks . . .

VAGRANT (*Passing along the ranks.*)
See what good training does. Attention! Sound the roll-call.
Soldiers, your country is sending you to war,
That you may fall. Two blades of grass
Are watching you.
Josef and Karel Capek, *The Life of the Insects*

Insects

In Rumania the caterpillar is thought to have originated in the Devil's tears, and in Switzerland there is a superstition that they creep into men's brains and drive them mad: the caterpillar in Lewis Carroll's *Alice in Wonderland* sits on a magic mushroom: illustration to *Alice in Wonderland*

floor of a London anti-aircraft site was thought to be covered with glow-worms but in the morning they were found to be fragments of decayed wood infected with a fungus.

The fly had a place in early forms of worship according to Pliny, Pausanius the Greek traveller and geographer, and Aelian the Roman teacher and writer. A Jewish legend relates that Elisha was recognized as a prophet because no fly approached his place at table. Among the Greeks an ox sacrifice took place annually at the temple of Zeus at Actium to honour him as an averter of flies. Apollonius of Tyana is said to have freed Constantinople from flies by setting up a bronze fly. Hera is reputed to have set a gad-fly to chase Io because of her amorous relations with Zeus and in Norse mythology Loki transformed himself into a fly to torment his enemies.

In the folktale motif of 'hiding from the Devil' the hero conceals himself first in a raven's egg, then in a fish and finally in an insect. There are affinities with the Irish myth in which Etain is transformed into a fly. Among Christians, flies were regarded as having devilish affinities but the legend of St Colman mentions a kindly fly which marked his place in a book when he went to take part in services.

In northern tundra regions mosquitoes and midges may occur in such numbers as to make life difficult. Throughout much of northern Asia and in Mongolia a tale, known in a number of variants, explains how these insects originated. The Ostyaks of western Siberia say that a cannibal demon woman in the far north created them. According to other versions a hero, sometimes said to have been born of a virgin, attacked a man-devouring monster and slew him. From his decaying carcass came clouds of mosquitoes to plague mankind. A different version tells of the monster being reborn again and again until his carcass was burnt; then the mosquitoes appeared from the ashes.

E. A. ARMSTRONG

John Webb/National Gallery

Inspiration

Breathing in: in Genesis God breathed into Adam to bring him to life: poets, prophets, oracles, diviners, medicine-men and shamans are frequently believed to be inspired by the presence of a god or spirit in them which enables them to discern truth: in Christian theology inspiration results from the direct action of the Holy Spirit: sacred scriptures are often believed to be divinely inspired and the Vatican Council of 1869–70 confirmed the old doctrine that the Old and New Testaments 'have God as their author'.

INTERROGATION OF THE DEAD

IN ISLAMIC TEACHING the interrogation of the dead begins when the burial is complete and the mourners have retired. Tradition describes this in detail, but it is not clearly spoken of in the Koran.

It is commonly said that two angels, Munkar and Nakeer, come to examine the dead. They make the dead person sit up, and question him. The righteous replies that his Lord is God, that Islam is his religion, that Mohammed is God's messenger, and that he has learned this from reading God's book and believing in it. A voice then cries from heaven that he has spoken the truth, that a bed and clothing from paradise are to be provided for him, and that a door is to be opened towards paradise. This is done, he is refreshed by the air and perfume, and abundant space is made for him.

The infidel is made to sit up and is asked the same questions, to which he replies that he does not know. A voice from heaven cries that he has lied, that a bed and clothing from hell are to be provided for him, and that a door is to be opened towards hell. Some of its heat and pestilential wind come to him, the grave closes in on him and crushes his ribs. He will remain there suffering severe punishment until the resurrection.

The Koran speaks clearly of a final judgement in which man has little chance to defend himself, for everything is recorded and so is a foregone conclusion; but sura (chapter) 16.112 mentions man's attempt to defend himself. Judgement takes place on the day of resurrection. There are vivid accounts of the terrors of the last day, when mankind will be raised up and stand before God to receive justice.

The Koran speaks of the books, or scrolls, to be produced containing the record of everyone's deeds. The righteous will receive their books in the right hand and the unbelievers will receive theirs in the left. This is followed by the reward of the Garden (paradise), or the punishment of hell. The evidence of the books makes interrogation unnecessary: 'When the scrolls shall be unrolled . . . then shall a soul know what it has produced.'

There is also reference to the balances. Several passages speak of those whose balances are heavy prospering and of those whose balances are light losing their souls. It is commonly held that the deeds are weighed, the good and the bad being in opposite scales, and men being judged according to which is heavier. On the day of resurrection the balances will be just, and no one will be wronged.

Tradition speaks of the *Sirat* (literally a road), which is a bridge over hell, 'finer than a hair and sharper than a sword', which all must attempt to cross. Believers will keep their footing, but unbelievers will slip and fall into hell.

The Koran does not speak of such a bridge, but attempts have been made to

According to Islamic tradition, after they have died believers successfully cross a bridge over hell, but unbelievers slip and fall: Indian miniature, c 1700, showing two of the dead crossing the bridge; below them unbelievers plunge into hell

show that it does. 'Not one of you but shall go down to it' (sura 19.72) does not really bear such an interpretation, for it is obviously addressed to the Meccans who rejected Mohammed's teaching about resurrection. The following verse says, 'Then we shall deliver those who have shown piety and leave the wrong-doers kneeling there.' It is evident that this verse refers to hell and not to a bridge over it.

Al-Ghazali, the famous theologian and mystic quotes sura 3.23 regarding the wicked, 'Guide them to a road to hell and stop them for they shall be questioned.' The word sirat is here used for 'road', but there is no indication that it is a bridge over hell. The wicked, although they are to be interrogated, are to be led on the way to hell before the interrogation seems to take place. It is striking that from a comparatively early period statements of belief include belief in this bridge.
(See also ISLAM.)

JAMES ROBSON

FURTHER READING: T. P. Hughes, *A Dictionary of Islam* (Gordon Press, 1980); A. S. Tritton, *Islam, Beliefs and Practices* (Hyperion Press, 1981).

INUIT

Until very recently, Westerners used to call the peoples of polar North America 'Eskimo', but that word is a form of insult, applied to them by a nearby tribal group, the Wabanaki, who liked to put down their neighbours by calling them eskimantsik, *'eaters of raw flesh'. Today Westerners do not call these people Eskimos but employ the name they have always used for themselves:* Inuit, *'human being'.*

PRIMARILY A COASTAL PEOPLE, the Inuit occupy an area extending from Greenland and Labrador in the east to the Bering Sea in the west; some groups live on the Siberian shore of the Bering Straits. In 1979 their numbers were estimated at around 92,000, of whom approximately half are to be found in Greenland, with the rest being fairly evenly divided between Canada and Alaska. Thanks to improved diet, hygiene and medical care, their population is now increasing, though only slowly. Speculation over their origins remains inconclusive; they have obvious affinities with the Mongoloid peoples of Asia, but culturally and linguistically they are a race apart.

Their dialects are variants of one distinctive, highly inflected tongue, which has nothing in common with any of the other archaic languages of the American continent. Until relatively recently, the Inuit have had little cultural contact with other peoples: only in Alaska (and to a lesser extent in Greenland) is there evidence of this. However, it has been pointed out that the Inuit culture is part of the great polar culture circle, stretching around the rest of northern Eurasia. The Inuit have been divided into about a dozen major groups, but resemblances between the groups are so well marked that there is every justification for speaking of Inuit culture and religion as a whole.

The first known Europeans to make the acquaintance of the Inuit were Eric the Red's Norsemen in the late 10th century. But it was not until the start of the Christian missionary activity in Greenland in the 18th century that their religious beliefs really came to the attention of the West, as the Danes renewed their long-forgotten interest in Greenland. Since then, prolonged contact with Westerners – especially with missionaries, varied government

The Inuit believed they had to placate gods and spirits if they were to find sufficient game when hunting in the harsh climate of the Arctic
Left Lithograph of a sea goddess by the Inuit artist Paulassie: sea spirits in particular are shown great respect because they control the main supply of food *Right* Unusual two-sided carving of spirits from Cape Dorset

NFB-Chris Lund

officials and traders – has had an almost revolutionary effect on Inuit culture. Many local ways have disappeared before they could be properly studied and recorded by outsiders. In most places all of their traditional beliefs and customs are gradually being submerged and generally forgotten.

Many Inuit now practise some form of Christianity, and it is uncertain to what extent the old religious beliefs and procedures can still really be called parts of a living culture and outlook to the majority, although a recent revival of traditional ways has somewhat reversed this situation. However, in this article we shall be concerned with Inuit religion as it was (as far we can tell) before the coming of Christianity and other Western ways. Although most of the beliefs and practices described here have vanished, the article is still written in the present tense, as if they had survived.

Ungentle Spirits
The traditional religion of the Inuit has, to a considerable extent, been shaped by the often extreme conditions of their environment, where death can come quickly to anyone who makes a mistake. Inuit have to contend with a variety of seemingly capricious, even malevolent, natural forces. They have to know how to counter, and control as far as they can, these forces if they are to survive and perhaps even to prosper.

The first need, if life is to be sustained, is food. The Inuit are a hunting or fishing people, according to locality and season, and one of the few gifts which the multitudinous denizens of the spirit world may give is plentiful game.

The spirits may provide game – but then again, they may not. Why, a hunter was asked, were there no bears in a certain place at a certain time? 'No bears have come,' he answered, 'because there is no ice, and there is no ice because there is too much wind, and there is too much wind because we mortals have offended the powers.' His reply combines the weather-lore of the experienced hunter and the awareness – even the resignation – of a man who knows that he has to contend with great powers.

The supply of food is ultimately controlled by the spirits, and, should they be offended in any way, they will withhold the bear, the seal, the whale and the caribou, until re-

compense is made. In practical terms, this means the observance of a variety of taboos.

It has been pointed out that the supernatural world of the Inuit is strangely timeless and static. Unlike many 'tribal' peoples, the Inuit seem to have little conception of a past – at least not of an ideal past. Everything is attuned to the present moment. 'Everything has always been as it is now.' Significantly, Inuit mythology is virtually without creation myths, and those that exist, in Alaska, have almost certainly been derived from the North-Western Indians.

Nor is there any reasoned account of the creation of man, save as a very incidental byproduct of the Sedna myth, which speaks of Inuit, other human beings and beasts as having sprung from the union of a goddess and a dog-man. The Inuit, it seems, have always been very much as they are today; so, too, have their gods.

It is tempting – at least for Western onlookers – to speak of the Inuit deities as a hierarchy; tempting, but unjustified, since the Inuit themselves certainly do not think of them as such. The Inuit are animists, and regard the whole world as the abode of spirits, with every natural object inhabited by some spirit. Over and above these are the animal spirits of the air and sea spirits, and other classes of spirits which do not fit neatly into any of these categories. The hierarchical aspect, to the Western theorist, emerges from the fact that the Inuit conceive of a Supreme Being, Sila (Silap Inua), who has all the characteristics of a High God (see HIGH GODS).

Miniature Spiritual Doubles
The Inuit word for 'spirit' is *inua*, which is the third person possessive of *inuk*, 'man', and thus means 'its man or woman' or 'his or her man or woman'. The inua is in effect a miniature double of the human being, animal, or object in which it lives: this is, of course, one of the basic ideas on which practically all animistic belief the world over rests. Silap Inua is the inua of the air, who may be male or female, who lives in, or may be identified with, the sky, and accordingly controls atmospheric phenomena.

To the polar Inuit 'Sila' is a synonym for 'weather', 'the universe' or 'the whole', but it is not normally the recipient of worship, nor the subject of a developed mythology. Sila is the only 'genuine' Supreme Being in Inuit

religion, although other deities can fulfill something of the same function.

Second in the rank of deities is the moon spirit (with various names, of which one is Tarquiup Inua), who controls all land animals and all fertility, human as well as animal, and as such is of incomparably greater practical importance than Sila. A widespread myth tells how the moon and sun were once a brother and sister who lived on earth. The two committed incest; although the girl did not at first know this, when she found out, she fled from her brother into the heavens. He pursued her, and his pursuit is continued for all eternity. A Greenland variation tells how the moon and his sister the sun live in a double house with a single entrance.

Not only must the moon spirit be constantly propitiated if he is to grant success in hunting, but, since he is the bestower of fertility, he can be entreated on behalf of barren women. It is believed in some areas that the shaman or medicine man can fly to the moon to obtain children for childless women, and may have intercourse with the woman in question as a further measure. The sun, as the moon's sister, is of comparatively little cultic importance.

Mutilated Goddess
Among Inuits who rely on sea hunting, the greatest of the spirits is Sedna (also called Nuliajuk, Nerrivik, Arnquagssaq) who 'owns' the seals, whales, walruses and all other sea creatures, and is worshipped (and feared) in Greenland and in the central areas of northern Canada.

The most elaborate Inuit myth tells how a girl named Avilayoq married a dog, and brought forth offspring – Inuit, white men and other creatures. The children made so much noise that the couple moved to an island, from which the dog husband had to be sent to the girl's father for food. This was put in a pair of boots hung round the dog's neck. One day, while he was away, a man came and took the girl away, revealing himself later as a petrel. Her father went to look for her, and took her away from the petrel's country in a boat.

But the petrel followed them, called up a storm and threatened to upset the boat. In terror, the old man threw his daughter overboard, and when she clung to the gunwale, cut off her fingers one by one. The upper

Since women were regarded as unclean in hunting contexts, absolute sexual continence had to be observed before and during hunting expeditions

joints became the whales, the second joints the seals, and so on. Eventually she sank into the sea, but only after her father had struck out one of her eyes. On his return home, the old man filled the dog's boots with stones, and he, too, sank. The daughter became one-eyed Sedna, ruler of the sea, who dwells with her father and dog husband in the depths of the ocean. She is both sea goddess and a goddess of the dead.

Ruler of the Sea

As ruler of the sea creatures, Sedna must be appealed to for success in hunting. This involves the observance of taboos and the intercession of the shaman when taboos have been broken. The shaman goes into a trance, during which his spirit is believed to fly to Sedna's realm; on arrival, he steps over the dog, and does his best to placate the sea goddess. This involves the combing of her hair, since it is believed that broken taboos cause filth to collect in her hair. He may be told that the hunt will not prosper because some secret offence or breach of taboo such as the eating of boiled meat.

All other things being well, Sedna is eventually placated, and the shaman returns to his body; he then tells the people what has happened, and in many cases spontaneous confessions result. A similar procedure is followed in respect of land animals guarded by the moon spirit. Again, the shaman is able to 'fly' to the moon and intercede for his people. Clearly, there is ample room for trickery on the part of the shaman – but his supernatural capacity is seldom questioned.

Other rituals are observed in connection with hunting, since all the spirits controlling the supply of food must be kept well disposed. So, for example, a seal which has been killed may be left a drink of water in order that its spirit may carry a good report to the spirit world. Mourning rituals are observed when an animal is killed similar to those for human deaths – again in order not to offend the spirit of the dead animal. Elaborate precautions are taken on the death of a bear or a wolf, since their spirits are thought to be more dangerous than those of other animals.

Bladder Festivals

In Alaska, there is an annual 'Bladder Festival', in which the bladders of animals killed during the year are offered in order to ensure future hunting success. There is a constant need to observe the taboos: for instance, since women are regarded as unclean in hunting contexts, absolute sexual continence must be observed before and during hunting expeditions. There are many ways of discovering breaches of taboo. The most obvious is the lack of game; another is to 'weigh' the head of a recumbent person by a thong passed round the back of the neck. Lightness or heaviness determines the degree of guilt involved.

Sky and sea deities may in some cases 'divide' themselves in such a way as to delegate their functions. On Baffin Island, the Kadlu are three sisters who produce thunder and lightning by rubbing skins together – probably an original function of the High God. Other minor deities are connected with the earth. One striking specimen is the 'Disembboweller' of Greenland, a female demon, cousin of the moon spirit, who disembowels anyone she can make laugh. Most local deities in fact are malevolent, and inspire solely fear.

An interesting group of spirits – not quite deities – are the *tornait*, from which the shaman's familiars are recruited. They

Left Even the most unlikely objects are thought by the Inuit to have their guardian spirits: drawing of cooking pot spirits by Kenojuak
Below left Spirit charm, part of the shaman's equipment, which enables him to communicate with the forces controlling sea-hunting
Right Wooden salmon mask showing both the physical form of the fish and the alarming spirit which lurks within it

Michael Holford

may be associated at times with the dead, and it is possible see in them distorted popular reminiscences of the people of the Thule culture (the earliest known Inuit culture), in the same way as the Celts of Iron Age Britain are believed by some to have become the 'little people' or fairies of folklore. The chief of the *tornait* is known as Tornarsuk, and treated in some areas as a Supreme Being.

The Wandering Soul

Like other tribal peoples, the Inuit believe that man has not one, but several 'souls', *inuas*, all of which are associated with the body only temporarily. There are many variations, but it is broadly true to say that humans can have three types of soul: the 'free-soul', an immortal spirit and source of power which lives on in another world after death, or may return as a ghost to plague the living; the 'life-soul' which animates the body and dies with it; and the 'name-soul', which attaches to the name, and which can be passed on to another human being.

It must not be thought, however, that these can be sharply distinguished from one another in most circumstances. An Inuit of the Great Fish River, when asked what he understood by the soul, answered: 'It is something beyond understanding, that which makes me a human being.'

The soul may be conceived of as a miniature of man, living in some part of his body; or there may be many such miniatures scattered around the body, and especially the joints. What is basic to Inuit belief, however, is the connection between the soul and power or life-force. Sickness, for instance, is often interpreted as loss of soul, and therefore to be cured by the catching and bringing back of the soul by the shaman.

Death and disease are quantitatively, rather than qualitatively, different and it is, perhaps, not altogether surprising to find in some quarters a belief in the powers of the shaman to raise the dead – to bring back the soul from the very borders of the realm of the dead. In no case does 'loss of soul' occur without a cause: either negative or passive (the breaking of taboos) or positive and deliberate (malevolent magical practices, black magic); it is the task of the shaman to eliminate the latter cause, by neutralizing the spirit force concerned.

Closely connected with these ideas is the

belief that the wandering soul of the dead man or woman is potentially dangerous to the living. Clearly the dead live on, because they are seen in dreams; clearly they are dangerous, because of the things that happen to the living, and for which an ultimate cause must be sought.

Unaffected by the bounds of space or time, the dead's only chance of making their wants known is through the person of the shaman, and human beings can only lead relatively trouble-free lives by acceding to their requests and demands. Ghosts may sometimes be seen: but this is a misfortune of the first order, exceeded only by the touch of a spirit, which brings instant death.

This is not to say that, in Inuit belief, the dead become malevolent ghosts. Most pass after death to a state in which they are at

least happy; it is only the few who have had the misfortune to meet death in an unsuitable way who are forced to wander.

There is little or no idea of post-mortem judgement on the basis of good and evil deeds involved. What really matters is whether or not the person in question has observed all the taboos during life, and the manner of his or her death. So the Inuit of the Bering Straits believed that the souls of shamans and those who have died by accident (especially in hunting), suicide, violence, starvation or in childbirth go to a land of plenty in the sky.

Football in Heaven

Some Inuit regard the Aurora Borealis as the spirits of the fortunate departed playing in effect a sort of football in the heavens.

Those who die a natural death descend to the underworld or to the underwater realm of Sedna, a land of gloom and deep darkness but accessible to the shaman so that he may succeed in releasing the unfortunate soul. The central Inuit distinguish between a sky heaven (Qudliparmiut) and a subterranean hell (Adliparmiut) – again on the basis of the kind of death, rather than as punishment or reward for a life well or ill lived.

For about four or five days – the length of the estimated journey to the land of the dead – the soul remains in the house in which the person has died, and may then stay by the grave until summoned to enter the body of a new-born child.

This is actually the 'name-soul' which is passed on as the child receives the name of the deceased, and which represents a kind of transmigration doctrine. The house in which the person has died is abandoned, and his or her possessions are deliberately thrown away to avoid any risk of contaminating the living.

Belief of this kind can lead to terrible consequences: a sick person may be removed from a house, and left to die in isolation; the burial shroud may be put on before the person is actually dead; and in extreme cases, the dying man or woman may be put in the coffin while still alive. Elaborate safeguards are also observed in order to prevent the ghost from returning to the death house. The corpse may be removed through a window, or through the smoke-hole, a temporary door, or some other inconvenient aperture; in fact through anything but the proper door, in order to prevent the host from finding its way back inside again.

Precautions against the Dead
When the dead man is a shaman, the precautions are intensified. A snare may be placed at the door to frighten the ghost, who might fear being trapped on trying to re-enter his house. The living, too, take precautions: they may plug their nostrils in order not to become prey to 'spirit infection'; they may keep a knife under the pillow at night; and a sledge may be set up either at the grave site or at the death house as a warning to unwary travellers.

During the period of mourning, various taboos are enforced. Some Inuit will avoid

Musées Nationaux du Canada

Left Christmas barely recalls the pagan festival which it usurped, celebrating the returning sun. Drums were used by shamans to help them undertake spirit-flights *Above* The Inuit make string figures when the sun begins to move away south, hoping thereby to trap it and delay the coming of the long winter

uttering the name of the deceased, perhaps for fear of attracting his ghost; almost all of them impose a ban on working with sharp instruments such as knives, needles and harpoons, lest they should injure the ghost (however unwittingly) and bring trouble on themselves. Hunting expeditions will in general be suspended for a few days, out of respect for the dead, or in order not to deprive the dead of their proper nourishment of wild animals.

Burial Practices

Burial beliefs and practices vary. As the ground is too hard for interment, the normal practice is surface burial, either covered by stones or uncovered, or in some cases cave burial or sea burial. In the Bering Sea area the covering is added to surface burial as a further protection against the ghost walking. Similar reasons may be suspected in instances of flexing and binding the corpse.

Most Inuit provide the dead with grave goods – food, water, tools, weapons, and so on – for use in the beyond. In most cases, the objects provided are broken, not, as has sometimes been assumed, to prevent theft, but to liberate the spirit essence of the pot, pan, kayak or paddle in question. Human sacrifice is thought to have occurred in the past, but only rarely. The need to neutralize the dead extended to the practice of periodic feasts, in which the dead were invited back to the land of the living in order to partake of the bounty of their descendants. In the Norton Sound area of Alaska there were three such 'ordinary' festivals annually; but these were eclipsed by the Great Feast of the Dead held every 10 or 15 years.

This feast lasted five days, with dancing, and the giving of presents to the representatives (normally the namesakes) of the dead. This feast should not, however, be confused with the 'Inviting-in Feast' of the Yukon, in which a similar pattern was observed, only this time with regard to the inuas who grant good hunting, if properly placated. In

both these cases, elements appear to have been taken over from the Indians of the North-West, including such customs as the wearing of masks.

Spirit Mediators

It is the medicine-man (*angakok*), mediator between the living and the spirit-world, who gives the everyday practice of religion much of its distinctive character and most of its point. He or she – for women might also fulfil this role – was known all around the polar regions, from Lapland to Labrador.

The qualifications for becoming an angakok were twofold: a most unusual aptitude, which could at times involve a certain mental abnormality, and training. For the angakok had to possess supernormal powers and be seen to possess them. He had to be able to enter into a trance, and to communicate that trance to others; he had to speak the shaman language (a version of archaic Inuit). Above all he had to learn to control the spirits, heal disease by restoring 'lost' souls, and obtain food for the people by propitiating Sedna and her like.

His equipment was simple, and centred on the drum on which he summoned spirits to help him undertake his spirit-flights. Exact details of his training are not known, for these matters were kept hidden, but we do know that it began at an early age (seven or eight), with apprenticeship to an older shaman, when he set out on the quest of a vision of his own familiar or guardian spirit. Dark tales are told of shamans, who are reputed to have brought about the death of infants in order to have these spirits at their call. But the angakok, although remarkably cunning at disguising his real intentions, was not evil; he worked for the people, not against them.

Sorcerers and Magicians

There are also Inuit sorcerers, workers of malevolent or black magic, but even less is known about these. So much is certain, however, that the practice of Inuit religion revolves around the shaman, and that any powers the ordinary individual may possess are subordinate to those of the angakok.

Not that the individual is altogether devoid of power. Power can be inherited or bought; an amulet may be traded for a kayak, and even a familiar spirit may be made the object of a good exchange.

Obviously this is done because probably the most important thing in the whole of life is the possession of power. For the world is full of 'negative power', derived from the spirits, but capable of attaching, like a virus, to any person or any object; and the only defence is similar power harnessed to one's own ends.

Amulets are carried and worn by most Inuit for this very purpose: a man's umbilical cord or afterbirth, teeth, toenails – any one of which might be used wrongly by sorcerers – animal bones and hair; carved stones and other objects. Almost anything will serve. The end justifies any means.

And what is the end? The continuing, ever necessary attempt to control and channel the natural and supernatural powers of the Inuit world. For their physical conditions are exceptionally harsh and unforgiving, and their gods can by no means be considered always, or even mainly, well-disposed. If the Inuit are not to be frozen out of existence, they must maintain a harmonious relationship with the terrifying forces, both natural and spiritual, which pervade their whole environment.

Indeed, much Inuit culture is aimed simply at dispelling fear: fear of gods, ghosts, spirits, shades, shamans, sorcerers. For the religion of the Inuit is often considered essentially a religion of fear. As the Danish explorer Knud Rasmussen (1879-1933) was told: 'We do not believe, we only fear. And most of all we fear Nuliajuk (Sedna) . . . Nuliajuk is the name we give to the Mother of Beasts. All the game we have comes from her; from her come all the caribou, all the foxes, the birds and fishes ... We fear those things about us and of which we have no sure knowledge; as the dead, the malevolent ghosts, and the secret misdoings of the heedless ones among ourselves.
(See also SHAMAN.)

ERIC J. SHARPE*

FURTHER READING: M. Lantis, *Alaskan Eskimo Ceremonial* (University of Washington Press, 1966); G.H.Marsh, *A Comparative Study of Eskimo-Aleut Religion* (Univ. of Alaska Press, 1954); W. Fitzhugh and Susan Kaplan, *Inua: Spirit World of the Bering Sea Eskimo* (Smithsonian, 1982); J.G.Oosten, *The Theoretical Structure of the Religion the Netsilik and and Iglulik* (Krips, 1976); D. J. Ray, *Eskimo Masks: Art and Ceremony* (University of Washington Press, 1967).

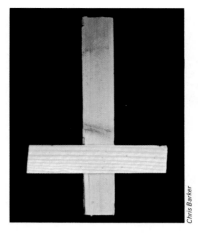

Inverted Symbols

Symbols which are upside down, backwards or the wrong way round, usually connected with evil; inverted crucifixes or other Christian symbols are used in black magic because they deny God and the accepted order of things, and state disorder, abnormality and evil; prayers are sometimes said backwards in the Black Mass and it was long believed that demons write backwards. See PACT; PENTAGRAM; and SYMBOLISM.

Chris Barker

INVISIBILITY

THE HERO who owns a ring or a cap, hood or helmet which makes him invisible is a familiar character in folktales and legends. A ring which makes its wearer invisible plays a crucial part in J. R. R. Tolkien's *The Lord of the Rings*. Perseus, the great Greek hero who slew Medusa (see GORGONS), had a cap of darkness which prevented anyone from seeing him.

The idea of the cap or hood of darkness may be based originally on the simple ostrich principle employed by a small child who hides from you by putting his hands over his eyes: if your head is covered so that you cannot see other people, then they cannot see you. There is something of the same principle in the symbolism of the taking of the veil by nuns, who retreat into 'invisible' seclusion from the life of the everyday world.

The Buried Head

Some invisibility magic attempts to make you literally invisible, even to yourself, but more often the aim is the slightly less ambitious one of preventing people from seeing you, as in the charm recommended by a 14th century Jewish work, the *Sefer Gematriaot,* which is to recite Genesis 19.11: 'and they struck with blindness the men who were at the door . . .' This depends on the principle that the power inherent in holy writ will cast an enchantment of blindness over those about you.

Similarly, the *Malleus Maleficarum* (15th century), in its day the leading authority on witchcraft, says that witches 'can take away the male organ, not indeed by actually despoiling the human body of it, but by concealing it with some glamour...' It cites the experience of a Dominican friar, who was visited by a young man who 'woefully said that he had lost his member.' The friar examined him and, finding no sign of the missing organ, asked him whether he suspected anyone of bewitching him. The young man said yes, he suspected a woman of his acquaintance, and the friar advised him 'to soften her with gentle words and promises.' The young man followed this advice and returned a few days later to show that he was whole again. 'First,' says the *Malleus,* 'it must in no way be believed

that such members are really torn away from the body but that they are hidden by the devil through some prestidigitatory art so that they can be neither seen nor felt.'

A process in the *Grimorium Verum* for becoming invisible says that you must begin the operation before sunrise on a Wednesday. You need seven black beans and the head of a dead man. Put one bean in the head's mouth, two in its ears and two in its eyes (which makes only five beans – presumably the other two are meant to go in the nostrils). Then trace a certain symbol on the head, and bury it in the ground, with the face turned up to the sky. Every day for nine days, before sunrise, water the buried head with good brandy. On the eighth morning a spirit will appear to you and ask what you are doing. You reply, 'I am watering my head.' He will ask you to let him do the watering but you must refuse until he shows you the same symbol that you traced on the the head. This proves that he is the spirit of the head and not a deceiving spirit. Let him water the head, and on the ninth morning you will find that the beans have ripened. Test them by taking one of them at a time, putting it in your mouth and looking in a mirror. 'If you cannot see yourself, it is good.'

What you have done, in effect, is to give the beans the deadness of the head (and you have also identified yourself with it by announcing, 'I am watering *my* head') so that when you put them in your mouth the invisibility of the dead and buried head is transferred to you. It is better not to swallow the

---

In the Abyss

Incantation for becoming invisible:

I have set my feet in the North, and have said: I will shroud myself in mystery and concealment. The Voice of my Higher Soul said unto me, Let me enter the path of darkness, peradventure thus may I attain the Light. I am the only being in an Abyss of Darkness; from the Darkness came I forth ere my birth . . . And the Voice of Darkness answered unto my soul, I am He that formulates in darkness, the light that shineth in darkness, but the darkness comprehendeth it not. Let the Mystic Circumambulation take place in the Place of Darkness.

Israel Regardie *The Golden Dawn*

---

beans because you can only become visible again by removing them from your mouth.

The link between invisibility, death and burial appears again in the frequent references to shrouds in a long invisibility ritual devised by the Order of the Golden Dawn. After certain preliminaries, the operator recites an 'Enochian Spirit Invocation' beginning: 'Ol Sonuf Vaorsag Goho Iad Balt, Lonsh Calz Vonpho. Sobra Z-ol Ror I Ta Nazps . . .', and continuing in this vein for some time.

The Blue-Black Egg

Next he invokes the Recording Angel, 'O Light invisible, intangible, wherein all thoughts and deeds of all men are written,' commanding him to 'concentrate about me, invisible, intangible, as a shroud of darkness, a formula of defence; that I may become invisible, so that seeing me men see not, nor understand the thing that they behold.' It is clear that the ritual is not intended to make the operator literally invisible but to allow him to pass unnoticed, inscrutable.

The magician continues by conjuring the Lady of Darkness to clothe him with ineffable mystery and to send the great Archangel Tzaphqiel to formulate about him a shroud of concealment. After further incantations, the ritual instructs the operator to 'formulate the black egg around you, the idea of becoming invisible. Imagine the results of success, then say, "Let the shroud of concealment encircle me, at a distance of 18 inches from the physical body . . ."' Next, the operator declares that he is formulating around himself the blue-black egg of Harpocrates (the Graeco-Egyptian god Horus the Child – see HORUS), 'as a shroud of concealment . . . that I may pass unseen among men to execute the will of my Genius.'

Presently, he repeats a fine incantation which states that he has formulated 'the light that shineth in darkness, but the darkness comprehendeth it not' (the reference is to John 1.5). Then, mentally formulating the blue-black egg with great force, the magician declares: 'Darkness is my Name, and Concealment. I am the Great One Invisible of the Paths of the Shades. I am without fear, though veiled in darkness, for within me, though unseen, is the Magic of the Light divine.'

Iridology is an unconventional diagnostic technique that purports to read vital bodily signs through the changing patterns of the eyes. It has been thought for many years that the eye, particularly the coloured part or iris, acts as a barometer of the body's general state of health.

IRIDOLOGY

ONE OF THE MOST APPEALING THINGS about iridology is that it is an entirely non-invasive procedure. In fact, the iris, that part of the eye which surrounds the pupil, was first named after Iris, the Greek goddess of the rainbow, because of the range of colours and markings that can be found on this organ. Hippocrates (c 460-377 BC), the celebrated Greek physician, once wrote that it is especially important to pay attention to the eyes when making a general diagnosis of a patient's health.

Iridology was not, however, really systematized until the beginning of the 19th century. It was at that time widely thought that a dark spot on the iris signified either an injury or illness, and that clear blue or clear brown eyes with no significant markings indicated a sound constitution and generally good health. About 160 years ago, a Hungarian boy called Ignatz Peczely noticed that when his pet owl suffered an injury, a mark appeared suddenly on the iris of its eye. When Peczely later qualified as a doctor, he remembered this childhood incident, and wondered if the same principle would apply to human eyes.

He took up a post in one of Budapest's hospitals, and began applying himself to research, examining patients' eyes both before and after treatment. He drew detailed 'maps' of their irises, and these form the basis of the iridology wall charts which hang today in the consulting rooms of iridologists. He discovered that each condition consistently appeared to cause markings on the same place on the iris. When the condition improved, the mark seemed to fade or even disappear altogether.

Peczely assembled this material and published it. Doctors in Germany became interested in the potential of what seemed to be a new and comprehensive diagnostic tool. From there iridology spread throughout western Europe, and in the early years of the 20th century was introduced into the US by the Swedish homoeopath, Dr Nils Liljequist. Half a century later, an American, Dr Bernard Jensen, developed the comprehensive map of the features of the iris still in use today. There are schools of iridology teaching these principles in the US, Britain and Europe. Examination is by a strong light and magnifying glass, followed by plotting on an iridology 'map' or photography of the irises by an adapted camera. Special video cameras are now also used.

One feature of iridology stressed today is its potential as a preventative diagnostic tool. The theory states that health conditions often show up on the iris before their more usually accepted symptoms are apparent, and therefore it acts as an early warning system. Hence practitioners claim to be able to spot and suggest cures for medical conditions that have not yet shown up. Even minor shocks or traumas will show up in the iris, it is claimed.

By contrast, other conditions which are totally natural, like pregnancy, do not show up on the iris. Strangely, practitioners claim that any injury or diseased organ or tissue which has been operated upon will not be recorded in the iris. If this is so, then this may well offer a clue to the exact working of the mysterious relationship between the iris and the rest of the body.

The basic range of eye colours is brown, blue and grey, with mixed colours such as green or brown-green. Markings on the iris can be drawn from a wide range of colours including orange, yellow, white, red and green. Fine white markings are thought to indicate stress, while dark patches signify a lack of energy in whatever organ or tissue associated with that part of the iris by iridology. Dark external rims around the iris are thought to indicate a toxic build-up in the skin caused by poor elimination. A typical iridological diagnosis might be that a dark and fuzzy rim around the right eye indicates poor faecal and toxin elimination, and a resulting poor skin tone. Alternatively a diet which is too rich, with too much coffee, drinking and smoking is thought to produce the same effect.

'Textures' of the irises are described by iridologists in rather flowery language, and classifications of the general 'grain' of the iris will range from 'silk', through 'linen' to 'hessian'. An iris with a fine 'weave' of colours is supposed to indicate a strong constitution, whilst an open grain appearance, rather like hessian, is supposed to indicate a much weaker constitution.

Strangely, iridologists consider the reverse is true of the emotional toughness or otherwise of the patient under examination. 'Silky' iris texture is more likely to indicate a person of a more highly strung nature, more likely to respond to stresses and difficulties, but better at achieving goals. On the face of it this sounds like gross stereotyping, on a par with some early systems of psychological categorisation.

Each sector or 'pie wedge' of the iris is divided by concentric circles which are seen by iridologists to divide the iris into a number of target areas. The 'wedges' are identified by the numerals of the clock face and these in turn are divided into different concentric bands. Ultimately, the iris is divided into 96 small components by a combination of radial, circular and segmental sections. The correlation between the sections of the iris and the other parts of the body and their afflictions correlate from the right eye to the left eye, in that they are an almost mirror image of each other, but marks will not necessarily show up on both eyes. For example the just past two o'clock to three o'clock sector (from an imaginary hour hand) of the left iris is attributed to the lungs, as is the nine o'clock to almost ten o'clock sector of the right iris.

There are exceptions to this apparent mirror image. For example, the liver is attributed to the 'quarter to eight' position of the right iris, but the corresponding 'quarter past four' position of the left iris is attributed by iridologists to the spleen. The kidneys appear to correlate with the 'quarter to six' position of the right iris, and the corresponding 'quarter past six' position of the left iris. The lymphatic and circulatory systems are mapped on to the outer edge of the iris, while the autonomic nervous system appears on iridological wall charts on the inner edge of the iris, next to the innermost ring which corresponds to the stomach and pylorus.

Although there are exceptions, people's eyes do appear to conform to the standard iridology 'map'. As, seen from the doctor's point of view, the liver is supposed to be sympathetically connected with the eight o'clock position of the right iris, chronic drinkers should show markings in this position. This they often do.

Another example might be the presence of a mark known as a 'radial platt' in the seven o'clock position of the left iris of a woman patient, corresponding to the supposed sympathetic site of the womb, sur-

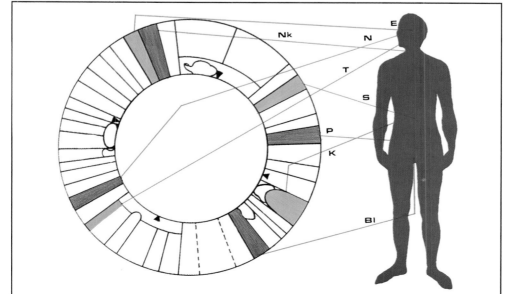

Iridologists still use wall charts which derive from those pioneered by Ignatz Peczely in the 19th century. This chart, which was devised as a guide for students of iridology, demonstrates how the different parts of the circle of the iris – schematically represented in the diagram – correspond with the parts of the body concerned. The section marked E (*top left*), for example, refers to the neck and section K to the kidneys (*bottom right*)

rounded by what iridologists describe as 'peppercorn markings'. This might suggest to the iridologist that it would be advisable for his patient to take a cervical smear test, and follow up its results through conventional gynaecological channels.

Much iridological diagnosis is concerned with the theory of toxic build-up, and the effects of poor living habits on the patient. The general state of the patient's metabolism is of great concern to the practitioner. Questions of childhood health conditions or exposure to chemical poisons such as pesticides, coal tars, caffeine, food additives, X-rays, alcohol and tranquillizers, are investigated in a fashion similar to naturopathy. Iridology attempts to reverse the effects of

conditions and events which might have occurred long ago in childhood, in a way that resembles, and may owe some theoretical framework to, Freudian analysis. Iridology also views the body in terms of degrees of well-being and general energy flow, in a similar way to yoga theory. This level of animation is thought to be indicated by the 12 o'clock position on both irises.

As iridology is essentially a diagnostic tool, treatment is supplied by other complementary therapies such as herbalism, naturopathy, Bach flower remedies, homoeopathy, or sometimes by acupuncture, osteopathy or reflexology. Where necessary, practitioners will refer patients to a conventional allopathic practitioner.

Iridology is still speculative, being in the position of a collection of observed relationships, rather than an established technique where the rationale behind the observed correlations can be explained and extrapolated into a scientific theory.

STEPHEN SKINNER

FURTHER READING: James and Sheelagh Colton, *Iridology, a Patient's Guide* (Thorsons, 1988); Dorothy Hall, *Iridology: Personality and Health Analysis Through the Iris* (Angus and Robertson); Theodore Kriege, *Iris diagnosis* (Fowler, 1969); Henry Lindlahr, *Diagnostic Methods,* (Lindlahr Publishing, 1922); Ignatz Peczely, *Discovery in the Realm of Nature and the Art of Healing* (original textbook).

IRON

THE TAMING OF FIRE opened the door to the mastery of metals, which in turn marked a vital stage in human progress. Iron was the chief agent of this transmutation, which helped raise human life from the primitive to the civilized. This would in itself have been sufficient in non-materialistic ages to have given iron a reputation for the supernatural – a reputation which it also acquired on the grounds that the first iron, having descended from the heavens in the form of meteors, was of celestial origin. It was called by the ancient Egyptians 'the metal from the sky' and by the Aztecs, who never learnt to work it, 'the gift of heaven'.

The earliest known iron implements date from the late second millennium BC, but even before that time iron in an unworked form had been regarded with awe. Ancient monarchs were won over with presents of iron or steel daggers and Achilles proposed a ball of iron as a prize in the funeral games instituted in honour of Patroclus.

The technical development of iron has now completely overshadowed its psychic aspects, although within living memory schoolchildren would still touch cold iron for luck and recite the magic charm, 'Touch wood, no good, Touch iron, rely on.' In the more distant past, humanity testified to iron's magical qualities by attitudes which on the surface might appear contradictory, for this metal was regarded as both dangerous and protective.

Iron was considered taboo in certain religions, no iron tool being permitted in the temples of ancient Greece, for example, while in the Temple of Solomon 'neither hammer nor axe nor any tool of iron was heard in the house when it was being built' (1 Kings 6.7). A relic of this old antipathy to iron survives in the custom which prohibits the use of scissors to cut a baby's fingernails until the end of its first year.

As long ago as 1350 BC, amulets of meteoric iron were placed reverently in the tomb of Tutankhamen to protect the sarcophagus against evil spirits, thus testifying to the ancient role of this metal as protector of mankind. The Romans believed that the association of iron with the war god Mars endowed it with its protective powers, but this must be regarded as no more than a

Iron has been credited with supernatural powers for many centuries, and in Italy it is still thought to afford protection against the Evil Eye: charm made from a lemon pierced with iron spikes

local version of what was even then an almost universal myth.

Long after the fall of the Roman Empire in the West, the magic of iron continued to influence the customs and beliefs of peasant life. In Italy iron pyrites were used as a charm against eye diseases; in China they kept dragons at bay; in Burma they intimidated crocodiles; while throughout Europe they guarded the home against lightning. In the 19th century, iron bars used to be laid across beer barrels to protect beer from thunder-storms. In India cold iron was essential in funeral rites; it was believed to counteract any ill-effect from spirits which succeeded in escaping from the corpse.

The power of iron over ghosts was proverbial and as recently as 1854, on the occasion of the evocation of the spirit of Apollonius of Tyana (a noted ancient necromancer), which took place in London, it was considered

expedient to create a magic circle of magnetized iron to neutralize all potential dangers from the ghost.

Medieval man approached the fairy kingdom fearfully and took elaborate precautions, many of which involved the use of iron. He who ventured into a fairy mound ensured his safe retreat by driving his knife into the earth by the threshold. Iron was also laid in the cradle of the new-born baby to prevent the fairies from substituting a changeling. It would appear that one group of supernatural beings alone was impervious to the power of iron – the Teutonic goblin, traditional miner and ironmaster of northern Europe, and forger of enchanted swords (see DWARFS).

The nightmarish forces that haunted the waking hours of ancient man were believed to be susceptible to iron's magic power, whether it took the form of the horseshoe attached to the cottage door or a knife secreted beneath it. According to the Roman historian Pliny, iron coffin nails on the lintel of the door provide protection against all wandering spirits. A form of white magic, employed against suspected witches until well into the 19th century, consisted of filling a bottle with pins and heating it intensely. This had the effect of so tormenting the hag that she was compelled to relinquish her hold upon her victim.

Equally potent and still observed in modern Italy is the custom of touching cold iron to counteract the Evil Eye (see EYE). A *jettatore*, an individual with the power to 'fascinate' or cast the Evil Eye, can also be overcome by the jangling of iron keys, since to a devil the very sound of iron is anathema. Even in this century the hapless King Alfonso of Spain, a notorious *jettatore*, was embarrassed by the constant jangling of iron keys wherever he travelled in Italy and was actually refused an audience by the superstitious Italian dictator Mussolini.

On the outer walls of some English cottages, large spiral ties may be seen as reminders of the old superstition that iron afforded protection against fire. Much of the magical aura of the blacksmith was largely derived from the fact that he was a worker of iron; in comparatively modern times the primitive smiths of the Celebes maintained a god of iron in their forges to guarantee the quality of the metal.
(See also AXE.)

IROQUOIS

Although the majority of Iroquois are now Christian, there is a remnant whose beliefs and culture are based on the visions of the prophet Handsome Lake

THE ORIGINS of the Iroquois, the most advanced group of American Indians north of the Pueblos, are lost in the confusion of archeological time. Their legends assume that they were always in their historical homeland of New England.

The Iroquois had many gods, who were essentially the powers of Nature. It was very apparent to the Indians that they were dependent upon the goodwill of powers beyond direct human knowledge; the wind and the rain, the passing seasons, the lightning and the sunshine, the forests and the rivers, all were active and seemingly alive. Thus it was felt that men must act so as to propitiate the living powers of the universe they saw around them.

It does not follow that life is dull and oppressive when people feel the gods are all around them; on the contrary there was a feeling of being part of the whole world of Nature. When Nature rejoiced mankind also danced and shared the happiness; when she was preparing for winter mankind also stored away the things of summer and rested hopefully for the coming of spring.

The gifts of Nature were maize and beans, wild deer and beaver, many kinds of timber, birch bark, apple orchards, maple syrup and honey. These things the Iroquois received with gratitude and cared for them, developing their usefulness as best they could. If a hunter killed an animal he made a little offering to its spirit so that more animals might be reborn. If a woman planted a maize field she walked naked around it, sharing her fertility with the food plants.

There were many tricky and dangerous spirits to be charmed away, and they were conjured with in the dances of the False Face society, so called because of the carved wooden masks worn by the performers (see FOOL). Unhappily there were cruel and deadly human enemies, and they were weakened by magic and defeated by the young warriors. The overshadowing presence above was felt mostly through the spiritual life-force known as Orenda, coming in varying degrees to human families.

Some families descended from great ladies whose magical powers were greater than most other ancestresses. Some chieftainesses had sons and nephews who were vehicles of the inner wisdom gleaned through contact with ancestral spirits. Some men were given great powers direct from the spirit world. Such men were like lone pines standing high among the forest trees. Such a one was Dekanawida, the law-giver and friend of his fellow philosopher and law-maker, Hiawatha.

The two great law-givers of the Iroquois lived at the time when Elizabeth I was ruling in England and the great Mogul, Akbar, was ruling in India. They were different from those civilized monarchs, however,

for their work was done among peoples dressed in skins and living in houses made from tree bark. In those days the life of those Iroquois was not unlike that of Europeans at the end of Neolithic times, about 4000 years ago. The tribes used arrow-heads of flaked stone, cultivated the ground with wooden hoes and cut down the forest with stone-bladed choppers.

Their villages consisted of a few hundred people living in two or three long-houses in separate family rooms in a vast apartment dwelling. The huts were surrounded by earthen defences surmounted by a defensive wall of wooden stakes. Inside the village were storehouses for dried maize and beans, which were always built on bluffs near a river so that water could be drawn up in

An Iroquois philosopher and law-maker, who later became a demigod, Hiawatha lived during the 16th century; in his narrative poem *Hiawatha* Longfellow used the name of this great Iroquois chieftain, but all other material is Algonquin: in this illustration to the poem, Hiawatha's grandmother Nokomis attempts to dissuade her grandson from setting off on a dangerous quest

buckets made of birch bark in times of trouble. Stores of nourishing pemmican, made from animal suet beaten up with wild berries, ensured a store of food rich in vitamins. It was used by hunters and traders, and was a reserve in time of trouble.

The five nations who spoke Iroquoian languages were always at war with one

another in those early days. It was because of the sorrows and stupidities of wars between related people that Dekanawida and Hiawatha came together. Like all innovators they were unpopular and treated with suspicion, but after a period of exile they persuaded the tribal councils to come in peace to a series of conferences.

Hiawatha was a Mohawk, but his work began among the Onondaga tribe. The opposition from the Onondaga chief Wathatotaro was so intense that he caused Hiawatha's daughters to be murdered. The teacher then went to the Oneida who persuaded the Mohawk to join them and to invite the Cayuga to the gathering. Then the three nations approached the Onondaga again, and this time Wathatotaro agreed provided that they would bring the Seneca to join them. the Seneca agreed and the whole five nations joined into a league of mutual friendship and protection which they called 'The Extended Lodge', meaning that the Council Lodges of each nation were now joined together.

The five nations now controlled the area from the shores of Lake Erie to the lower reaches of the Hudson River, the greater part of New York State. Yet a century later, at the time of their greatest power, their total population was only about 16,000.

Dekanawida was traditionally of Huron birth, but his parents tried to drown him because of a prophecy that he would cause trouble to the nation. He survived, and later left home to live among the Iroquois, where he was the great law-giver and was

also regarded as a prophet and magician. He is ranked by the Iroquois among the demigods.

Among the laws he established was the one which ended the blood feud among the Iroquois. It laid down that a human life was valuable, and a death by violence was to be atoned for by the payment of five strings of wampum. However the man who had committed the crime had also forfeited his own life, and that was worth five strings of wampum also. Hence the next of kin of the slain man was to receive ten strings of wampum from the killer. Wampum was a high unit of value and such a penalty was a great discouragement to homicide. It was largely instrumental in preventing the recurrence of inter-group wars among the people of The Extended Lodge.

Wathatotaro has become also a demigod of a thoroughly terrifying demonic character in more recent Iroquois belief. He was regarded as having strange powers in his own day, and was renowned for pride, sexual prowess and strength, as well as a subtle mind. These qualities made him a very great chief and in spite of his stubborn resistance to the idea of a union of the tribes he was able to gain a predominant position for his Onondaga people within that group. They had 14 hereditary chieftainships in the council of the confederacy whereas each of the other four nations only had ten each. The chief holding Wathatotaro's position was to be the only one empowered to summon a meeting of the confederation.

Thus the three most important chiefs who

were concerned with making the league became demigods in tradition and entered the realms of the legendary while still remembered as historical persons.

History Told in Beads

While the Iroquois had developed agriculture and the communal hunt for food production, and had evolved an advanced social system based on inheritance in the female line, they had not reached the point where money was necessary for trade, and their writing was still in the primitive symbolic stage. They engraved pictures of events on pipe-stems to record an adventure, and they used strings of wampum beads often made up into belts with symbolic patterns as historical reminders.

The wampum was made from the thick valve of a spondylus shell. The valve was broken off and polished on a stone, then it was slowly bored through from end to end. The resulting beads, some white and some purple, were carefully polished and strung on sinew. The message on a wampum belt could not be read in our way but it was a reminder of a story, in much the same way as a page of pictures may remind a child to recite the appropriate nursery rhyme. Each nation had an official Keeper of the Wampum, who on ceremonial occasions could bring out the belts in his possession and recite remembered verses telling of the event which the belt commemorated.

The coming of European settlers and military forces was a disaster for the Iroquois. At first there were minor squabbles

The many gods of the Iroquois Indians were essentially powers of Nature, for it was clear to the Indians that they were dependent on the goodwill of powers beyond direct human knowledge – wind, rain and sunshine *Left* Food crops were thought to be blessed by protective feminine spirits: watercolour showing the corn, bean and squash maidens, by Earnest Smith, a Seneca Indian *Right* The products of the earth were used for ceremonial costumes, emphasizing the close relationship between man and Nature: mask made from maize leaves. Husk Faces, wearing these masks, guide evil away from the house

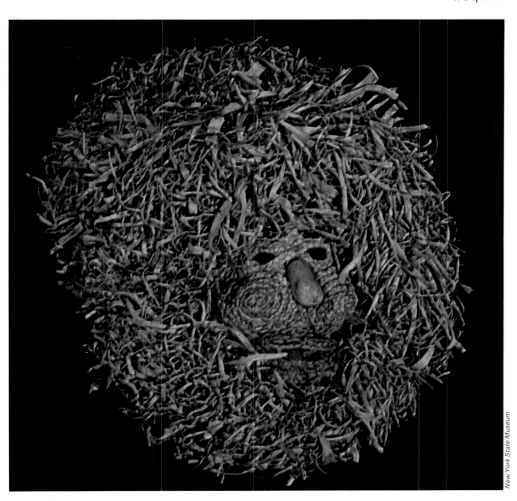

New York State Museum

at the same time as a good deal of trade; but later the rivalries between the great powers of the day brought the Iroquois as mercenaries into the wars of the colonial epoch. Mostly they fought on the side of the English, because they had been attacked by a party of Canadian Indians under French command and they resented the insult.

The wars altered the way of life terribly. Villages were raided and burnt and the people massacred. Money was paid for scalps of captured enemies, and there were reports of Europeans occasionally assisting the tribesmen in the ghastly tortures of captured enemies which had for long been part of the war honours system of the tribe. The wars brought no happiness to the Iroquois; they were fought by foreigners for overseas possessions rather than for the benefit of the Indian inhabitants of the land. Sometimes honourable men insisted that the treaties signed with the Iroquois must be kept, but more often the pressure for land and power drove the white man to dispossess the Indians and drive them from their native soil.

The Visions of Handsome Lake
In this period of increasing uncertainty the Iroquois were threatened with total disruption. Some of them opposed the American Revolution and eventually removed over the Canadian border, while others remained on their reservations, trying to preserve something of the past. The old religion was much weakened, and the missionaries persuaded most of the people that there was another way of life with regard to the spiritual powers behind the world of Nature.

The Iroquois now have a heroic and persistent little saint of their own in Kateri Tekathawitha, who suffered much to ease the ancient barbarism. She was a member of the Catholic group of the Iroquois who had settled at Cauhnawaga in Canada.

Other missionaries worked in the United States among the Iroquois, and most of the people became Christians, though there was always a minority opinion against the preachers who persuaded them to accept the many injustices which they suffered at the hands of the master race. The minority became the followers of Handsome Lake, the brother of the famous chief Cornplanter. In June 1799 a vision came to Handsome Lake; he saw three noble beings who told of happier days to come. Later he was introduced to a fourth who was the Creator, who had taken pity on the suffering Indians.

The new religion was a serious effort to reorganize the ancient Iroquois beliefs and preserve old customary ceremonies, while adapting to the new knowledge which had become available. It was rather strict, and stood firm for abstinence from alcohol. This followed another vision in which the prophet saw a lake full of Indians in their canoes, who were trading good food for liquor handed out by an evil being in the guise of a trader. This was the Devil leading the Indians to self-destruction.

Handsome Lake's prophetic mission was to bear its fruit much later, but he had given his people a new focus of unity in the revival of old tradition and in the re-creation of a mystical unity in the long-house which symbolized the meeting-place of the founder nations of the Federation.

The prophecies of Handsome Lake are unusual in the history of prophetic visions among peoples suffering from cultural oppression, because they gave rise to no insurrection. They rather led to a withdrawal from close contact with the white man on the part of the older and more conservative among the Indians. This continued to be the case for nearly a century, so that the traditions remained alive only through a small minority of the Iroquois. Since the first accounts of the prophecies were transmitted by word of mouth there grew up a disagreement on what was actually said, and there were two later attempts to codify the system. It is now printed and the consensus of opinion is that the tenor of the original revelation has been faithfully preserved.

The present codified state of the Handsome Lake beliefs is well adapted to the needs of a new kind of Iroquois community living within a highly organized modern state. It is more important than the actual membership would suggest, because it has become a focus for the preservation of the Indian basic culture. The majority of the Iroquois however go to one or other of the Christian churches.

Early treaties gave the Indians the right to move freely between their reservations and in modern times they have fought politically to keep their freedom of movement across the frontiers. Their struggle against giant corporations which would make good use of their lands has also been intense, not because of any obstructionist will to resist, but because there were constant threats to override the rights of the communities as guaranteed by past treaties, and sealed by the exchange of wampum belts. The struggle has become a political one, not against the white man but against the covetousness of commercial interests.

Fertility and Healing Dances
Some of the ancient customs have survived, half as ritual, and half as folklore. They have altered less than the Godiva rides and may-pole dances of Europe; the False Face society still knows healing rituals and the Husk Faces, who wear masks made of plaited maize leaves, still whisper and guide evil away from the house. An ancient happy occasion used to be the Naked Dance in which the young people used to dance

British Museum

entirely naked and a chosen couple brought fertility to the plantations in sexual intercourse while the others danced around. Now the original purpose of the dance is commemorated in the name Shaking the Branches (really the maize plants shaking in the wind and fertilizing the seed in this way); the dancers, now clothed, dance waving imaginary leafy plants in their hands. The overt sexual magic is no longer there.

Dances are seasonal affairs, and the New Year Dance is perhaps the most important nowadays. In this the heralds of the festival are the Husk Faces. They bring in the other dancers and open and close ceremonies, whispering like the breath of the wind and teaching by signs. The formal dancers are masked and wear modern clothing. By tradition men and women exchange clothes and, like European mummers, pretend to be of the opposite sex. It could be that this may have come from contact with the early settlers who preserved many of the folk customs of their homeland; but the basic idea was Iroquois. One can imagine the difficulties of the young warriors trying to dance in girls' long skin gowns.

The False Face dancers at this ceremony did not have to show their healing magic.

Wampum beads constructed from shells were made into belts with symbolic patterns that served as reminders of Iroquois tribal history; each of the nations that spoke the Iroquois language had a Keeper of the Wampum who recited the stories commemorated in the belts on ceremonial occasions

They represented diseases and had the power to take disease away with them. In old times the members of the society cut their masks from a living tree, but now they are made of wood from the timber yard.

Apart from the New Year festivities the False Face society used to hold special dances for healing sickness. The patient was laid down beside a wood fire. The dancers wearing their hideous masks and carrying rattles capered around chanting an appropriate song. They scooped up hot ashes from the fire and rubbed their hands in the hot embers, showing no signs of pain. Then they would turn the patient and rub hot ashes into selected parts of his body. This was magic, they thought, taught to the first members of the society by an ancient giant who had been subdued by the Great Spirit.

The giant was the giver of illness, and he was forced to teach the healing ritual to counteract his powers of evil. In fact, the heat and massage stimulated nerves and internal organs and could have a beneficial effect. However the more precise powers of modern medicine have in most cases driven the False Faces into being symbols of bad luck who, by their dance, can charm ill fortune away from the household where they perform. In due course their ritual will be simply a folklore frolic like the Helston Furry Dance.

In the modern world the Iroquois people have become normal citizens, with special treaty rights securing their home reservations from total assimilation into the national states. Many of their younger men earn big wages as steel erectors. In this dangerous trade they have earned a reputation for fearlessness and skill. This appears to have replaced to some extent the ancient initiation into warrior societies; and it is in fact far more dangerous. After nearly four centuries of contact with the civilized world, and much suffering, the Iroquois have managed to retain a tribal organization, some old customs, and a homeland in the shape of a group of reservations.

C. A. BURLAND

IRVING

Radio Times Hulton Picture Library

Edward Irving, founder of the Holy Catholic and Apostolic Church: he believed that he was the leader of a faithful group of worshippers whom God was gathering together as the end of the world drew near

A misfit in the grim severity of Scottish Presbyterianism, Edward Irving went to London to attract the fashionable world by his stirring oratory. His belief in the imminence of the Second Coming was taken up by his followers after his death

SUNDAY SERVICE for a Victorian Presbyterian was a long, serious and hardly colourful affair. Yet for those who had followed the fashionable Scots preacher, Edward Irving, Sunday worship became three hours of ritual, intricately performed with incense and holy water by nearly 50 clergy and servers, all clad in colourful liturgical vestments. It was indeed a rather startling product for the dour Scots' Church of the time and hardly reflected its Calvinistic origin. No wonder that these erstwhile Presbyterians had chosen for themselves the name Catholic Apostolic Church, while the world tended to continue to call them Irvingites.

At the age of 30, Edward Irving had had a rather unsuccessful ministry in Scotland and was on the point of leaving for the mission field when the Caledonian Church in London's Hatton Garden invited him to be their minister. His congregations in Edinburgh had found their young minister's sermons rather bewildering and even a prominent divine of the day was prompted to compare them to 'Italian music — only appreciated by connoisseurs'. Nevertheless, Irving was a success among the poor, bringing a simple Christianity into the slums and entering each home with a blessing 'Peace be to this house'. He had an impact on the lives of ordinary people which derived from the two opposite sides of his character: he was both dramatic and sincerely humble at the same time. It was this contrast within his powerful personality which was to bring the crowds to Hatton Garden.

London in 1822 presented Irving with a challenge much more suited to his taste than had his Scottish ministry. He went to the Caledonian Church with the avowed purpose of attracting the fashionable world. He believed that he could find a way to their hearts by speaking to them in the words that they used and drawing his illustrations from the current plays, novels, and newspapers. Here would be the audience of connoisseurs which he needed.

His assessment was right. The Londoners of the Regency were inveterate sermon tasters and a fashionable preacher would draw congregations from all quarters, almost irrespective of denomination. Irving's remarkable oratory was soon mentioned by George Canning, then Foreign Secretary, in a speech to the House of Commons. Society took Canning's hint and the chapel in Hatton Garden was soon too small to accommodate all who wished to hear Irving. In 1827 the congregation moved into a new building in Regent Square where Irving continued to attract the crowds.

His success was due largely to his ability to project his personality, but also to the ringing modernity of his tones. He was a great controversialist and sharply critical of the current fashions, so that the publication of a volume of his sermons became a real literary event, drawing the fire of all who had suffered from his denunciation. He strove to be a fashionable preacher and his personality needed the limelight, yet he continued to combine publicity-seeking with a real humility and undoubted sincerity.

Sense of the Dramatic

By this time Irving's teaching had become highly personal rather than Presbyterian. The fashion for his preaching began to fade and as it did so his opponents began to question the validity of his views and the orthodoxy of his doctrines. He had been increasingly influenced by Adventist beliefs and his sermons were made the more immediate by his growing insistence that he and his congregation were living in the last days before the Second Coming of our Lord. The mystical works of Coleridge and of a Roman Catholic priest who wrote under the pseudonym Ben Ezra influenced Irving considerably and he began to point to the portents which heralded the end of the world. His willingness to acknowledge spiritism, faith healing, and 'speaking in tongues' as signs of this Second Coming was too much for the Presbyterian Church and in 1833 he was deposed from the ministry by his home presbytery of Ancrum.

Yet it was the London presbytery which had made the first move when, three years before, it had excommunicated Irving for teaching that Christ's human nature was not perfect but liable to sin. The validity of this charge is difficult to assess. His doctrinal position was inconsistent and changed with remarkable rapidity. He would often allow his sense of the dramatic to make him overstate a perfectly legitimate point, and it would seem that it was not so much what he said but the way he said it which was under attack. Irving's followers were certainly extremely orthodox in their teaching on the historic doctrines of the Church and it does seem likely that the London presbytery had picked on some loose language in order to be rid of a minister and his flock who seemed generally to be moving further and further away from what they knew as Presbyterianism.

As a result of growing hostility, the Irvingite members left Regent Square in 1832 and moved to a dark chapel in Newman Street, where they set themselves up as the Holy Catholic and Apostolic Church. Irving was beginning to see himself as the leader of a faithful remnant whom God was gathering together as the end of the world came near. His Romantic views which, as a young man, had meant that he had carried a volume of Ossian's poems about with him, had been further strengthened by his contact with Coleridge and he was more and more convinced that the new Apostolic Age was about to burst upon the world. Further proof of the imminence of the Second Coming came during a tour of Scotland when spirit manifestations and speaking in tongues were recorded. The stage seemed set for a Pentecostal revival, with perhaps a few Romantic additions suited to the temper of the age and Irving's own predilections. Yet when Irving died in December 1834 he left behind him no distinctive body of doctrine, no blueprint for a Church, no liturgy or ministry; and every expectation was that the fledgling Catholic Apostolic Church was destined to an early oblivion.

Awaiting the Second Coming

This, however, was to reckon without the remarkable influence which Irving's personality had had upon his followers. Meeting at the home of a banker named Henry Drummond, the leaders of the Catholic Apostolic Church drew up a constitution for the new body. They were preparing a suitable vehicle for the gathering together of God's elect for his impending coming. From the Church emerged 12 apostles who were to be the interpreters of God's mysteries. They appointed 12 prophets who were to explain the Scripture and exhort the people to holiness, and 12 evangelists to teach doctrine. There were also 12 pastors to care for the people and seven deacons to aid them. Each of the apostles was assigned a tribe and the Apostolic College was set up at Albury in Hampshire, where Henry Drummond had his seat and where he built a fine church in the Gothic style.

The movement was under way and all vestiges of spiritism and speaking in tongues were soon removed. The followers of Irving differed from the High Church members of the Church of England in their assurance that the Second Coming of Christ was near and in their conviction that they would be among the first to welcome him. Their services became more and more elaborate and in 1842 the liturgy of the new Church was compiled, based upon Roman, Greek, and Anglican models. Regulations for daily prayers and services were laid down and on Sunday the Solemn Eucharist would take nearly three hours. The distinction between priest and preacher meant that equal emphasis was placed upon the sacraments as upon preaching; and the Catholic Apostolics believed in the real presence of Christ as fervently as any Anglo-Catholic.

Small, Pious Group

The new Church prospered financially. Besides Drummond, a number of rich men belonged and all its members paid a tenth of their income to the church. A tenth part of this tithe went to the headquarters at Albury and the rest was used for the upkeep and growth of the movement. It grew rapidly. Soon there were seven churches in London besides others in many of the main provincial towns and the Irvingites spread overseas, particularly to Germany and the United States.

There was however no provision for the continuation of the hierarchy. The Advent of Christ was so firmly expected that although the apostles, who were alone able to ordain, were manifestly mortal, the Irvingites faced the likelihood of the Church's dissolution with equanimity. The ritualist movement within the Church of England meant that there was increasingly no real need for the Catholic Apostolics. They became a small, pious group, very orthodox in belief and less and less insistent upon the Adventism which had been their one distinctive trait. Their churches passed into the hands of other bodies which needed them: Anglican, Roman Catholic, and Orthodox. Individual members made their submission to Rome or to Canterbury and finally in 1963 the great cathedral church in Gordon Square was leased to the Church of England as their chaplaincy to the University of London. The last apostle died in 1903 and there are now no clergy left, although some services from the Irvingite liturgy are still read in Gordon Square. The Church, now dedicated to Christ the King, stands as a magnificent memorial to a movement founded by a small group of connoisseurs whose lives Edward Irving had changed.

J. S. GUMMER

ISHTAR

Ishtar was a radiant goddess rapt in beauty, terrifying and tempestuous, 'lady of resplendent light': eight-pointed star, symbol of Ishtar, from a boundary stone, c 1120 BC

ISHTAR was the Semitic name for the old Sumerian goddess Inanna, the most powerful goddess in Mesopotamia. Representing the full potency of womanhood and maidenhood, and possessed of subtle powers in shaping the fortunes of man, she was worshipped for more than 2000 years. Doubtless many facets of her character altered during this period; and different aspects of the goddess were venerated in different cities.

For the appraisal of Ishtar there is no more revealing source than the Sumerian hymn, *The Exaltation of Inanna*. Composed in about 2350 BC by Enheduanna, the daughter of King Sargon of Agade in Akkad, in the north of Babylonia, this long poem describes the struggle for her supremacy over Nanna, the moon god in the southern city of Ur, and her final acceptance in the city of Uruk (Erech), also in the south, by the high god, An.

Reading between the lines, we can see how King Sargon, a usurper, set the divine seal to his empire over Sumer and Akkad by equating Sumerian Inanna with Akkadian Ishtar. Here is a glimpse of the kind of political and religious struggle so frequent in the long history of ancient Egypt, but more rarely revealed in Mesopotamia.

This poem, which begins with the description of Inanna as the lady who possessed all the attributes of divinity, tells of her many accomplishments. Following the description of the dramatic struggle against the older divinities and against the wicked collusion of the older gods in Ur and Uruk, we end in a hymn of praise, through which the high priestess and her goddess emerge triumphant.

Inanna is the radiant lady rapt in beauty, terrifying and tempestuous, but she is also seen as a lady of resplendent light, beloved of heaven and earth. Inanna-Ishtar is also the dread goddess, who can, if she will, accurse vegetation and command fear in mankind. Not only is she possessed of sexual potency, able to control both fertility and sterility, but she is also a mighty goddess in battle, and this martial quality of Ishtar was as pervasive as any in the later development of her character.

Terrifying Seductress

In the hymn, she is described as 'the lady mounted on a beast' and as 'lent wings by the storm'; and in art she is frequently shown mounted on a lion or lioness, or leading both together. For example, on the high rock carvings of Maltai in Assyria, she occupied a prominent place in the procession of the gods; she was mounted on a lioness, and no doubt gave her blessing to the Assyrian armies as they marched through the defiles which separated Assyria from Iran, on their annual campaigns.

The description of her as having been 'lent wings by the storm' recalls the goddess's many sinister images, among which one of the most striking is the great terracotta, known as the Burney relief, in which the naked, winged goddess, usually called 'Lilith', with feathered legs and birds' talons, mounted on lions, appears in the guise of a seductive vamp of terrible aspect. Here she is seen to be of 'terrible countenance', in the words of the poem. In the early poems another side of Inanna-Ishtar's character is revealed, namely, of the goddess who presided over divination, incubation and oneiromancy, the interpretation of dreams.

She was invested with all the great powers of womankind, and while possessed of seductive beauty and charm, could, if so moved, turn rivers to blood.

Inanna-Ishtar presided over one of the most important ceremonies of the year – the ritual marriage of the god, in the course of which the king was wedded to the high priestess and in this way induced for his people the promise of agricultural prosperity. Indeed, on the famous stone vase from Uruk, c 3300 BC, Inanna herself may perhaps be recognized, taking part in the spring festival. There is certainly evidence from later periods of the king's special relationship to Ishtar, the goddess who in the words of A. L. Oppenheim 'becomes the carrier, the fountainhead, of his power and prestige'.

For the people of Agade, Ishtar was an incarnation of the planet Venus, which was known as Dilbat. In military history, Ishtar of Nineveh and Ishtar of Arbela are prominent in battle and ensure victory for the Assyrian armies. A famous war poem of Tukulti-Ninurta I, referring to an event in the 13th century BC, tells how Ishtar intervened at a critical point in the battle as a result of which the Assyrians triumphed over Kashtiliash, King of Babylon.

Ishtar was also invoked as a healer; indeed she made a memorable journey in about 1375 BC from Nineveh to Thebes, in Egypt, in order to lay hands on the aged and ailing King Amenophis III. This was not the first occasion on which her powers had been so used. But the most sinister episode in the mythology concerning this goddess is the

account of her descent into Hades, a tale of early Sumerian origin, in which Inanna strives dangerously with her sister, the queen of the underworld, and only narrowly succeeds in escaping from it.

Lady of the Dawn

Ishtar, however, is often thought of as an erotic goddess concerned with sexual intercourse, and later in history her hierodules or prostitutes were to earn a licentious and evil reputation, especially in the city of Uruk, where there was an elaborately organized college of priestesses of Ishtar, the head of which was the high priestess herself. This cult enjoyed a considerable expansion elsewhere, and finally emanated in the lewd practices of the Phoenician Astarte, and Hebrew Ashtaroth, so much condemned by the Old Testament prophets.

There is evidence that organizations similar to the one in Uruk existed first in Ashur, and then in Babylon. In Ashur, the religious capital of Assyria, the remains of a temple which belonged to Ishtar *dinitu*, 'the lady of the dawn', or the 'lighting up' have been excavated. What happened within the sacred precincts may be deduced from a series of lead discs and tokens found elsewhere in the same city. These plaques showed men, and women who were probably hierodules in the service of the goddess, enjoying sexual intercourse on the brick pillars of the temple. Other figures are also engaged in an erotic dance.

This practice has an interesting counterpart in Herodotus's account of a strange marriage practice in Babylonia, in the course of which eligible women sat in the temple and intending suitors cast a coin in their laps, invoking the name of the goddess in settlement and witness of the marriage contract.

(See also ASTARTE; GILGAMESH; MESOPOTAMIA; PROSTITUTION.)

M. E. L. MALLOWAN

The Eyes of Death

In a Sumerian poem, the judges of the underworld pronounce death on Inanna:

The pure Ereshkigal seated herself upon
    her throne,
The Annunaki, the seven judges, pronounced
    judgement before her,
They fastened (their) eyes upon her, the eyes
    of death,
At their word, the word which tortures the
    spirit . . .
The sick woman was turned into a corpse,
The corpse was hung from a stake.

S. N. Kramer *Sumerian Mythology*

FURTHER READING: W. W. Hallo and J. J. A. Van Dijk, *The Exaltation of Inanna* (AMS Press, 1979); S. N. Kramer, *Sumerian Mythology* (University of Pennsylvania Press, 1972); A. L. Oppenheim, *Ancient Mesopotamia, Portrait of a Dead Civilization* (Univ. of Chicago Press, 1964).

ISIS

THE GREAT GODDESS of the ancient Egyptians, Isis was the wife of Osiris, the god who died and was restored to life. He had been king of Egypt, but his evil brother Seth, whom the Greeks later identified with the monster Typhon, had killed and dismembered him and buried the pieces in various places. Isis searched for and found the pieces, put them together and revived him. Osiris became king of the underworld and their son Horus, called Harpocrates by the Greeks, became ruler over Egypt.

As Queen of Egypt, Isis' hieroglyphic symbol is the throne. She is also the exemplary mother who has taken infinite

pains to nurse, protect and bring up her son Horus and she is frequently depicted suckling him. With care and incantations she protected him from all diseases, and after the death of Osiris she saved him from Seth who wanted to murder him. When Seth brought a lawsuit against Horus before the court of the gods, intending to become king of Egypt himself, Isis intervened and enabled her son to win the case. Isis therefore did everything that a good woman can do for her husband and child, and became the model for all Egyptian women.

Her sacred animal is the cow, the mother of calves and provider of milk, 'the fruitful image of the all-producing goddess'. For Isis gives life, fertility and prosperity to people, animals and fields.

As man fertilizes woman, and Osiris Isis, so did the annual flooding of the Nile fertilize the soil of Egypt; coming in the middle of the hot summer, this inundation was looked upon as a miracle and attributed to Isis. When the river dried up in the summer, it meant that Osiris was dead, killed by Seth-Typhon, the hot wind of the desert. But Isis searches for the dead Osiris and finds him on the day of the Nile flood in the river's holy waters. The water, Osiris, flows over the withered earth, Isis, and fertilizes it.

The Nile flood coincides with the first appearance of Sirius, just before sunrise, and this was interpreted as a causal event; Sirius (Egyptian Sothis) was seen as the star of the Nile flood and the star of Isis.

The day of the rising of Sirius and of the river's flooding became the sacred New Year's Day of the Egyptians.

After the conquest of Egypt by Alexander the Great in 331 BC the country was ruled by Greeks for 300 years, and during this period the cult of Isis became completely Hellenized. When the Romans took over the government in 30 BC they relied on the support of the Greek middle class in Egypt and the language of administration remained Greek; during this era, the goddess's cult spread over the entire Mediterranean basin. It was only when Constantine the Great, after his victory at the Milvian bridge in 312 AD raised Christianity to the level of the national religion, that the Isis cult lost its importance and was subsequently prohibited.

Seeking the Dead Osiris

The Greeks identified the Egyptian Isis with their Greek goddesses: Isis, the provider of corn, was the Greek Demeter; Isis, the goddess of love, was Aphrodite; Isis, wife of the king of the gods, was Hera; Isis, the goddess of magic arts, was Hecate, and so on. By depicting Isis as the prototype of the human woman, she was put on a par with the Greek heroine, Io, who was loved by Zeus and had been changed into a cow, the Isis animal. A gad-fly sent by Hera chased poor Io over land and sea until, after a long and frantic flight, she came to Egypt. There, on the banks of the Nile, Zeus changed her back into a woman. This myth was a consolation for everybody who was hunted throughout life as Io was; at the same time it demonstrated the close connection between Greece and Egypt.

Isis was also compared with other goddesses such as Artemis, Persephone and Nemesis, and especially with Tyche, the goddess of fortune (the Roman Fortuna), and with Providence. These various identifications are the expression of living religious feeling. The great goddess appears in many different forms and always reveals new aspects. She is called *myrionymos,* 'the one with ten thousand names', and a Latin inscription is translated as: 'Thou, the one who is all, goddess Isis.' Her whole being is impenetrable, but behind her many faces and names there is one and the same divine Unknown.

Next to Isis are always her husband Osiris and her son Horus and she can never be viewed individually, without her family. However, during the Greek period of Egypt a change set in as other sides of the nature of Osiris were given prominence, and he was given the name of Osiris-Apis, abbreviated to Serapis. Apis was the sacred bull of Memphis, the old capital of Egypt, and Serapis was the god of this city. However, he also became the god of the new capital Alexandria and of the new Greek dynasty, the Ptolemies.

Isis' ancient role as throne goddess, the Queen of Egypt was perpetuated among

Isis was the mother of the god Horus, with whom the pharaoh was identified: in this wall painting from a tomb the goddess is shown embracing Prince Amun-kher-khopsh, son of Ramses III: 12th century BC

the Greek kings; Cleopatra appeared on official occasions in the costume, one might even say in the guise, of Isis. The Isis religion therefore had a political element, it was the national religion of the Egyptian state: those who worshipped Isis and Serapis acknowledged their loyalty to the reigning royal house.

This fact encouraged the spread of the Isis and Serapis cult in the Greek ruling circles of the Ptolemies, in Cyrene, Cyprus, Crete, the coastal towns of Asia Minor and the Greek islands whose religious centre was Delos. On the other hand, for political reasons, an expansion beyond the sphere of influence of the Ptolemies was not regarded favourably anywhere. There were only branches of the Isis cult in seaports, such as Athens, Salonika and on Euboea. But even in Egypt itself, linking the royal cult with the Isis-Serapis religion was in many respects a disadvantage as pure religious feelings cannot arise when the practice of a religion is welcomed and rewarded so distinctly by those in high places.

The political decline of the Ptolemies, which started in 200 BC, followed by the complete loss of autonomy that resulted from Egypt's incorporation into the Roman Empire, provided a real opportunity for the Isis religion to expand. Having lost its political aspect, it became possible for the religious and ethical aspect to be strengthened. On Delos, for instance, the Isis cult became purely religious, and as Delos was an important centre for trade with Italy, the Delian cult even reached that country.

The transformation of the cult of Isis into a religion of Mysteries first occurred in the Roman Empire. Because there was no longer a political aspect to worshipping the goddess, the cult now appealed to people as individuals: each one was personally offered salvation, and promised regeneration after death. If a man entered into the service of Isis it was his own personal decision.

The consecration ceremonies of the Isis Mysteries during the Imperial period are described in detail in *The Golden Ass* of Apuleius. There was a wealth of rites: the morning opening of the temple, the vigils, the abstention from wine, meat and love; the rites of cleanliness which included wearing white linen clothes, shaving the head and ablutions. Novices lived for a time within the precincts of the temple; the statue of Isis was contemplated, there was ecstatic prayer and obligatory tears were shed. The worthiness of the candidates was tested at a kind of hearing, and anyone who had sinned gravely was rejected. Sins were confessed and forgiven through immersion in water, and worshippers pledged themselves under oath to the service of the deity and to secrecy. With every new variation the sacred myth of Isis was restated, the seeking and the finding; in each procession Isis sought the dead Osiris, and found him every time the holy water was drawn.

The initiation into the Mysteries was in three stages and consisted of a voluntary ritual death and revival. The initiate stepped on to the 'threshold of Proserpina' (the Greek

Roger Wood Studio

Persephone) and went on a journey 'through all the elements' for which mechanical appliances were probably used. As in the case of Freemasons, there also seems to have been a coffin ritual, and perhaps a baptism of fire. In all probability, a 'sacred wedding', a sexual union, was an integral part of the initiation. Finally, the initiate received a new name and the mystics then partook of a communal meal, with music and dancing.

Garden of Religion

There was an entire vocabulary of religious symbols: the life of man was a pilgrimage or a sea journey, the sinful world was the sea, the religion of Isis was the ship and the haven, and Isis herself the mast and the sail. Her priests were the fishermen who rescued the souls from the sea, the evil world, or bird-catchers who caught the souls (birds or butterflies) with their lime-twigs; the mystics were soldiers on holy military service for Isis, or gardeners who laboriously cultivated the garden of religion. The Isis priests were the true philosophers, who attained the perception of God, and the functionaries in the religious organization of the community were the legitimate 'consuls'; the community itself was called Ecclesia, like the Greek general assembly and later the Christian Church.

The wheel was the symbol of Isis, the sponge indicated the purification of the mystics, and the ladder their spiritual advancement. The anchor symbolized the religion that granted security, the bosom the all-providing goddess, the amphora, a two-handled vessel, the holy water; the lamp stood for the night-feast of the goddess, and the yardstick, justice. The winnow, in which the grain is separated from the chaff, represented the cleansing of the soul in the initiation, the palm the 'victory' of the mystic and his rebirth.

Great pilgrimages were undertaken in the service of Isis, from Rome to Egypt, and indeed as far as Syene, now Aswan, where the source of the Nile was said to be, and where the holy water was drawn when the Nile was in spate. Above all, outstanding festival cycles took place in the service of Isis. One of these was the festival of the goddess as mistress of navigation on 5 March. This was a spring festival, when the beginning of the navigation period was ceremonially inaugurated by the 'voyage of Isis'. The goddess's worshippers walked through the town in a long procession, wearing masks, and accompanied by music and choirs, and the first ship was then put to sea. The festival was also called *ploiaphesia*, which can be roughly translated as a 'launching'. Isis herself inaugurated the navigation for the year, as according to the myth she had been the first to set sail on a ship. There were two other important festivals, one on 24–25 December and the other on 5–6 January, dates which were also important holy days in the competing Christian religion.

The abolition of all frontiers in the Mediterranean area under the *Pax Romana*, with trade and communication among countries restricted less than at any time in history, encouraged the spread of the Isis

Mysteries. Like the Jews and the Christians, the Greeks from Egypt formed small communities in all the towns of Asia Minor in order to practise their native cult, and also helped one another in other ways. Anyone who came into an Isis community did not suffer materially; he would have friends and helpers.

It is clear that the 'church' of Isis had a 'mission' during the Imperial period, and that Memphis and Rome were the holy cities. At four places in Greece and Asia Minor, when Isis sanctuaries were being excavated, identical sacred texts were discovered, depicting Isis proclaiming her power. There is therefore no doubt that propaganda was being spread. It may be assumed that there were Isis sanctuaries or shrines in all the Mediterranean ports, and also in many inland cities and towns.

The cult's growth was partly because of its rather exotic nature: the strange and mysterious rites were an attraction, and at the same time it was Hellenized to such an extent that people quickly became accustomed to it. On the other hand many Egyptian concepts still clung like tiresome and disregarded eggshells to the Isis religion. This was particularly the case with regulations concerning priests. They had to be born into the caste, as they could not be elected, they had to cut their hair, wear only linen garments, refrain from eating various kinds of food and on the whole observe many taboos. Only a native Egyptian could be considered for high office in the priesthood; a large-scale mission was impossible and in view of the tolerant nature of the religion was probably never envisaged. In any case a type of lay clergy had evolved in Greece and Rome, the 'bearers of the shrine', who held leading positions in the religious community. In Egypt itself they were a group of laymen who were called in to act in a subordinate capacity without being accepted into the priest-caste.

Mistress of the Elements

In the Roman Empire the Isis and Serapis shrines had characteristic features in common. The temples were built in the Greek style; but instead of the old roof construction they often had vaulted roofs. Most of the statues were in the Greek style but there were also those in the style of Egypt, or simply stiff-limbed statues imported from Egypt. There were also representations of Apis, the son Horus with a hawk's head, the servant Anubis with a dog's head, and the sacred animals.

Several hymns were written in honour of Isis, but *aretalogies*, reports of the miraculous deeds of Isis and Serapis which were recorded in the temple, are the most characteristic feature of the literature that developed through the worship of the goddess. For fishermen who were dying with thirst on the high seas Serapis changed the salt water into fresh water; he helped one of his priests on Delos in a critical legal dispute; and he also lengthened the life of a servant by causing a stranger to become drunk and die in his place, for this god was able to 'change the clothes of destiny'.

Michael Holford/British Museum

The exemplary mother of the ancient Egyptians, Isis was later identified with various Greek and Roman goddesses; her cult eventually became a religion of Mysteries: glazed porcelain bust of Isis *(above)* and *(facing page)* relief of the goddess; she wears a disc set between cow's horns on her head-dress

According to a recent theory, the literary form of the love story developed from these accounts of miracles. Several classical novels such as the story of Psyche and Cupid by Apuleius, would therefore be coded texts of the Isis religion.

During the period of the Roman Empire the Mysteries of Isis were strongly influenced by Greek philosophical theories. Isis is 'provider of all things in Nature, mistress of all the elements'. She embodies all contrasts: light and dark, day and night, fire and water, life and death, beginning and end. Whoever enters her service as a slave will achieve true freedom. Apuleius describes Osiris as Creator of the world.

The psychology of the Mysteries was apparently quite Platonic: the soul is not bound firmly to the body but comes from the Beyond; it plunged into the sinful body and must try to free itself and return to God. The whole life of man is governed by the goddess. The many external vicissitudes of life, all mishaps and trials, appear to be afflictions of wayward chance, of the goddess Fortuna. But if a man becomes converted and enters the service of Isis, it will be seen that all the vicissitudes were caused by Providence only in order to lead mankind to salvation. Fortuna and Providence therefore come together in Isis. The influence of the stars, blind Fate, so much feared by the people of late antiquity, was broken by Isis; her servants were confident that the goddess was standing above the stars and, as Providence, was guiding both them and Fate.

R. MERKELBACH

Roger Wood Studio

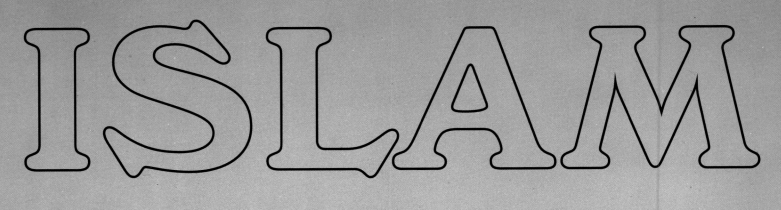

ISLAM

The faith of Islam encompasses both a simplicity that a child can understand and a complex mysticism far beyond the grasp of the ordinary Moslem. The creed 'God is the only God; Mohammed is God's messenger' is whispered in the ear of a new-born baby, repeated throughout life and traditionally is the last utterance of the dying

ISLAM (PROPERLY AL-ISLAM), a word which means submission to God, is the name given to the religious system derived from the mission of the prophet Mohammed in Arabia in the 7th century AD. One who submits to God is a Moslem, a title which includes nominal adherents. A distinction is made in the Koran between submission and belief or faith; belief is not a mere acceptance of doctrine but involves a whole pattern of behaviour.

At about the age of 40 Mohammed began to receive revelations in Mecca from God, but he faced much opposition there from Arab pagans and his new religion did not become really established until after his move to Medina about 12 years later, in 622. There he found more followers and gradually built up a powerful Moslem community. This was a form of theocracy in which he, as God's representative, had to be obeyed. Islam has never distinguished between the secular and the sacred; it regards all aspects of life as being under God's control.

There are several divisions within Islam, but the majority of Moslems belong to the

The Koran, God's eternal and uncreated word, revealed to Mohammed, is regarded as infallible ... it threatens severe punishment in the hereafter, or promises delights in the garden of paradise

body commonly called Sunnites, who developed a system with four bases.

First, the Koran, God's eternal and uncreated word, revealed to Mohammed from time to time during the Meccan and Medinan periods, is regarded as infallible. It gives guidance on many subjects; it summons man to submit to God and to do God's will; it threatens severe punishment in the afterlife to the wicked, or promises delights in the garden of paradise to those who worship strictly and pay legal alms; at times it expresses mystical thoughts in language of great beauty. But, as Islam expanded, many problems arose with which the Koran did not deal, so another authority was sought.

This was eventually provided in Tradition, traced to Mohammed, or at least to some of his companions. During the first two centuries much energy was expended in collecting such material, but only in the 3rd century of Islam were the collections of Tradition, which became canonical, finally written down.

In the collections, each tradition is preceded by a chain of transmitters, and marks are commonly added about the quality of its reliability. An elaborate science developed regarding the transmitters, types of traditions, methods of receiving and transmitting. This chain, while an important element in deciding reliability, was not the only one.

Schools of the Sunnites

The third basis is agreement by recognized authorities, even perhaps by the general community, for a tradition represents Mohammed as saying 'My people will never agree on an error'. This basis has an element of vagueness, for Islam has had no councils for formulating doctrines or reaching decisions. But with the passage of time means of agreement were evolved.

The fourth basis is deduction by analogy (*qiyas*). In earlier times, some authorities gave decisions on the basis of their own opinion, or held that a certain procedure was for the good of the community. This was too subjective so eventually qiyas prevailed; now qualified authorities form decisions by seeking an analogy in the other three bases.

According to Sunnite theory, these bases provide guidance on all subjects. Many schools of thought developed in Sunnite Islam, four of which survived. The Hanafi is

traced to Abu Hanifa of Kufa who died in 767, but the real founders of the school were two of his pupils. It later became the dominant school of the Turkish Ottoman Empire and the Indian subcontinent. The Maliki school is traced to Malik ibn Anas of Medina (d.795) who compiled a law-book, and whose ideas were developed by followers. It is now found mainly in North Africa.

The Shafii school goes back to Mohammed ibn Idria al-Shafii (d.820), an outstanding authority, whose writings exerted great influence. He studied with Malik and spent some time in some other centres, eventually settling in Egypt. This school has been predominant in southern Arabia, Indonesia, Upper Egypt and East Africa. The Hanbali school is traced to Ahmad ibn Hanbal (d. 855) who had at one time been a pupil of Shafii. In some respects it is noticeably stricter than the others. It is now found in central Arabia, and has had some influence on certain reformers in Egypt.

These schools are not sects, for there is no serious difference on matters of theology; but their views differ regarding a number of details of legal practice. The law, called *sharia* (path), is a divine law, given by God and developed from this in matters of detail

Facing page: Devout Moslems perform formal acts of worship five times each day: muezzin calling the faithful to prayer. *Below* Allah is the only God according to the Islamic faith: design using the letters of his name in a mosque in Istanbul. All pictorial representation of Allah is forbidden in Islam

under divine control. It deals with all subjects, for God's law applies in every sphere.

The Five Pillars

There are five pillars of practical religion. The first is the recitation of the attestation of belief: 'God is the only God; Mohammed is God's messenger.' This stresses God's uniqueness and Mohammed's mission as the final prophet. It is whispered in the ear of the newly born child; it is continually repeated throughout life; it should be the last utterance of the dying; and mourners chant it as they carry the bier to the grave.

The second pillar is worship. The formal worship (*salat*) is performed five times daily, preceded by ceremonial ablution and an expression of one's intention. The times are before sunrise, after midday, in mid-afternoon, soon after sunset, and when night has finally fallen. Worship is performed facing Mecca, the focal point towards which all prayer is directed being the *Kaaba*, God's House, in Mecca. Various postures are adopted: standing, bowing, kneeling, prostrating, and sitting back on one's heels. Koran verses, expressions of adoration, and some petitions are recited. Worship is essentially adoration, which may be followed by private supplications.

A certain number of sections (*rakas*) are prescribed for each period, and some supererogatory prayers are normally recommended in addition. These are said individually without a leader; but the prayers said in company with others – be it in a mosque or elsewhere – must have a leader (*imam*) who is followed by the company in words and postures.

One need not pray in a mosque, or even in company, but if a group worships together, one member must stand in front as imam. Mosques have their regular imam, but he is not to be compared with a clergyman; Islam allows no priest to stand between man and God. Attendance at the mosque is customary for midday worship on Friday, when a sermon is preached; afterwards people are allowed to resume their business, for Friday is not a sabbath in a way comparable to the Jewish or Christian sabbaths.

Legal almsgiving (*zakat*), the third pillar of religious duty, is now largely neglected because of other, more onerous, methods of taxation, but there are many who still pay it gladly. It is a tax on property possessed for

The Blue Mosque in Istanbul: it is customary for Moslems to attend a mosque for midday worship on Friday, but apart from this it is not considered necessary even to pray in company; although worship is led by an imam, who stands in front of a group of worshippers, he cannot be compared with a Western clergyman, as Islam allows no priest to come between man and God

one year, provided it exceeds a prescribed minimum. Assessments vary according to the nature of land and whether the agricultural land is irrigated or depends on rain (the latter bears a higher tax). Other criteria for the tax are animals, money and general possessions. It may be paid to a collector or directly to one of the classes who are entitled to benefit. In paying it, the intention must be expressed aloud, otherwise it becomes just a voluntary charity.

The fourth pillar, fasting, applies mainly to Ramadan, the ninth month of the Moslem lunar year, when one must abstain from food, drink and other bodily satisfactions from early morning, when one can distinguish a black from a white thread, until after sunset. Travellers and invalids are exempt, but, when the journey or the illness is over, they should make up for the days of abstention missed. The lunar year is 11 days shorter than the solar, so Ramadan moves backward round the seasons over 33 years. This means that the observance is severe in hot countries when Ramadan occurs during the summer months.

A sincere Moslem carefully observes the fast, the only modification being that, in a country at a high latitude with long days in summer and short in winter, he may calculate an average length for a day. Some Moslems, however, are content to fast at the beginning and end of the month, and others pay little heed. Fasting on a festival is forbidden. The two main festivals are the day of Sacrifice during the Pilgrimage and the period following Ramadan, when the holiday often lasts four days. Ascetics have observed additional fasts, but Tradition states that three days at a time are the limit. Some misdemeanours or sins of omission are expiated by fasting (see FASTING).

Pilgrimage is the fifth pillar of practical religion. In the pre-Islamic period, rites were observed at the Kaaba at different times, and at some places within about 12 miles from Mecca in the twelfth month of the lunar year. The purely Meccan rite is called *umra* and the other *hajj*. The umra may be performed at any time; the hajj, which has specified days in the twelfth month, is a duty which should be performed once in a lifetime by adults who are sane and have sufficient means. Women must be accompanied by a relative. If a person has the financial means to observe the hajj, but

Sonia Halliday

is incapacitated, he or she may pay the expenses of a deputy to perform it on his or her behalf; the deputy acquires no merit for himself, however.

Kissing the Black Stone
Pilgrims must halt at a station outside the sacred area and don the pilgrim garb (*ihram*). Men wear two garments, one thrown over the left shoulder and tied at the right side, the other tied round the waist and reaching below the knees. Women wear a long robe and commonly, though not necessarily, cover the face. In donning the ihram one must express one's intention. If careful about the wording, a person entering Mecca some time before the hajj may remove the pilgrim garment after the umra, and resume it later in time for the hajj.

The umra consists of going round the Kaaba seven times, kissing, or at least saluting, the Black Stone fixed in the wall, praying at certain holy spots, and running seven times between two hillocks, al-Safa and al-Marwa; a rite connected with Hagar's search for water when Abraham sent her away with Ishmael.

A sermon giving instructions about the hajj is preached on the seventh day of the twelfth month, the eighth day being the first day of the hajj proper. The people go out to Mina, but some go straight on to Arafat where, from after midday till sunset on the ninth day, the people stand on or round a sacred hill, this being the high point of the hajj. The pilgrims next stampede to Muzdalifa and go on the following day to

Interior of the Blue Mosque: engraving by Thomas Allom of the scene when crowds gathered there in 1839 to see the Sacred Standard of the Prophet, which was being displayed in the mosque

Mina where there are three pillars, at which they throw stones: it is said they are stoning Satan, but the origin of the practice is not clear. Animals are sacrificed, a rite observed that day throughout the Moslem world.

This is the great festival. The head should be shaved, or the hair cut, after which ordinary clothing is assumed. For three days the pilgrims throw stones at the three pillars in the valley of Mina, at one on the first day, at all three on the others. Then they go on to Tanim where they don pilgrim dress before performing a farewell umra.

Many come to Mecca hoping to die there, bringing their shrouds which they dip in the sacred well Zem Zem; pilgrims commonly take some of the water home with them. Many also go on to visit Mohammed's tomb at Medina as a natural act of piety, for it is not a religious duty.

Theological Differences
Islam has had its theological differences. The Koran is not a theological treatise, for Mohammed was primarily a preacher, and like many preachers he was inclined to overemphasize the point he was making. This is clear in references to God's omnipotence at one moment and to man's responsibility at another. If one chooses one's texts from the Koran, ignoring those which con-

tradict them, it is possible to argue that man is responsible for his actions and able to do right more or less unaided, or alternatively that God is the only active agent, with man being almost an automaton.

Mohammed obviously did not believe the latter for, if so, it would have been useless to urge men to obey God. But some of his first listeners, who felt that he did, turned the argument against him by saying, 'Had God so willed we should not have served anything apart from him' (sura 16.37). To this, Mohammed's only reply was that their fathers had spoken similarly. Discussions soon took place and factions developed.

Out of these discussions an important movement arose, which used rational arguments to uphold its views. It was called Mutazilitism, coming from a root meaning 'to withdraw'. The orthodox explanation speaks of them seceding from the community, but there is reason to question this. The Mutazilites called themselves the people of unity and justice, stressing two important doctrines. They believed so strongly in God's unity that they rejected the doctrine of the eternity of the Koran, as this suggested an eternal being co-existing alongside God. For the same reason, they denied that God has attributes, for this indicated multiplicity; when it was said that God's attributes were in his essence, this seemed worse than the Christian Trinity. They held the attributes were God's essence. The insistence on justice means they held that God does what is best for his creatures, and this involves man's free will.

Many Moslems come to Mecca hoping to die there, bringing their shrouds which they dip in the sacred well Zem Zem

Some early Western scholars thought the Mutazilites were free-thinkers, but further research has discredited this. They were sincere Moslems and, although some of them indulged in speculation, insistence on God's unity – the fundamental Islamic doctrine – coloured all their thinking. It was unfortunate that the Caliph al-Mamun issued a decree in 827 stating that the Koran is created, or not co-eternal. There was violent opposition, and an inquisition was set up, but so persistent was the opposition that some 20 years later the Caliph al-Mutawakkil declared official the doctrine of the eternity of the Koran, and instituted a persecution of the Mutazilites in turn.

Sunnite Orthodoxy

The doctrine of al-Ashari (d.935), who had been brought up in Mutazilite teaching but eventually abandoned it, and of similar thinkers, was propounded by rational methods learned from them. Sunnite theology hardened under the scholastic theologians, among their chief doctrines being the eternity of the Koran, God's decrees, an acceptance of Koranic anthropomorphic phrases without asking how they could be used of God, and acceptance of items of eschatology, such as the bridge over hell (see INTERROGATION OF THE DEAD).

An attempt at mediation was made regarding the decrees by a doctrine called *kasb* (acquisition). This states that while God is the only active agent, man can acquire freedom of action. It has been said this means little more than that man is the place where God's actions occur. 'God will not burden any soul beyond its power. It will be credited with the good it has acquired and debited with the evil it has acquired' is the basis of this doctrine. Some argue that if God is the only agent, it matters little where his actions occur.

The famous mystic and theologian, al-Ghazali (d.1111), argued that tyranny can occur only when someone interferes with another's property. As all property is God's, what he does cannot be called tyranny. This may do justice to God's omnipotence, but it suggests a low conception of man. But despite these doctrines, not all Moslems are fatalists. There is an element of fatalism, especially among the common people, but no one can really be a practical fatalist. Many Moslems stoutly uphold man's free will.

The Path of the Sufis

There were ascetic tendencies in early Islam which gave rise to a significant mystical movement. This was Sufism, a name derived from *suf* (wool), referring to the coarse woollen garments of ascetics. Sufis have similarities to mysticism in other religions, but their beliefs are in fact closely related to the Koran and Mohammed. Those who wished to join the Sufis normally attached themselves to one spiritual director. He demanded implicit obedience as he guided them in following the Sufi Path, and so controlled any excitable tendencies.

From the 12th century, Sufi orders developed, linking themselves to one particular great Sufi. In addition to prescribed prayers, they have their own rituals observed both by those who spend their lives in worship and by others who visit their centres to join in their worship. A typical practice is the *dhikr*, which may consist of repeating the name Allah, or some other sacred phrase; it is often associated with music, which has no place in normal mosque worship. Many Moslems have found something evil in music, especially stringed and wind instruments, called the Devil's pipes. A dance may also be associated with the dhikr, the Mevlevi dervishes being noted for this (see DERVISH). The dhikr may lead to a state of trance, novices being under the supervision of a spiritual director.

The Sufi Path has as its goal direct union with God, and some Sufis have proclaimed beliefs that orthodox Moslems consider blasphemous. A notable example is the teaching of al-Hallaj, who said, 'I am the Truth'. For this utterance he was crucified in 922. There are suggestions of pantheism in Sufism, especially connected with their doctrine of the Oneness of Being. This teaches that God is the only absolute reality. But Sufism found a place within Islam, thanks largely to the influence of al-Ghazali, the teacher who resigned his chair in Baghdad and devoted himself to solitude for 11 years.

Belief in the virtue of saints developed quite early and still has a firm hold on the common people. There are different categories of saints, from those who sustain the world to saints connected with Sufi orders and finally to local saints. They can convey blessing (*baraka*), so their tombs are often visited and their prayers sought. Each saint has a special season when people gather at the tomb for the annual visit, the *ziyara*, when a fair is held.

In North Africa *marabouts* (hermits and monks) exert great influence, both alive and dead, and are consulted in time of need. In Shiite Islam, pilgrimages are made to the shrines of the *imams* (hereditary semi-divine rulers) at Meshed, Karbala, Najaf and Kazimayn; and so important are the imams that many feel such visits are equivalent to the hajj to Mecca. In the early period, the caliphate's role was also important, although the caliph never had the right to determine matters of faith. He should not be compared with the pope, but was simply the defender of the faith and head of the community.

The Imams of the Shia

There is, however, within Islam a party which considers a leader of paramount importance. This is Shiite Islam, the official religion of Iran and the religion of important communities in Iraq, India, Pakistan and elsewhere. The Shiites speak of an imam whose role as a leader is more comprehensive than that of a mere caliph. The movement, with political origins as is common in Islam, developed among supporters of Ali, Mohammed's cousin, who, they felt, should have been the first caliph.

In the course of time some doctrines, differing from those of the Sunnites, began to develop. The Imamites, the main body of the Shia, believe in 12 imams, the first being Ali, the next two his sons al-Hasan and al-Husayn, and the remainder in direct line of descent from al-Husayn who, with his followers, was killed at Karbala, an event which is remembered annually. The imams are held to be sinless, and it is believed that a divine light passed from one to another. The 12th imam, Mohammed al-Muntazar, withdrew from human affairs in 878, but is believed to be still ruling the world. At its opening early this century the first parliament in Iran was said to be held under the auspices of this hidden imam.

The imams are invested with an almost divine aura, not implying any idea of incarnation, but rather that they are endowed with divine qualities. The 12th imam, who is to return at the end of time, is believed to have absolute power. Love of the imams is necessary for salvation, according to the Shiites. It is believed that, on the bridge

which all the dead must attempt to cross, one of the barriers is love of the imams. No one lacking this can cross.

Shiites have their own collections of traditions, transmitted through imams, but there is no place for the analogical deduction and consensus of recognized authorities of the Sunnites. Instead there are *mujtahids*, 'men who exert effort', agents of the imam, who have complete knowledge of the Koran and the Traditions and so can guide the people. In doctrine Shiites teach free will, and they differ from Sunnites in minor details of ritual, as well as adding a phrase to the call to prayer. A temporary marriage with a specific date for its termination is allowed. A Shiite may dissemble his beliefs when in danger because of them.

The Ismailites are a smaller branch of Shiites, but became prominent earlier than the Imamites. They believe in seven imams. A dynasty was established in Tunisia in 910 headed by Ubaydallah, called the Mahdi, a reputed descendant of Mohammed's daughter Fatima. This was the Fatimid Caliphate which conquered Egypt and ruled there till overthrown by Saladin in 1171. During its rule, Egypt was a great centre of Islamic culture, and many fine Fatimid buildings and works of art remain.

There have been splits also among the Ismailites themselves. The Aga Khan, head of one section, is invested with an element of near-divinity. The Nusayrites in north Syria broke off from the main stream, a notable feature of their doctrine being their belief in Ali's divinity.

'The Only True Moslems'

Another early split in Islam was that of the Kharijites who had fought on Ali's side against Muawiya, but objected to the dispute being put to arbitration. They were originally warlike and puritanical, and a thorn in the side of the caliphate. They taught free will, insisted that faith must be proved by works and felt they were the only true Moslems. They admitted no superior class or hereditary claim, holding that anyone, no matter what his origin, was eligible to become caliph, provided he was a sincere Moslem and possessed the requisite qualities. If a caliph proved unworthy he could be deposed. For them, fighting to spread the faith was a missionary task.

Today they are represented by the Ibadites in Oman, East Africa, and parts of North Africa, but are not uncompromising like their ancestors. They are prepared to intermarry with other Moslems. They do not believe the Koran is uncreated (eternal) and hold that serious sinners will go to hell for ever, contrary to the Sunnite view that Mohammed will intercede for his people and that all who have even a grain of faith will eventually be freed from hell.

Early Islam saw much fighting, first in Arabia, then farther afield. The word *jihad* (striving) has been used for what is called the holy war, but it has a wider connotation. The Koran rebukes men who failed to go out to fight, but Mohammed was fighting against Arab pagans. In later times, many Moslems have argued that jihad is not primarily an armed conflict, but means

The basis of the Islamic faith was founded on revelations received from God in about 610. However, the movement was not truly established until some 12 years later; even then there was strong opposition in many quarters to the teachings. Fierce battles were fought with the unbelievers. These miniatures from the Topkapi Museum in Istanbul show some of the major events in the history of Islam. These include some interesting battle scenes, in which the enemy forces, most unusually, employ elephants in their cavalry

striving in general, especially against one's lower nature. But Islam was certainly spread by the sword in many regions. Extensive territories, stretching from Spain to the borders of China, were gained by fighting; but the fighters were more interested in spreading the sphere of Islam than in forcing conversion. Jews and Christians, the other two 'peoples of the book' (the Old Testament) were allowed to retain their religions while paying extra taxes. In many regions the extension of Islam has been due to the influence of traders, notably in Malaya, the Philippines and Indonesia, as also in East, Central and West Africa. In addition Islam has conducted much missionary work in Europe and America.

By the last decade of the 20th century Islam ranked second only to Christianity among the world religions in the number of its adherents, with a total approaching the 1,000 million mark in 70 per cent of the countries of the globe. The main Islamic block of countries with a Moslem majority

Moslem worship is essentially adoration of God, and is performed facing towards the Kaaba, the house of God in Mecca: the worshippers recite verses from the Koran, expressions of adoration of God, and sometimes pray for God's help: Moslems praying in Dakar, West Africa

Picturepoint London

population extends from Turkey and Morocco, across Iraq, Iran and central Asia to Pakistan and north-western China. Bangladesh and Indonesia are outliers. Sunni Moslems account for about 83 per cent of the faithful, but the Shiites are strong in the Middle East and are in the majority in Iran and Yemen.

The whole question of Islam's relationship with the West and Western ideas and tendencies has recently become acute. The 19th century saw strong westernizing tendencies at work in Islam, notably in India and Egypt. Moslem intellectuals called for Islam to absorb the best in Western science and attitudes. The most drastic attempt to westernize a Moslem country was made in the 1920s in Turkey under Mustafa Kemal

Ataturk, who turned the former heartland of the Ottoman Empire into a secular state. These westernizing tendencies, however, provoked a formidable backlash in Islamic fundamentalism. Reversing the pattern as understood in the West, Moslem revolutionaries look not to the future but to the past. They believe that the original perfection of Islam has been corrupted and seek to restore its pristine purity and rigour; they are often fiercely hostile to Western ideas and especially to the influence of the United States, which is often denounced as 'the Great Satan'.

The century's first real fundamentalist organization was the Muslim Brotherhood, which was founded in Egypt in 1929 to overthrow the British-inspired secular constitu-

tion and restore a religious state enforcing Moslem law. The Brotherhood helped depose King Farouk in 1952, but afterwards fell out with the new republican regime. It and similar groups have played an important role in the Middle East and elsewhere in the Moslem world, including the new state of Pakistan, which was declared an Islamic Republic in 1956.

The Iranian revolution in 1979, which deposed the Shah and established another fundamentalist Islamic republic, was carried out in the name of Shia martyrs and led by the Ayatollah Khomeini, who maintained that 'true Islam lasted only for a brief period after its inception.' Some of his followers believed that he was the long-awaited Twelfth Imam; extraordinary scenes of grief accompanied his death and burial in 1989. As the 1990s wore on, the West became increasingly alarmed at the spectre of Islamic fundamentalism as a new aggressive force in the world after the collapse of Soviet Communism.
(See also DRUSES; MAHDI; MOHAMMED; SUFIS.)

JAMES ROBSON*

FURTHER READING: N.J.Coulson, *A History of Islamic Law* (Columbia Univ. Press, 1964); D.D.Duncan, *The World of Allah* (Houghton Mifflin, 1982); R. Levy, *The Social Structure of Islam* (Cambridge Univ. Press, 1957); F. Rahman, *Islam* (University of Chicago Press, 1979); Caesar E. Farah, *Islam – Beliefs & Observances* (Barrons, 1982); M.Z. Ullah, *The Islamic Concept of God* (Routledge and Kegan Paul, 1984).

Isles of the Blest

Or Fortunate Isles, a happy otherworld of lovely flowers and trees, music, feasting and beautiful women, to which souls go after death; usually located in the far west where the sun sets; St Brendan voyaged to the Isle of the Blest or Earthly Paradise; shown on medieval maps somewhere in the Atlantic.
see BRENDAN.

Ismailis

Sect of Islam, named for Ismail (d. 760), eldest son of the sixth imam or spiritual leader of the Shia Moslems, excluded from the succession by his father. In the 9th century Ismaili preachers proclaimed the imminent return to earth of Ismail's son as the Mahdi, or Messiah: the Fatimid rulers of Egypt from the 10th century were Ismailis and so were the Assassins, the terrorists of Persia and Syria in the 12th and 13th centuries: the present imam of the Ismailis is the Aga Khan.
See ISLAM; MAHDI.

Popperfoto

The witches of Italy were famed as masters of their craft. They were heirs to a tradition which reached back to the time of the Romans and Etruscans and which continues today, particularly in Sicily and the south

ITALIAN WITCHCRAFT

LA VECCHIA — the Old Religion — is still the title given to both black and white witchcraft in Italy and Sicily. Since these practices have their foundations in the beliefs of the ancient colonizers, the name is highly appropriate.

Greek, Etruscan and Egyptian rites were incorporated into the official Roman religion; and astrology, augury and divination were employed in imperial policy making. Yet it is important to understand that pagan authority condemned the dark side of magic just as zealously as the Inquisition of Christian times. Frequently, all sorcerers were driven from Rome, accused of harming state or emperor with their evil spells. Nocturnal ceremonies to invoke the infernal deities, the making of wax images and the tying of knots to cause pain, death or sexual impotence, and of course the manufacture of poisons (employed to speed up the supernatural processes) were offences punished by crucifixion or being thrown to the wild beasts.

The Roman poet Horace (1st century BC) among other classical writers described the feared magical practices in minute and horrifying detail. Apuleius (2nd century AD) gave an account of old and ugly crones and their gruesome art in *The Golden Ass*, a story about a young man who is turned into an ass through dabbling in witchcraft. The similarity between their exploits and those revealed under hideous torture during the witchcraft trials, some 1400 years later, is quite startling. Another of his works, the *Apologia*, made a careful distinction between harmful and helpful magic, the

The people of southern Italy, perhaps more than anywhere else in Europe, still retain their belief in witchcraft. Villagers in a remote district of the Campania burn a lamb in a ceremony designed to keep witches at bay

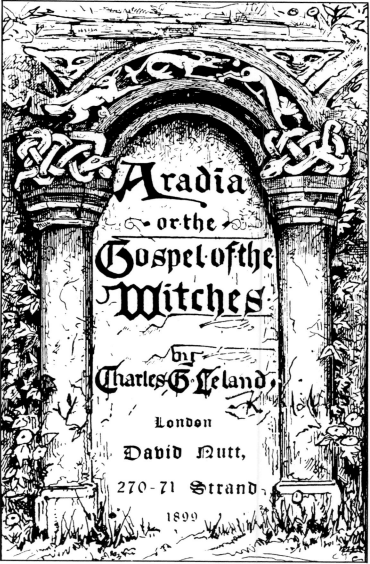

Mansell Collection

John Freeman

latter including astrology and the conjuration of demons to give the sorcerer advance knowledge of future events. The Roman witch, therefore, named *strix, saga* or *volantica* – nocturnal bird, wise woman or night flyer – was the forerunner of the Italian *strega*, the peak of whose dreadful persecution endured from the 15th to the 18th century.

In the first years of Christianity all private magical rites were forbidden and only public augury permitted. The Ostrogoths, who invaded Italy under their leader Theodoric in the 5th century, were Arian Christians; they classified divination as paganism, and therefore an offence to be punished by death. In 500 AD all sorcerers were driven from Rome. When in the following century the Lombards reached Italy they sold magicians as slaves outside their province, irrespective of whether the magic was successful.

Pagan Under the Skin

Only fragmentary evidence exists of witchcraft during the Dark Ages. While feudal rulers fought to gain control of the new kingdoms left vacant by the collapse of the Roman Empire, the Church was involved in consolidating her own supreme authority over temporal powers and destroying the

Above left Pope Urban VIII: in the early 17th century, three friars, a cardinal's nephew and a notorious sorcerer were convicted of casting spells and holding a mortuary mass in an attempt to shorten his life *Above right* Title page from *Aradia,* the book in which Charles Leland described the practice of witchcraft in Italy and Sicily; Aradia, or Herodias, was the daughter of Diana, goddess of witches

early heresies. It took many centuries for the majority of simple folk to absorb Christian tenets. Gradually pagan temples were rededicated, and St Apollinarius presided over the healing spring which had once belonged to Apollo. For a long while Christianity must have been only a veneer covering far older customs, especially since the priests were often not much better informed than their ignorant flocks. The evidence produced by the Inquisition shows that paganism and Christianity merged into a curious paradoxical faith.

Though virtually at the heart of Christian Europe, Italian peasants adhered to their ancient rites and beliefs. In the lonely glades and woodlands set aside for such pre-Christian revels they continued to honour Venus, Bacchus or Diana Herodias. The last goddess was the evil spirit said in later

centuries to lead countless bands of witches on flights through the night. It is reasonable to assume that the pagan gatherings survived in the form of the notorious witches' sabbaths.

Two strands must be distinguished in Italian witchcraft. The wise women dealing in love and healing potions, and their destructive opposites, who told simple fortunes, gathered herbs by moonlight and muttered charms, were only to be found in country regions. Although sometimes subjected to village lynch laws the pastoral witch, on the whole, remained unharmed until the hysterical outburst against witchcraft provoked by the Inquisition at the beginning of the 15th century.

Her urban counterpart, associated with the major cities of Rome and Naples, was a more sophisticated exponent of magic, a descendant of the classical sorcerers. Such people studied astrology and divination, and their interests extended to alchemy, medicine and astronomy in pursuit of a wider knowledge of the universe. Their clients were not an illiterate peasantry but the educated members of the ruling class.

The Church's attitude to sorcery was imprecise and depended upon the varying opinions of her leaders. Among the educated

Illustrations taken from 17th century Italian editions of the *Compendium Maleficarum,* showing typical scenes at a witches' sabbath; accounts of such practices extracted at Italian witch trials differed little from those obtained in other parts of Europe *Top right* Children are boiled and roasted; witches were often charged with child murder and cannibalism *Centre right* Presentation of children for the first time at the sabbath *Bottom right* Dancing at the witches' sabbath

there was a passion for knowledge and desire to see into the future, using part-magical, part-scientific processes. Popes, kings and learned men studied astrology and thereby indulged in the same grisly practices ascribed to sorcerers. To the superstitious anyone seeking to probe the unknown was disobeying God's laws, approaching heresy or in league with the Devil.

Poisons and Potions

Throughout history the particular Italian failing seems to have been making and using poisons. With their potions the witches were apparently following the national tradition. One of the earliest examples of secular legislation against such practices was instigated by the 12th century Norman king of the Two Sicilies, Roger II. He stated that the concoction of love potions, whether they worked or not, was a crime. In 1181 the Doge Orlo Malipieri of Venice also passed laws punishing poisoning and sorcery.

Emperor Frederick II of Sicily (1194–1250), known for his wide learning as 'stupor mundi', 'the wonder of the world', employed Saracen diviners and invited to his court the Scottish sage, Michael Scot, who was reputed to be a wizard. With Frederick's permission his astrologers practised the forbidden augury, using flights of birds and victims' entrails, but the Emperor had no real belief in sorcery, despite the reputation his clerical adversaries gave him. He upheld the law made by Roger, and set down that anyone tampering with food or drink to provoke love or hatred must be executed if the recipent died or lost his senses; if nothing happened the would-be sorcerer faced a year's imprisonment.

Throughout the 13th century sorcery was in Italy an offence punished in the secular courts. Astrology was not included among the forbidden arts, and papal decisions were sometimes made with the aid of astrologers. Every royal court in the kingdoms which made up Italy had its resident astrologer. But such practitioners, even though they were respected and believed, walked on thin ice. If, like Peter of Abano and Cecco d'Ascoli, they were led by their studies into heresy, they were in as much danger from the Inquisition as the sorcerers.

The witch mania which swept through Europe reached Italy in the mid-15th century; the northern territories, nearest Germany, were particularly affected. The more the Inquisition sought, the more cases of witchcraft came to light. Papal Bulls, like the one issued by Innocent VIII in 1484, turned the persecution of witches into an uncontrolled epidemic. In the first year of its publication 41 people were burned in

Federico Arborio Mella

Como after the zealous investigations of the Dominican Inquisitors.

Fear, ignorance and superstition, fanned by the desire to stamp out heresy, sent countless innocent people to the stake. Anything out of the ordinary was thought to indicate witchcraft. A woman, neither young nor pretty, who inspired love in a man, would be suspect. The village wise woman who healed, procured abortions or made love philtres was naturally assumed to have the Evil Eye and to work in conjunction with demons. When children became sick their hysterical parents sought a scapegoat and confused, lonely old women were accused of witchcraft. The most terrible tortures were then employed to extract confessions. Details of witches' sabbaths obtained in this way varied very little from those found in the rest of Europe, which suggests that the Inquisitor, wherever he might be, asked the same questions until the required answers were given.

La Volta

One particular characteristic of Italian witchcraft was the dance called La Volta. This was described as having such fantastic leaping steps as to make it incredible to the onlookers. At Como and Brescia children between eight and twelve years old, who had attended sabbaths but been reclaimed by the Inquisition, performed this dance. It appeared so difficult and skilful that the learned men concluded it could not have been learned from human beings.

It is not really surprising that reports were soon circulating which suggested that witches would outnumber the faithful. In 1510, 140 witches were burned at Brescia, and 300 in Como four years later. Fantastic stories spread that at least 25,000 people attended a sabbath near Brescia. At Valcanonica 70 more people were burned and the Inquisitor claimed to have another 5000 under suspicion.

Venetian secular authority protested vigorously because the area was threatened with depopulation. In theory, the secular court was supposed to carry out the sentences if they agreed with the findings produced by the Inquisition. In 1521 Leo X issued a Bull which gave the real state of the law, and showed that the secular court was expected to do no more than confirm the proceedings. The Inquisition was given the right to use excommunication and interdict if sentences on witches were not carried out.

The Venetian Council of Ten bravely produced a most enlightened reply and suggested proper legal regulations for future trials. They pointed out that the witch-hunters' greed for money prevented anyone from being found innocent, adding that if so many of the ignorant peasantry were in error they had need of really good preachers rather than persecutors. Such sensible attitudes were ignored.

More sophisticated magicians turned hurriedly to astrology to prevent being charged with witchcraft, but the Italian sorcerer's reputation was known far afield. When in 1439 a French baron, Gilles de Rais, had wanted to procure gold by supernatural means he had sent to Florence for a priest and necromancer named Francesco Prelati (see GILLES DE RAIS).

Despite his thirst for knowledge the cultured man of the Renaissance was extremely superstitious. The new classical studies revived interest in magic. Omens were studied. There was a widespread belief in ghosts, and in ceremonies that could evoke devils to do man's bidding. Such attitudes among literate people increased the witch-hunting atmosphere.

Devils in the Colosseum

In his autobiography, the great goldsmith and sculptor Benvenuto Cellini wrote of a learned Sicilian priest who invited him to take part in some magical ceremonies to conjure up the spirits of the dead. Accompanied by some friends, Cellini went to the Colosseum. The priest donned sorcerer's robes, drew circles on the ground and heated perfumes. The rites continued for an hour and a half, in which time Cellini said the Colosseum was filled with legions of devils.

In a notorious case in 1633 the pope himself was the victim of sorcery. A certain Giocinto Centini was told by a prophecy that his uncle, Cardinal d'Ascoli, would be the next pope. In order to shorten the life of the present pope, Urban VIII, Centini hired an Augustinian friar and notorious sorcerer, Peter of Palermo. Two other friars helped cast spells and celebrate a mortuary mass. Their attempts failed and they were all arrested.

A picture of a typical sabbath emerges from the evidence at a witch trial in 1646 when an old woman known as La Mercuria was arrested at Castelnuovo. Long suspected of being a witch, the woman was charged with the offence that, instead of swallowing the host at two Communions, she held it in her mouth to use afterwards for some devilish purposes. It was also alleged that her spells had caused a young noblewoman to miscarry. Under torture La Mercuria named other witches who in turn were tortured. One, Domenica Gratiadei, described the sabbaths at which they feasted, danced and worshipped Satan. They smeared themselves, she said, with ointments made from dead babies, among other equally appalling ingredients, and then had sexual relations with the Devil, to whom they also gave the hosts they had purloined. When the trial ended in 1647, eight people were beheaded and their bodies burned.

In 1789 Giuseppe Balsamo, known as Count Cagliostro, and his wife set up as sorcerers in a house in the Piazza Farnese in Rome (see CAGLIOSTRO). His illustrious clientele included princesses and priests. Three years later the Inquisition condemned him to death. Pope Pius VI commuted the sentence to life imprisonment and shut Cagliostro's wife in a convent.

At the end of the last century Charles Leland wrote a book entitled *Aradia*, in which he described practices that were still rife in Italy and Sicily. In most cases witches claimed to be descendants of families where the craft had been practised for generations. At their sabbaths they wore no clothes, said incantations over meal, salt, honey and water, and worshipped Diana and her daughter Aradia, or Herodias, as the female messiah. After supper they danced, sang and had sexual intercourse. Stones with natural holes through them were valued as having special powers, and the witches dealt mainly in the preparation of love philtres.

Almost more than anywhere else in modern Europe, the people of southern Italy and Sicily still retain the customs of La Vecchia. The Evil Eye is feared and the phallic sign invoked to destroy its power. Wax hearts and images are stuck with pins, and wise women consulted for charms to make people fall in or out of love, and to gain lucky lottery ticket numbers.
(See also EUROPEAN WITCH PERSECUTIONS.)

SANDY SHULMAN

Ithyphallic

'With an erect phallus': male gods are sometimes depicted in this way to emphasize their virile fertilizing and creative power; ithyphallic figures appear in prehistoric cave paintings and are connected with religious and magical rites in many parts of the world, including India, Central and South America, and Greece and Rome; in some ancient Egyptian ceremonies ithyphallic statues were carried in procession. See PHALLIC SYMBOLISM.

Roger Wood

Ivy

Powerful magical plant, associated with holly and with Christmas; as an evergreen, connected with the Roman Saturnalia and other winter festivals to mark life's continuance and coming rebirth in the spring; plant of the Greek god Dionysus and the Roman Bacchus; the god was often depicted wearing an ivy wreath and his worshippers, the Bacchae, were said to chew ivy as an aid to attaining frenzy; also connected with inspiration and poetry, and believed to diminish drunkenness.
See HOLLY AND IVY.

Axel Poignant

JACK

AS LONG AGO as 1414 it was recorded that anyone called John was likely to be nicknamed Jankin or Jack, and Jack also very early became a general term for an ordinary man, one of the common people. In the Coventry Mystery Plays and the Towneley Mystery Plays, both dating from the mid-15th century, the names Jack and Jill are used to mean any boy and girl.

Jack is the central character of several nursery rhymes. One of them is 'Jack Sprat', which in a version of 1639 also contains Jill – 'Jack will eat no fat, and Jill doth love no lean'. Another is 'This is the house that Jack built', first printed in 1755, in *Nurse Truelove's New-Year's-Gift: or, the Book of Books for Children.* But the rhyme is probably much older and has equivalents in many European languages. Then there is 'Jack and Jill' itself, which seems to date from c 1600–1650, though it has often been suggested that it contains older mythological and folklore themes, partly because the top of a hill is the last place to which anyone would normally go for water. One theory is that it is based on a Scandinavian myth in which the two children are kidnapped by the moon while they are drawing water. They can still be seen in the moon, with the water-bucket hanging from a yoke on their shoulders.

The Wise Fool

Jack is also the hero of many folktales, well-known in Britain and the United States, and with parallels on the Continent where the central character's name is Hans, Jean, Juan or whatever is the local equivalent. Jack is sometimes the wise fool, the young man whose rustic naivety is really an openness to experience that brings him rich rewards, rewards that are denied to the more cynical and materialistic. Sometimes he is the crafty, aggressive opportunist who tricks the stronger but stupider giant (and the popularity of the stories may owe something to the underlying motif of the common man turning the tables on the rich and powerful).

An example of the 'wise fool' role is the story of 'Jack and his Bargains', in which Jack is the son of a poor farmer who is heavily in debt and sends Jack to sell

Jack in the Green – a man hidden inside a framework covered with green boughs – figured in the old May Day festivities, often representing the spirit of the reviving vegetation

a cow at the fair. This happens three years running and each time, to his father's despair, instead of selling the cow for a good price, Jack exchanges it for something magical, first a wonderful stick which beats people on command, next a dear little bee with a lovely singing voice, and finally a beautiful fiddle that plays by itself. But all turns out for the best, because Jack and his three magical possessions are the only things which can make the king's daughter laugh, for she has never been known to smile. So Jack is given her hand in marriage, 'an' if they ain't dead, they're livin' yet.'

The famous tale of 'Jack and the Beanstalk' begins in much the same way, with Jack being sent by his poor widowed mother to sell a cow, but he exchanges it for five magic beans which, planted in the evening, have grown by morning into a towering beanstalk which reaches to the sky. The insatiably curious Jack promptly climbs up it till he comes to the sky, where he finds an enormous woman in an enormous house. She is the wife of an ogre who loves to eat 'boys boiled on toast', and when the ogre

appears she hides Jack in the oven. The ogre sniffs the air and says:

> Fee-fi-fo-fum,
> I smell the blood of an Englishman,
> Be he alive or be he dead,
> I'll grind his bones to make my bread.

The ogre's wife puts him off the scent and while he is asleep, Jack steals a bag of gold and takes it home. On later visits he steals a hen that lays golden eggs and a golden harp which plays by itself. Eventually the ogre catches Jack red-handed and chases him down the beanstalk but Jack cuts the beanstalk down with an axe. 'Then the ogre fell down and broke his crown and the beanstalk came toppling after' (there is a parallel line, of course, in 'Jack and Jill'). Jack and his mother become very rich on the giant's treasures, he marries a princess and they all live happily ever after. The version current in the hill country of the American South follows the same pattern but the objects Jack steals are a rifle, a skinning knife and a coverlet with gold or china bells on it.

In this story Jack turns from wise fool at the beginning to crafty trickster by the end, and one begins to feel rather sorry for the giant. Again, attempts have been made to discern mythological themes under the surface. According to one not very probable theory, the bag of gold stands for raindrops, the hen for the sun and the harp for the wind, and the whole story is about the restoration of the fertilizing activities of the forces of Nature to the earth.

The Giant-Killer

Jack's greatest fame is as a slayer of giants. One version of 'Jack the Giant-Killer' is set in Cornwall in the time of King Arthur and Jack kills the giant of St Michael's Mount, who in early Arthurian legend is slaughtered by Arthur himself. This giant, named Cormelian, is 18 feet high and 9 feet round. Jack digs a pit outside the giant's cave, camouflages it with a covering of sticks and earth, and then sounds a blast on his horn. Cormelian rushes out, falls into the pit and is finished by a blow from Jack's axe. Jack is awarded the giant's treasure.

Later, putting up for the night at a house, Jack discovers that it belongs to another giant, who welcomes him in. But in the night Jack hears the giant singing to himself, 'Though here you lodge with me this night, you shall not see the morning light; my club shall dash your brains outright.' So Jack puts a log of wood in his bed. The giant creeps in and batters the log with his cudgel. Astonished to find Jack alive and well in the morning, the giant gives him a hasty pudding for breakfast. Jack puts it in a bag and hides it inside his coat. Offering to show the giant a clever trick, he stabs the concealed bag with his sword and the pudding tumbles out. The giant tries the same trick, plunges a sword into his vitals and expires.

There are many versions of the giant-killing story, differing in detail and containing many motifs known in folktales. They are part of the widespread general theme of the human hero who outwits a giant, kills him and so obtains his treasure.

(For Jack in the Green, see GREEN; for Jack-o'-Lantern, see WILL-O-THE-WISP.)

FURTHER READING: K. M. Briggs, *Dictionary of British Folk Tales in the English Language* (Pantheon Books, 1980); I. and P. Opie, *Oxford Dictionary of Nursery Rhymes* (Oxford University Press, 1951).

Jackal

In Indian folktales, a shrewd and cunning animal, like the fox of European folklore which it resembles; as a scavenger and eater of carrion, often associated with death; Anubis, the Egyptian guardian of cemeteries who guided the dead to the judgement of Osiris, was depicted as a jackal or dog: traditionally a timid creature, and Bushmen would not eat the heart of a jackal in case they should become cowardly themselves.

See HYENA AND JACKAL.

William MacQuitty

JADE

THE TOUGHEST STONE on earth, jade has been used since prehistoric times for the making of tools, ornaments and weapons. It has also, among certain peoples, been credited with mystical significance and medicinal properties. The English word 'jade' comes, through the French, from the Spanish *piedra de ijada,* the 'stone of the loin'. The mineral acquired this name because Europeans first encountered it not, somewhat surprisingly, in their contacts with the Far East, but when the Spaniards invaded Mexico early in the 16th century. The Aztecs offered their unwelcome visitors objects and pebbles of jade which they themselves regarded as of the highest value, not only for their beauty and rarity but because of their powers of healing.

Jade was considered effective for curing and warding off ailments of the groin and kidneys. (Hence it was also sometimes called the 'kidney stone', which ultimately led to the use of the word 'nephrite' for a variety of jade, from the Greek for kidney.) Sir Walter Raleigh, writing his *Discoverie of the Empyre of Guiana* in 1596, tells how the 'Amazones' would barter gold for jade to treat disorders of the spleen. It may be that as jade was harder than all other stones, it was thought it would break up gallstones and kidney stones. It seems that the original inhabitants of Central America treated these ailments by laying jade against the skin near the affected part, encouraged

Hamlyn/Sir Isaac Wolfson

Axel Poignant/British Museum

Left Chinese jade figure of the late 17th century, thought to represent an attendant presenting an offering to a deity *Above* Hei-tiki amulet from New Zealand *Right* The Chinese regarded jade as the most precious of gemstones, using it for their most sacred objects and finest works of art: horse's head of the Han dynasty

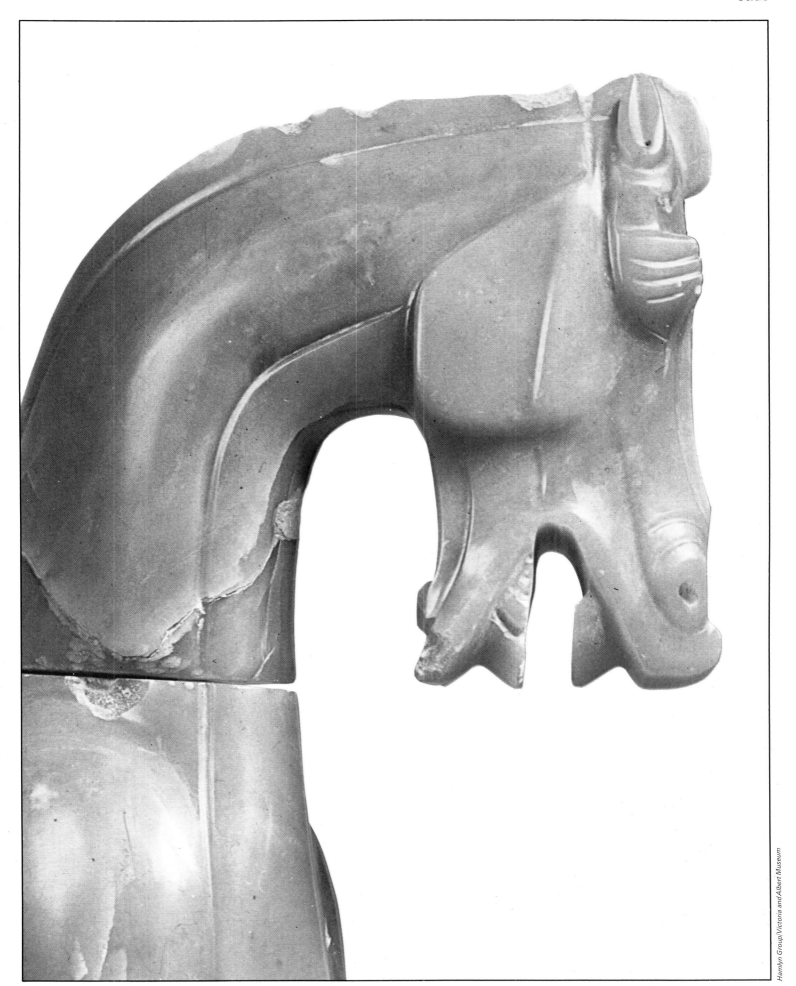

sometimes by the stones being similar in shape to the diseased organs. However, 50 years after the discoveries of Cortez, European doctors were recommending jade, crushed and powdered and mixed with water, as a specific not only for spleen and kidney troubles but for a variety of more common ailments, including biliousness and swollen feet. We may be sure, however, that quacks and charlatans took advantage of the simple-minded and did not scruple to use other ingredients when claiming to prescribe jade. Perhaps this was as well, since powdered jade taken in any significant quantity would be harmful, if not fatal.

Some experts make a similar point about the Chinese use of jade for medicinal purposes; they suggest that what their doctors claimed as jade may in fact have been a form of marble, similar to Parian marble, which can often look very like off-white jade and is less harmful when taken. Chinese physicians prescribed 'liquor of jade' for manifold disorders, from weak blood to asthma, and pronounced it good for the voice and for shining hair. They believed that the material grains of jade passed through the body, while its immaterial virtue remained to do its healing work. The Chinese also believed that jade could prevent, or at least retard, the decomposition of corpses. The nine orifices of the body were stopped with jade plugs or had amulets of the mineral laid upon them — a cicada on the tongue and almond-shaped discs on the eyes. The Aztecs and certain Pacific islanders had similar customs.

Stone of Emperors

Jade objects have been regarded in many parts of the world as talismans of good luck — a belief that survives to the present day, even in 'advanced' countries. The most intriguing examples of these talismans are the *hei-tiki* of the Maoris of New Zealand. (There are quantities of jade in the South Island.) Hei-tiki are curious amulets or pendants resembling a little man. Some believe them actually to picture the human embryo and to be symbols of fertility but others consider they represent a more abstract idea of continuing life force. The objects are handed down in families or from friend to friend. Eskimos and North American Indians also regarded jade as lucky but did not appear to attach mystic or medicinal significance to the stone.

It is the Chinese above all who have held jade in the greatest veneration. The Chinese word for jade, *yu*, also signified beauty of spirit or body and the stone was a symbol of the five cardinal virtues of charity, modesty, courage, justice and wisdom. The ideogram or written character also signified jewel and treasure. Jade was considered the most precious and beautiful substance of all. The emperor wore jade sandals, worshipped at a jade altar and carried a jade seal and sceptre. The stone was used for badges of high rank and for the most prized grave ornaments, as well as for the loveliest works of art.

The most sacred Chinese objects made of jade, from the earliest times, included symbols of heaven and earth and of the deities of the four cardinal points of the compass. Heaven was represented by the *pi*, a circular disc with a hole in the middle, and earth by the *ts'ung*, a vertical cylindrical tube, square on the outside. The god of the east was symbolized by a green tablet, that of the north by a ring, the deity of the south by a red sceptre and that of the west by a tiger tablet. These objects are frequently of astonishing beauty and are among the supreme achievements of Chinese, or indeed of human, art. A typical example of the more practical side of the Chinese genius is the use of a jade plate as a tiny gong. Records of the 23rd century BC show that jade's ability to produce a pure musical tone was known even at that early date.

Jade Queen of the West

It is interesting that jade is not found in China proper. For thousands of years all the jade worked in China came from the far west, from what is now the province of Sinkiang. It was not until 1784 that a regular trade in Burmese jade began. An ancient Taoist legend reflects the distant origin of jade. It tells how the beautiful Jade Queen lived in a fabulous palace in the inaccessible Mountains of the West. She was sought out by the emperor, who reached her fastnesses in the course of a single night by riding eight bewitched stallions in turn. Another ancient Chinese tale relates that the moon is the home of Yu-t'u, the Jade Hare, who brews the elixir of life from crushed jade.

Jaguar

An animal which plays an important part in South American Indian myths, being regarded as a brother-in-law, as man's rival in killing game, and as a rival in sexuality: some tribes believe that the hero who gave them their culture was a jaguar and that a Celestial Jaguar will one day make an end of the world: in Brazil it is thought that the sun takes the form of a jaguar at night and shamans are possessed by the jaguar spirit, sometimes turning into were-jaguars at death. See BRAZIL.

Constantino Reyes-Valerio

Non-violence is carried by the Jains to an extreme; this small but influential Indian sect go to elaborate lengths to prevent the accidental killing of even a fly or a mosquito, or the harming of atoms in wind or water

JAINS

THE RELIGION of the *Jains*, or *Jainas*, an Indian community some 1,700,000 persons strong, is of great antiquity. It derives from the same school of thought which produced Buddhism and the Sankhya philosophy (a branch of Hinduism). Whereas Buddhism, whose origins roughly coincide with the growth of Jainism, became a world religion, the latter remained confined to India. The onerous demands its austere doctrine makes on its adherents as well as its uncompromising atheism may have militated against its spread to other countries and restricted its appeal even within its homeland.

The name Jainas is derived from the title *jina*, 'the conqueror', given to Mahavira, the last of the prophets or saviours of the Jain faith. Mahavira, a historical figure and contemporary of Buddha, born about 540 BC, has sometimes been described as the founder of Jainism and his was certainly a prominent role in the development of the community and its ideology. But Jains regard him not as the first but as the last of a long line of saviours, a line believed to stretch far back into primordial times. The traditional number of these saviours is 24. They are said to have attained complete liberation from the world. They are transcendent, cleaned of temporality, omniscient, actionless and absolutely at peace.

The 23rd Saviour

The penultimate saviour, Parsva, is supposed to have attained liberation 246 years before Mahavira, that is, about 743 BC. There is reason to believe that Parsva actually lived and taught a doctrine approximating to the historic Jain ideology. His life story as preserved in Jain tradition is a prototype for the lives of all Jain saints. In his previous incarnation he ruled as the god Indra in the 13th heaven, and when the time for his return into the human world came he descended into the womb of Queen Vama, the wife of King Asvasena. He grew to be a prince of great beauty and strength, but showed no interest in mundane pleasures and ambitions. He renounced the world and achieved a state of omniscience by overcoming his *karma*, the accumulated results of deeds in previous existences (see KARMA). After this enlightenment he lived for many years teaching and moving among mankind until he died at the age of 100. Parsva, like the previous 22 saviours, revealed by his example and teaching the Jain religion, which is believed to be eternal, having existed throughout the ages from the very beginning of time.

Vardhamana Mahavira, far from being the 'founder' of Jainism, was the son of pious Jain parents and worshippers of Parsva, who were of Kshatriya caste and lived in Bihar near the present town of Patna. He married and had a daughter, but like the Buddha he left his family and possessions and led the life of a wandering monk, preaching and gathering many disciples. Though Mahavira and the Buddha moved through the same country at the same period, and both attained great fame in their lifetime, there is no record of any meeting of the two great religious figures.

The disciples of Mahavira were organized in communities of monks and nuns, to which their leader gave a constitution and a code of laws. According to tradition his followers consisted of 14,000 monks, 36,000 nuns, 150,000 laymen and 358,000 lay women. At the head of these communities were 11 chief disciples; there was great emphasis on discipline and a rigid regime of austerities, penances and fasts, besides meditation and daily routine duties.

For some two centuries the Jains remained a small community of monks and followers. But in the 4th century BC they gained strength and spread from Bihar to Orissa, then to South India and westwards to Gujarat and the Punjab, where Jain communities became firmly established, particularly among the mercantile classes.

Clad in Space and Whiteness

In South India, and notably Mysore, Jainism attained considerable importance, and it was there that the sect divided into separated branches known as the Digambaras ('space-clad' or naked) and the Svetambaras ('white-clad'). The monks of the former branch dispensed with all clothes, and went about as completely naked as Mahavira is believed to have done. The members of the other sect owed their name to the white clothes which they wore. This difference in appearance gradually led to opposition between the two branches of the Jain community. The Digambara sect denied the ability of women to attain liberation, arguing that because in the context of Indian society women could not completely dispense with clothes, they also could not reach the necessary degree of asceticism.

The two sects, Digambara and Svetambara, have separate sets of ceremonial books. An oral literature was passed down

Richard and Sally Greenhill

from the days of Mahavira, but when the recollection of the original texts became unreliable, a council was called to reconstruct as accurate a canon as possible. Only the Svetambaras accepted this as authentic, and at the end of the 5th century AD it was committed to writing at a council in Kathiawar. But by that time many texts had become corrupt and new material had been added.

Jain philosophy is as pessimistic as that of Buddhism, but in its content it is very different. It is characterized by a strictly mechanical materialism in its simple view of the universe, which is regarded as eternal and indestructible. It functions through the interaction of six constituents. First there are the countless life-monads *(jiva)*

The doctrine of non-violence and reverence for every part of creation is central to Jain beliefs. Jain monks wear a cloth in front of their mouths, to avoid damaging any of the atoms of the air, and carry brooms with which to sweep the ground before them, in case they should inadvertently crush some small insect

or living souls, each of which is uncreated, imperishable and endowed with infinite energy. Though intrinsically all alike, they have been modified and diminished by perpetual contact with the non-living entities *(ajiva)* which comprise space and everything other than life-monads. The third constituent of the universe is *dharma*, a word having many meanings and in this context standing for the medium through

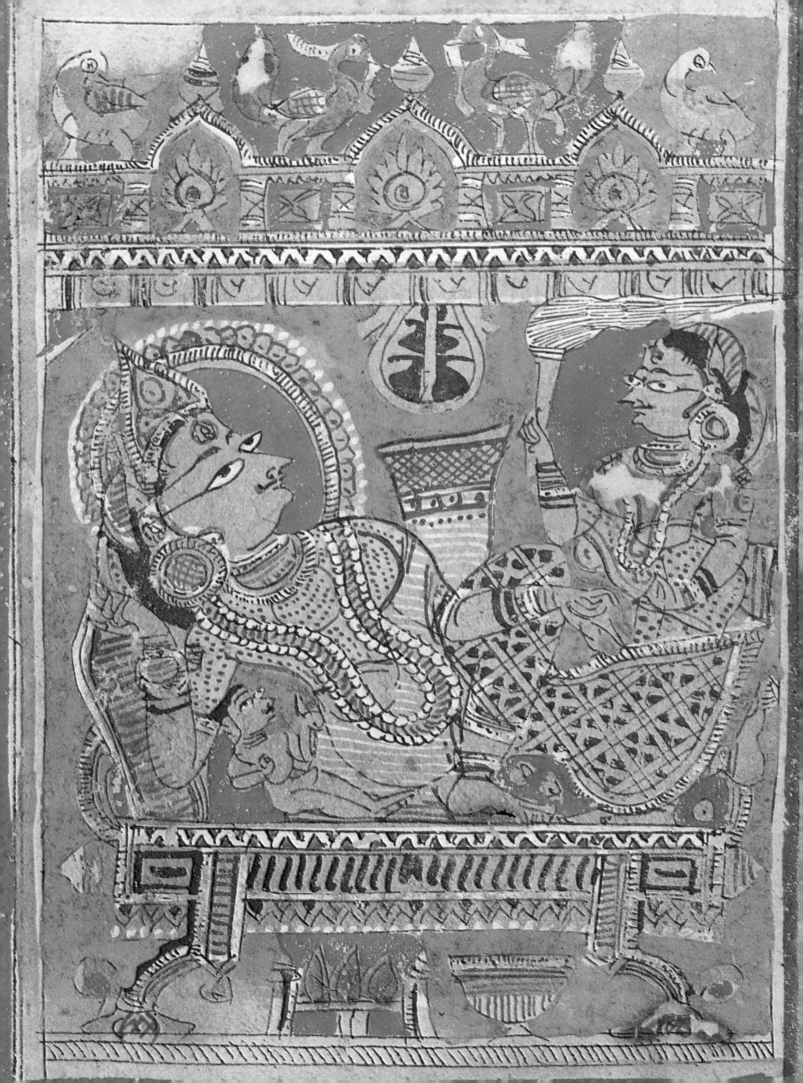

The birth of Parsva, the 23rd saviour of the Jain faith and an incarnation of the god Indra: his mother, Queen Vama, had seen a serpent by her 'side' one night during her pregnancy and the child was accordingly named Parsva, meaning 'flank'

which movement is possible; it is comparable to water in its relation to the fish which move through it. The fourth constituent is *adharma*, the medium which makes immobility possible; the fifth is *kala*, time, which facilitates change, and the sixth and last constituent is *pudgala* or matter composed of minute atoms.

The life-monads, which are eternal, take on innumerable transient forms of life as so many masks. According to Jain philosophy even the gods are nothing but life-monads wearing temporarily favourable masks in fortunate circumstances. Jains believe in the freedom of the individual: thoughts, words and deeds, if virtuous and unselfish, lead the life-monad to enlightenment, but if bad and unconsidered fling it into darker, more primitive conditions. This belief in the effect of accumulated merit and demerit on the fate of the individual in a future reincarnation, Jainism shares with Buddhism and Hinduism. When a life-monad or soul is freed from all bondage created by previous actions, it obtains release from the cycle of births. It then achieves *moksha* of complete deliverance and enters Nirvana (see NIRVANA). But Jains believe that the escape from transmigration, by shedding all the subtle matter adhering to the soul in fine

atomic form, is a difficult process. Many souls will never accomplish it and will continue to transmigrate for all eternity. Full salvation is not possible to the layman. To attain Nirvana a man must abandon all material fetters, and consequently a monastic life is essential for salvation.

Jainism is characterized by an extremely severe practical discipline and vigorous standard of conduct, not only for the ascetic but also for the layman. It emphasizes enlightenment, faith and right knowledge as well as a long list of acts of self-control and restraint. Purification of the mind through meditation is insisted upon as the starting point of all ethical life. Anger, conceit, intrigue and greed are regarded as the cardinal sins, and central to the ethical system is the doctrine of *ahimsa* or non-violence, which involves a deep respect for all life including the lowest forms of animal life.

Value in all Living Things

Jains carry non-violence to an extreme. Even lay-followers must take care lest they cause unnecessary inconvenience to their fellow beings. They must not drink water after dark, for some small insect may be swallowed and killed. They must not eat meat of any kind, or kill flies and mosquitoes which annoy or bite; indeed credit may be gained by allowing them to settle and have their fill of blood. Bed bugs may not be killed, and wealthy Jains employ special persons to lie on their beds and attract the bugs before they themselves go to sleep.

The ban on even the incidental killing of

any living being rules out many professions. Agriculture, involving such activities as ploughing or hoeing the soil, is incompatible with Jain ethics, and Jains are mainly engaged in trade, certain crafts, banking and money-lending. While laymen have to avoid only violence affecting living beings, the obligation of non-violence imposed on a monk goes even further. He must not snap his fingers or fan the wind, for that disturbs and causes damage; if he falls into a river he must not swim with violent strokes but should float gently in order not to injure the water atoms. The Jain community, therefore, preserves in an extremely fundamentalist form the doctrine of universal piety and respect for all forms of life, which first came into existence in the first millennium BC, and which has since gone through numerous changes in the civilization of India.

Jainism encouraged the commercial virtues of honesty and frugality, and the Jain lay community became largely mercantile at an early period. The wealth of its members was utilized for the construction of impressive temples, such as those on Mount Abu, and the raising of colossal rock-cut images, such as the 10th century statue at Sravana Belgola in Mysore. Although there was no real compromise with theism, Hindu gods were accommodated in Jain temples, and the Jain community adjusted itself to the Hindu social order by dividing into distinct castes.
(See also HINDUISM.)

C. VON FÜRER-HAIMENDORF

The word 'janitor' is derived from the name of Janus, the mysterious two-faced Roman god of gateways and passageways, who was also the protector and promoter of beginnings

JANUS

THE PRECISE ORIGIN and earliest character of Janus eluded even Roman savants. His name denotes any passageway, usually the classical arch, and yields the common Latin word for 'door' *(ianua)*. The god was considered present in every door or gate. Nevertheless he remains best known for his function in certain public arched gateways which did not belong to a fortification system. It is not clear whether *ianus* primarily meant the passageway itself or its god. Equally unclear was Janus's function within the passageway.

The month of January and invocation of Janus by the Salian Brothers, an ancient priestly group, authenticate Janus's longstanding worship. The Salian Brothers, serving the god Mars, and the month were traditionally instituted by Numa Pompilius, Rome's second king, around 700 BC. Although over five centuries later it became the first month of the civil year, January was reckoned the eleventh month of the

Roman coin with a double-headed Janus: the god facing both ways was believed to be present in every gate, door and passageway

liturgical year. The reasons for making January the first month were entirely secular but the Romans interpreted the choice as a sign of Janus's protection of all beginnings, which had developed from his supervision of entrances. On 9 January Janus received his only regular state sacrifice, which took place in the Regia, the chief pontiff's house in the Forum, where Rome's priest-king offered a ram. Ceremonies on his behalf must have been observed at the famous arched gateways and his few temples on diverse occasions. Scraps of the very old Salian Hymns contained special prayer-songs to Janus. These were sung in March at planting time when Janus seems to have aided vegetation: rather curiously, since a god particularly concerned with passageways seems to have little relationship with a vegetation deity.

The Good Creator
In the 2nd century BC, Janus appears in connection with two private sacrifices. One was made to Ceres, goddess of the growth of crops, and took place before the harvest. This association recalls the Salians' invocation of Janus as 'the good creator', for Ceres meant no more than 'growth' before her apotheosis. In the harvest ceremony Janus was invoked along with Jupiter and Juno. The second ceremony was an agricultural rite of Mars which required preliminary

Reverse side of a Roman coin, with Janus as a bearded man with a double face; this was the most usual way of representing him

invocation of Janus and Jupiter. Preliminary invocation of Janus in these and a few other ceremonies is assumed to derive from his function as protector and promoter of beginnings. However, his name does not stand first in most prayers and rites. In the oldest surviving records the god belongs to a group of vegetation deities and deserves the name of good creator. The passageway does not occur in such invocations.

According to Roman belief Janus was exclusively Roman. Early in the 2nd century Rome's first specialist in the calendar stated that the name January came from Latium, a region surrounding Rome, and had not originated at Rome itself. The Romans also recognized Janus in a cult image taken in 241 BC from Falerii, a town of the middle Tiber valley. The Faliscans were related by language to the Latins and by culture to the Etruscans and Sabines. Rome remained the paramount centre of Janus's cult. Some of her oldest coins carry the usual and famous representation of Janus *bifrons*, 'two-faced'. Occasionally a four-faced Janus, *quadrifrons*, is mentioned. The former anthropomorphic Janus belonged to the simple passageway and the latter to the gateways comprising two intersecting paths, where Janus faced in the direction of each of the four ways.

Some of the god's epithets were thought to indicate his divine functions; Patulcius and Clusivius (or Clusius) pointed to Janus being open or closed (from *patere* and *claudere*), while Consivius was related to the root of the word for sowing seed,

conserere. These old interpretations are subject to the linguist's doubt. Both Patulcius and Consivius seem to be found in Janus's Salian song. Other epithets are Junonius, Curiatius and Quirinus. The first recalls Janus's association with Juno in the harvest ceremony. The altar of Janus Curiatius was paired with an altar of Juno Sororia. Curiatius must be referred to the *curiae*, primitive divisions of Rome. His rites may have comprised purification of adolescents on their coming of age and entrance to their ancestral curia. Quirinus belonged to the same civil system and his name also derived from this word. However, Janus Quirinus was worshipped by all the curiae and was a state god. (See FOUNDING OF ROME; MARS.)

The Closed Doors of Peace
Janus Quirinus possessed the most famous 'temple' of Janus, situated off the Forum. The origin of the shrine is clouded in antiquity overlaid by folktale. The small rectangular building had double doors at each end, which caused this Janus to be called *geminus*, 'twin'. The side walls did not reach the roof, but were surmounted by grates. A statue of the two-faced god stood within this bronze enclosure that was presumably a monumental gateway on the street leading from the civic centre. This unusual temple stood as a symbol of war or peace to the Romans. Many Latin writers confirm how the open Janus betokened war and the closed Janus peace, the opposite of what might be expected. In explanation of this anomaly, students in modern times have argued that Janus was imbued with the vigour of war and therefore was closed in peace and open in time of war. Except for the connection with Mars, who was also an ancient god of vegetation and fertility, Janus shows few signs of belligerence. Moreover, when Augustus Caesar closed Janus Quirinus to herald a new era free from civil war, he mentioned only one closing in 235 BC, some six years after the first war with Carthage. There is very little truly old evidence for understanding the occasion of opening and closing Janus, when one normally expects a gate or passage to be closed during war. A recent study attempts to solve the problem by arguing that a *ianus* had originally been a bridge with a simple structure of two uprights and a crossbeam at both ends which was dismantled and thus 'open' during war. This theory depends upon a close topographical connection of ianus to water crossings; since archaic Rome was covered by a network of streams of which very few needed a bridge convertible to defence, this ingenious thesis cannot be proved.

Janus appeared unwarlike to the Romans, and so they stressed his role in peace. Such a divinity of peace does not recall the modern aspiration for peace. Rather the closed Janus put the mark of success and security upon the Roman empire and its policy of peace through armed intimidation. Putting aside his relation to agriculture, ancient and modern authors have laid particular emphasis on Janus in an original capacity of lord of beginnings. This capacity owes much to the accident of January's position in the civil calendar.

R. E. A. PALMER

Michael Holford/British Museum

Morris Newcombe

JAPAN 日本

Morris Newcombe

Peter Garston

Buddhism was the dominant religion of Japan for 1000 years, but the older, native Shinto cults survived, mingling happily enough with Buddhism. Later, in the 19th and 20th centuries, Shinto was used to help inspire aggressive Japanese nationalism. Since 1945 there has been a vigorous growth of new sects in Japan, many of them modernized adaptations of Buddhism and Shinto

DURING THE LAST HUNDRED YEARS, JAPAN has experienced a rapid, drastic and stressful change of character. An isolated, inward-looking country, living by farming and fishing, turned into a formidable military and expansionist nation which conquered huge areas of eastern Asia. It then survived a catastrophic defeat in 1945 to recover and re-emerge as one of the world's strongest economic powers. This transformation and the accompanying westernization, industrialization and materialism have weakened the two traditional Japanese religions – Shinto and Buddhism. Yet Japan is the only major country on earth with a monarch still revered by many of his people as a god.

Little is known of Japanese history before the 6th century AD, when Buddhism first arrived from Korea and China. The old indigenous religion, which previously needed no name, then began to be called Shinto to distinguish it from the new, imported faith. Shinto centred on the veneration of *kami*, or supernatural powers and influences, which included but were not limited to gods and goddesses. Animals and birds, trees and plants, mountains and

weapons, anything which was out of the ordinary and which seemed possessed of mysterious power, could be considered kami, including unusually gifted and formidable human beings – not only the emperors, but chieftains, warriors, sages or athletes like the great wrestling champion Sukune, who became the god of Sumo wrestling. The first Christian missionaries to Japan were particularly shocked by the absence of any dividing line between the divine and the human.

The two principal Shinto deities were the sun-goddess Amaterasu, the principle of fertility and nourisher of all life on earth, and her brother and polar opposite, the ferocious storm-god Susa-no-o, the principle of violence and destruction. Life in the world depended on the interplay of these two deities, but there were many other divine beings, including local gods and the ancestors of clans and families. The kami were originally worshipped in natural sanctuaries, on mountain tops, by a rock or a tree, or in any place felt to have a supernatural atmosphere, and there were rarely any images of them. Shamans went into ecstatic trance states in which they were believed to speak with the voices of the gods. In time, shrines, or 'palaces', were built for the more important deities.

Shinto was fundamentally a down-to-earth religion, not given to philosophizing, concerned with getting the best out of life and protecting its adherents from harm and misfortune. Fear of pollution was an important element and there were rituals for

Above left The Bunraku theatre in Osaka presents puppet drama of great artistry. This form developed in about 1600 from puppet plays performed at shrines and temples, presenting scenes from Buddhist and Shinto legend **Above right** The language, costume and settings of the the classic No theatre have not changed since the 16th century. The Japanese dance-drama derived in part from religious dramas performed at shrines. Masks are worn by the principal characters and movement and speech are very stylized. The plays, which frequently involve Shinto or Buddhist gods or other supernatural beings, are charged with symbolism and Zen mysticism

cleansing the polluting consequences of contact with death, disease or spilled blood.

Rites of Cleansing

When an emperor died, his capital was considered to be polluted by his death and a new capital was chosen for his successor. Most Japanese in mourning still prefer not to cross the boundary of a sacred site, which their presence would pollute according to the traditional rules. To this day precautions are taken to keep the sacred island of Miyajima in the Inland Sea, with its famous and beautiful Itsukushima shrine, free from pollution. No one is permitted to die or be born on the island, and no dogs are allowed on it.

Worshippers brought simple offerings of rice, fish, vegetables and fruit to the Shinto deities, and also cloth – now symbolized by strips of paper – and asked for help with

Kukai regarded all phenomena as activities of the Buddha's body, voice and mind; these three aspects of Buddha he termed 'the three secrets'

their problems. Fertility was a major concern; into the 19th century sacred prostitutes served important Shinto shrines.

The gods, and nowadays swarms of tourists, are still entertained with traditional processions, plays and singing and dancing at the leading shrines. Celebrations in the spring coax the deities to make the rice paddies fertile, and in autumn give them thanks for the harvest. At home favourite Shinto deities and the spirits of the family ancestors are honoured at modest household shrines, though these have become rarer in Japan since 1945.

The imperial dynasty, which united Japan and traced its line back to the legendary first Emperor Jimmu, claimed to be the direct descendants and chief priests on earth of Amaterasu, the sun-goddess. Jimmu, according to Shinto mythology, was her great-great-great-grandson and the three sacred and profoundly venerated items of the imperial regalia – the mirror, the sword and the curved jewel – came from her. These symbols are kept at the goddess's great shrine at Ise, south of Nogura, in buildings which are concealed from profane eyes by four concentric fences. The goddess herself is said to have selected this spot in the far, mythic past. For many centuries the high priestess at Ise was always a virgin princess of the royal house. The two shrines sacred to the sun-goddess and the rice-goddess are of cypress wood roofed with thatch, like traditional rice storehouses. They are rebuilt every 20 years. In each case, an exact replica is built next to the existing shrine, the goddess is then ceremoniously transferred to it and the previous structure is dismantled.

The Coming of Buddhism

Mahayana Buddhism (see BUDDHISM) is said to have first come to Japan in 538 AD, when a Korean king sent the imperial court a small image of the Buddha. The new religion was taken up in Japanese ruling circles, out of genuine conviction, but it was also better suited to a single, unified state than Shinto, with its innumerable local deities and spirits. Under a vigorous regent, Prince Shotoku (572-621), and a succession of Buddhist rulers, Buddhism became the state religion of Japan.

It was Shotoku, an enthusiastic student of Mahayana, who built the famous Horyuji temple to Yakushi Nyorai, the Buddha of Healing, which now contains the oldest wooden buildings in the world. Shotoku was an admirer of the advanced civilization of China and at this time Buddhism in Japan was fundamentally Chinese in character. Chinese and Korean monks came to Japan to teach and serve temples and monasteries, while Japanese monks went to study in China. In the 8th century the Emperor Shomu established Buddhist temples in every province in Japan, with the Todaiji temple at his capital of Nara at their head. The Daibutsu, or Great Buddha, the colossal bronze statue installed there in 752, draws visitors today from all over the world.

Buddhism in Japan was initially part of a wholesale adoption of Chinese culture. It employed Chinese rites, costumes, temple architecture and even the Chinese language. It flourished at court and among the aristocracy and the Shinto priests naturally wished to come to terms with it. The Buddhists on their side were generally tolerant by inclination and the two religions began to blend together. The great Buddhist Todaiji temple at Nara, for instance, contained a shrine to the Shinto war-god, Hachiman, while an image of the Buddha was given a place of honour in the Shinto sun-goddess's hallowed precinct at Ise.

The Lotus and the Three Secrets

Early in the 9th century, two Buddhist sects of a distinctively Japanese character emerged: Tendai and Shingon. Both of them were founded by Japanese who had studied in China and both gave an impetus to the blending of Buddhism with Shinto. The two sects dominated religion and culture in Japan for many centuries.

The founder of Tendai was a monk named Saicho (767-822), who after his death was honoured under the name of Dengyo Daishi (Propagator of the True Religion). He revered the *Lotus Sutra* as the greatest of the Buddhist texts and believed in meditation as the supreme path to enlightenment, but his system was broadly comprehensive and he regarded the Shinto kami as manifestations of the Bodhisattvas and great spiritual beings of the Mahayana tradition. Amaterasu, the sun-goddess, for example, was identified with Vairocana Buddha as 'the Great Sun'. Saicho's movement was embraced by the imperial regime. After his time Tendai endured many splits and schisms, and most of the later Japanese sects were descended from it.

Shingon was founded about the same time by one of the most remarkable and revered figures in Japanese history, a monk named Kukai (774-835), posthumously known as Kobo Daishi (Propagator of the Law), who was strongly interested in Chinese esoteric and magical teachings, and in Tantric lore (see TANTRISM). Kukai, like Saicho, identified Shinto and Buddhist deities. He taught that the entire universe is the body of Dainishi, the great cosmic Buddha, and so it follows that everything that exists, down to the tiniest particle of dust, has in it something of the divine nature. Buddhas and Bodhisattvas and Shinto deities and nature spirits are all emanations of the cosmic Buddha. Kukai regarded all phenomena as activities of Buddha's body, voice and mind; these three aspects of Buddha he termed 'the three secrets', concealed from most of humanity. By arduous training, however, by the use of magical signs and verbal formulae, and above all by meditation, a person could understand these secrets and make himself Buddha in this world and this life.

Kukai was credited with miraculous powers. Innumerable pictures and carvings are attributed to his masterly hand and his followers maintain that he did not die, but retired into the innermost sanctuary of the monastery which he founded on Mount Koya, south of Osaka. There, in profound meditation, he awaits the coming of Miroku, the Buddha-to-be. There are more than 100 temples on the mountain and the tomb is a major place of pilgrimage to this day.

The remarkable coalescence of the two religions created what is known as *Ryobu Shinto*, or Dual Aspect Shinto, a term actually coined by Saicho himself. Buddhist rites were performed in Shinto shrines, Buddhist priests conducted Shinto ceremonies, Shinto kami were given images in the Buddhist tradition and Shinto acquired the moral code of Buddhism. Many people had both a Buddhist and a Shinto altar in their houses and prayed to both Buddhist and Shinto deities for fertility, recovery from disease and general good fortune.

It was in this tolerantly eclectic form that Buddhism grew into a popular religion in Japan. It became the custom to have a

Japan

One of the chief surviving functions of Buddhism in modern Japan is to bury the dead and hold memorial services. Priests of the Nichiren sect, one of the main branches of Japanese Buddhism, celebrate San-Ju-San Kaiki, the 33rd anniversary and final official service for the departed; previous ceremonies will have been held on the 1st, 3rd, 7th, 13th, 17th and 23rd anniversaries (1) Priests pray in the cemetery before beginning the service (2) The relatives also pray before the tombstones; on the left are stacked boards inscribed by the monks with wishes for the dead (3) Within the Homyo Temple on the outskirts of Tokyo, priests offer up prayers in front of the gilded altar before (4) the chief priest takes the lead in conducting the ceremony. He burns incense (5) and the mourners step forward to pray at the altar and offer incense in their turn (6); the boards bearing wishes for the dead will be implanted beside their tombstones after the ceremony is over. A great bell, rung by swinging a wooden beam against it (7), sounds the end of the service

5

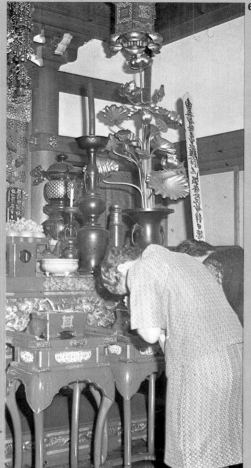

6

7

Shinto wedding and a Buddhist funeral, and the majority of Japanese today are still nominally followers of both Shinto and one or other of the main Buddhist sects.

From the late 12th century a succession of warlords ruled Japan with the title of *Shogun* (Commander-in-Chief) or *Rikken* (Regent), while the emperors were relegated to a state of glamorous but ineffectual pomp. New Buddhist sects now developed, which have a following in Japan today. Unlike Tendai and Shingon, these groups were exclusive, each claiming to know the true path and rejecting all other varieties of Buddhism, and there were sometimes violent clashes between their armed monks.

The Pure Land

Pure Land Buddhism came to Japan from China and was naturalized in its new home by some of the Tendai priests. Unlike the more demanding routes to salvation, which required profound meditation and philosophical understanding of the universe to attain the extinction of the ego in Nirvana, it believed that simple faith in a saviour and earnest, incessant repetition of his name would carry the believer after death to personal survival in idyllic happiness in Jodo, the Pure Land, a paradise in the west. The saviour was Amida Buddha (the Japanese form of the Indian Amitabha, the personification of 'infinite light'). Closely associated with him was the merciful goddess Kannon. The Japanese equivalent of the Chinese goddess Kuan Yin, she was once another Indian Bodhisattva, Avalokitesvara, but is now claimed as a manifestation of Amida.

The Amida Hall of the Byodoin Temple in the southern suburbs of Kyoto is a superbly impressive legacy of the cult. The whole building, which seems to float on the water of a pool, as if about to take flight, and the image of Amida Buddha in quiet contemplation in the centre of the hall were deliberately planned to suggest an earthly paradise. Founded in the 12th century, the Pure Land sect had mass appeal and was even more popular in the form advocated by a 13th-century monk named Shinran (1173-1262), who taught that the believer had no need to lead a good moral life. All that was required for salvation was a single moment of sincere belief and Amida's boundless compassion would save even the wickedest human being. The sect he founded, *Jodo*

Shinshu (True Pure Land), became the most popular traditional variant of Buddhism in Japan.

The Way of Austerity

The last major import from China was *Zen*, which again was developed in Japan by Tendai priests. The Rinzai sect was founded in 1191 by a monk named Eisai, who traditionally also introduced the tea plant to Japan and recommended tea drinking for one's health. Rinzai monasteries had an important influence on the Japanese tea ceremony. The other main Zen organization, the Soto sect, was founded in Kyoto in 1223 by Dogen. In 1244 he established the mountainside monastery of Eiheiji, which remains the sect's centre, where the monks still lead lives of quiet austerity as best they can among today's tourists.

By the 14th century, Zen had developed into the most influential form of Buddhism in the country and it became virtually the state religion of Japan. Engaging in lives of abstract contemplation and silent meditation, its monks aimed to achieve an intuitive perception of spiritual truth. Zen demanded the detachment of the self from transitory phenomena and the abandonment of all concern for personal gain. This strict self-discipline gained it admiration and adherents among the Samurai, the warrior class, who found it admirably suited to the life and ideals of the fighting man. Bushido, the Japanese code of chivalry, was powerfully influenced by Zen principles.

Another development was the work of a pugnacious Tendai monk named Nichiren (1222-82), who rejected all paths except his own and insisted that the Lotus Sutra contained the only true teaching. Expelled from his Tendai monastery for his intolerance, he denounced the policies of the government of the day and spent many years in exile for his pains, but founded a popular movement which is still going strong. His followers chant Namu Myoho Rengekyo ('Hail the Miraculous Law of the Lotus Sutra') to the beating of drums and gongs.

Pure Land and Nichiren Buddhism were always far more popular in Japan than Zen, which was essentially an austere and aristocratic minority sect, dedicated to attaining enlightenment by individual effort. Christianity made its appearance in 1549, when St Francis Xavier and two other

Jesuits arrived in Japan in Portuguese ships, being soon followed by Franciscan and Dominican missionaries. They had some success in making converts among the Japanese, who thought the new faith was some new variety of Buddhism, but Christianity was completely banned in 1614. Foreign priests were deported and only a few small groups of Christians survived, worshipping in secret while pretending to be practising Buddhism or Shinto, and disguising pictures of the Virgin Mary as representations of the goddess Kannon.

State Shinto

After a devastating century of anarchy and civil war from the 15th century to the 16th, Japan was reunified and a feudal system established under authoritarian Shoguns. They promoted Chinese Confucian ideas and ideals to underpin their tyrannical regime, while keeping Japan firmly closed to the outside world. Buddhism remained popular in its various forms with the masses and new sects continued to appear.

In the 18th and 19th centuries, powerful nationalistic feelings began to enthuse some intellectuals. They wanted a revival of Shinto as the true and original Japanese religion, which should be cleansed of the foreign Buddhist and Confucian accretions of the centuries, to serve the nation again as it had in the glorious past. This was one of the impulses behind the upheaval of 1868, when the Shogun was ousted and direct imperial rule theoretically restored under the young Meiji Emperor.

The seeds of the aggressive Japanese nationalism of the 1930s had been sown much earlier by influential writers like Moto-ori Norinaga (1730-1801), who had preached that Japan was the land of the gods, ruled by descendants of the sun-goddess and in need of no foreign ideologies.

Under the Meiji regime of 1868 to 1912, Japan was rapidly and efficiently westernized and industrialized, and Tokyo was made the capital. Buddhists were disapproved of, but retained freedom of worship.

Aki-no-Kami Taira-no-Kujanori encounters the apparition of the fox-goddess Koki-teno: print by Kuniyoshi. The fox figures extensively in the folklore of Japan as a cunning and dangerous animal skilled in magic, often having ability to take the shape of a beautiful woman

Victoria and Albert Museum

Courtesan engaged in the Tea Ceremony: 18th century print by Kitagana Kikumaro. The elaborate Tea Ceremony, a central feature of Japanese culture, developed out of the ritual drinking of tea in Zen monasteries

Christian missionaries were let into the country again, while a new organization called State Shinto was established to promote loyalty to the emperor and the nation. Shinto shrines were purged of Buddhist infiltrations, which involved the expulsion of Buddhist priests and the destruction of much Buddhist art. Handsome new imperial shrines were built. By the 1930s State Shinto had become the ideological bulwark of an aggressive nationalistic policy which emphasized loyalty to the sacred person of the divine emperor, Japanese superiority to all other peoples of the world and the destiny of the Japanese and their gods to rule the world. All Japanese, including Buddhists and Christians, were required to take part in patriotic State Shinto cere-

monies and the majority of foreign missionaries left the country.

The Divine Emperor

The Meiji system disguised the fact that the emperor did not rule the country but was merely the puppet of his ministers, behind a veil of fervent reverence deliberately inculcated as a focus for national unity. Ordinary people were not allowed to look at the emperor, who was too sacred for their crude gaze, and pictures of him were revered in

their own little shrines in people's houses. During the Second World War, unquestioning loyalty to the emperor and obedience to orders to the death, starkly exemplified by the kamikaze pilots who flew suicide missions against American warships (see KAMIKAZE), made a crucial contribution to Japanese successes.

After the dropping of the atomic bombs on Hiroshima and Nagasaki, however, and the Japanese surrender in 1945, State Shinto was dismantled by the American occupying forces and the Emperor Hirohito, the Meiji Emperor's grandson, who had been on the throne since 1926, was forced to inform his people on the radio that he was not divine after all. His announcement had to be followed by a translation from the emperor's

Tenri-kyo teaches that there is no evil, nothing more than types of dust that lodge on the soul and represent hatred, greed, arrogance and other reprehensible dispositions

court Japanese into colloquial Japanese, otherwise his subjects would not have been able to understand it.

Large numbers of Japanese, especially of the older generation, were, in any case, not convinced by the announcement. The emperor continued to live largely out of public view in a seclusion suitable to divine status and to perform the traditional Shinto rites of his office as the nation's high priest. When Hirohito died in 1988, those sections of the elaborate funeral ceremonies which involved his status as a god were tactfully curtained off from the view of the distinguished guests from the outside world, but they were carried out.

Statistics of religious affiliation in modern Japan are very confusing, because so many Japanese are real or nominal adherents of both Buddhism and Shinto that, when the figures are added up, the total of believers is more than the total population of the country. It is estimated, however, that 70 per cent or more of Japanese today do not class themselves as actively religious. Jodo, Jodo Shinshu and Nichiren are the largest Buddhist sects. Buddhist festivals are still observed, Buddhist monasteries still attract a few monks and the temples a few worshippers, while most funerals are still conducted by Buddhist priests, but old-fashioned Buddhism is in decline. Shinto, too, has been largely relegated to a background, heritage role – although people still like to be married at a Shinto shrine – and the postwar ban on public funding for religious institutions hit all but the most prestigious shrines hard. The main Japanese religious impetus since 1945 has been channelled into new sects and movements. (See also AMIDA; NICHIREN; SHINTO; ZEN.)

Modern Japanese Sects
Since 1945 – a year which marked the total disruption of traditional life, of political authority and of the nationalist, ethnic and religious myth fostered before the Second World War – many new sects have sprung up. Except for Nichiren Shoshu, most of them have had little impact on the outer word, apart from in a few Japanese expatriate communities. To the shock of defeat was added the diffusion of American values by the occupying forces and the establishment of religious tolerance. Sects that had earlier suffered state prohibition revived:

their values being different from those of the discredited government. New sects also emerged.

Most of the sects active in modern Japan have adapted important features of Buddhist and Shintoist belief, combined with other elements, so that many of them offer a new philosophy in which certain strains of traditional Japanese culture are still evident. The older sects, founded in the 19th century, betray more magical elements, while the newer movements display radical values drawn from American ideas: freedom of expression and the overcoming of inhibitions formerly denied by Japanese culture. It is hard to say how many new sects there are in Japan. After the war Japanese tax laws exempted religious movements, so a number of astute Japanese businessmen registered their premises as places of religious worship.

Emphasis on Healing
One of the longest established of the new sects is *Tenri-kyo* (Divine Teaching), which originated in the mid-19th century. A middle-aged farmer's wife, Nakayama Miki, was possessed by a god in 1837 and subsequently became convinced that ten deities had forced themselves upon her. Miki was clearly a mentally disturbed woman, who had once attempted to commit suicide. The emphasis of the cult which evolved through her agency was on healing and painless childbirth. As is typical of religious movements in non-Western societies, Miki did not immediately demand that her followers should avoid other places of worship. Towards the end of her life, she wrote down all her revelations. Like many other cult leaders, in later years she held herself aloof from her following. This enhanced her reputation for saintliness and facilitated the accumulation of legends concerning her miraculous powers.

The Tenri-kyo Church arose only after Miki's death at the age of 90 in 1887, a period when the new movement was experiencing some harassment from the Japanese government which, at that time, was promoting the Shinto religion. Fear of government persecution led to the modification of Tenri-kyo doctrines and practices to gain protection as a Shinto cult. A similar adjustment was made during the Second World War, when Miki was claimed as a great

Japanese patriot by her followers. After the war these tendencies were quickly reversed and older forms of worship were restored with a new emphasis on the then fashionable principles of democracy.

Tenri-kyo has been likened to Christian Science by some commentators, although it evolved quite independently and, indeed, rather earlier. It teaches that there is no evil, nothing more than types of dust that lodge on the soul and which represent hatred, animosity, greed, arrogance and other reprehensible dispositions. From Buddhism, Tenri-kyo acquired a belief in reincarnation, but the movement has been increasingly influenced by Christianity in more recent years, and has come to emphasize joyful acceptance of voluntary labour in menial tasks as a way of overcoming greed and learning humility.

Much of this voluntary work is undertaken in public parks and prisons, and in relief work for the needy. Miki stressed the importance of showing generosity to the poor, but in recent decades the leaders of the movement have preferred to collect benefactions from their followers and to distribute them from headquarters rather than to encourage spontaneous local charity. This development may be seen as an example of the bureaucratic trend typical of established religious movements, but it also reflects in part the fascination of the Japanese with their newly learned facility in voluntary organization.

Understandably, given its origins in the mind of a 19th-century farmer's wife, Tenrikyo has retained an inheritance of primitive magical concepts: animal deities and fertility symbols abound. These elements were closely associated with the preoccupations with the miraculous of the founder and her early followers.

There is also a belief – generally rather uncommon in the Far East – in a millennium, when heavenly manna will fall and usher in an age of joy and human brotherhood. This optimistic vision is a central theme in the sect's extensive propaganda, which is now disseminated by modern mass communication. Tenri city, which is the sect's headquarters both administratively and ceremonially, is a place of pilgrimage for believers. The Tenri-kyo movement today claims to have a total number of followers approaching three million.

Japan

Morris Newcombe

Left Trees festooned with unwanted fortunes. At one of the many Japanese shrines slips of paper telling your fortune are on sale; if the fortunes are not favourable, they are hung on a tree in the hope that the ill luck will blow away *Right* The Todaiji Temple at Nara, which contains the magnificent 53-foot-high image of Buddha Vairocana. Built in the 8th century by the Emperor Shomu, the temple testifies to the advance in cultural achievement which accompanied the adoption of Buddhist beliefs by the Japanese

following had fallen away, however, and it has remained small. The sect has an elaborate set of teachings. The spirit world is emphasized and man's eternal life there. An interesting teaching, curiously parallel to the Mormon doctrine of baptism of the dead, is that ancestors who died unsaved might be saved by the faith of their successors.

Offshoots of Omoto

Several sects were founded by former members of the Omoto religion. One of these, *Ananai-kyo*, was founded in 1943 by Nakano Yonosuke, who had been a fellow pupil of Onisaburo as a young man. Nakano claimed to have experienced revelations long before he set out to found his own religion. Although he followed an independent path, he remained on good terms with Omoto, in keeping with a tenet of both sects: the kinship of all religions. Nakano taught that there would be a world catastrophe but that men might escape it by obtaining God's spirit by special meditation and by the saviour that God would send. This movement emphasizes a return to pure Shinto faith. It also teaches that religion and astronomy are one and at one time built several observatories. In common with the Bahai faith, a movement of Persian origins, it organized international conferences at which the unity of all religion was the central theme.

In 1930, a 38-year-old man named Masaharu Taniguchi began to have revelations. He had been a scribe to Onisaburo and a devotee of Omoto; later he had become an adherent of *Ittoen* (Garden of Light), a movement that emphasized hard work as the way to nobility. Taniguchi recorded his revelations and soon after started a magazine that proved to be the beginning of a sect, *Seicho no Ie* (House of Growth). Initially he denied that his movement was a religion: it was rather a philosophy of life. In its early days it was more like a publishing concern, but eventually it claimed that it was indeed a religion. It teachings are highly eclectic, embracing ideas from Omoto, Ittoen and elements the the founder acquired from his study of Christian Science, Spiritualism and orthodox Christianity.

Seicho no Ie teaches that the individual may attain absolute freedom, conquering pain and disease. One of its messages is 'Do not love your enemy – because there is no enemy.' Another, reminiscent of Christian Science, urges believers, 'Drive the disease-idea out of your mind and you are sure to recover health at once.' The sect suffered in the years immediately after the war because Taniguchi had been a vigorous nationalist,

Great Honourable Goddess

A sect of quite different origin, *Tensho Kotai Jingu-kyo*, was also founded by a farmer's wife, Kitamura Sayo. Very much in the style of Miki, Mrs Kitamura claimed, in 1945, to speak with the voice of God, and she was thereafter referred to by her followers as Great Honourable Goddess. Like Miki, she believed that God had come to dwell inside her body, but she refused, at least until the early 1960s, to build a church. Her teachings were simple and little formalization occurred since Mrs Kitamura, as a supreme charismatic leader, always resisted such a development. She preached that there are six roots of evil: to regret; to desire; to hate; to covet; to love or to be loved intensely or beyond reasonable limits. The world is peopled by evil and benign spirits. Mrs Kitamura did not claim to expel evil spirits but to redeem them, and this she did by chanting a short prayer. Her sermons were often chanted, interrupted by hand-clapping and scrubbing motions to sweep away evil.

The most renowned aspect of Tensho Kotai Jingu-kyo was its emphasis on dancing and it was sometimes called 'the dancing religion', although dancing occurs in many modern Japanese sects. The importance of the dance for this sect was that if one had sincerely confessed one's sins and accepted with gratitude others' assessments of one's faults, then one had been brought to the gates of heaven: the dance of non-ego, *Muga no Odori*, would dance one through the gates. Estimates of Mrs Kitamura's following vary because of the lack of formal organization, but they were never very large.

A third woman, whose personal unhappiness was responsible for a formerly important sect, *Omoto* (the religion of the Great Source), was Mrs Nao Deguchi. The decline of the sect has been caused by schisms which have given rise to several offshoots, today counting many more adherents than Omoto itself. Nao had eight children when she became a widow. Two of them went mad and another was killed. In her distress she turned to the Shinto sect, Konko-kyo, but in 1892 she had a revelation of a messiah soon to come and she left the Konko-kyo movement. Soon after her vision a wandering religious enthusiast, Ueda Kisaburo, who later called himself Onisaburo Deguchi, arrived at her village claiming to have had identical revelations, and he was eventually recognized by Nao as the promised messiah. He married Nao's daughter and organized the Omoto cult into a separate sect which, until Onisaburo was persecuted by the government in 1921, grew rapidly.

An immensely active man, Onisaburo sought to establish a World Federation of Religions; he dictated 81 volumes of his experience of the spirit world; and he recruited some two million followers to the faith. The government moved against Omoto again in 1935; Onisaburo was imprisoned for seven years. Only in 1945 was the sect permitted to practise again, and Onisaburo reorganized it under the name *Aizen-e*, (Garden of Divine Love). Its

but the recovery of Japan in the 1950s produced a more favourable climate for his demands for the restoration of traditional education. The sect, which is among the strongest proponents of emperor worship, has a following estimated at over three million members in Japan, with branches in North and South America, Europe and Africa. It has a strong appeal to the more prosperous and to some intellectuals.

The best-known of the Omoto sects is *P L Kyodan*. Its very name reveals strong Western influences since P L stands for Perfect Liberty (Kyodan stands for Church). Under other names, this movement existed long before the Second World War, but took its present name after the leader's release from prison in 1945. Persecution by the Japanese wartime government was, at this time, a great advantage to the renewed sect, which adopted American attitudes.

The pre-war ethic of *Hito no Michi* (the name by which the sect had then been known) was reasserted with these modern trappings. That ethic had encouraged virtue in family and work relationships and promised rewards for right conduct. The 21 precepts of the faith were re-established. They assert that life is art, that the individual, as a manifestation of God, should live radiantly, equally with others, revealing himself by effacing his ego. The environment is said to be a mirror of the mind, but everything makes for progress and development. To forget that one is an artist is held to encourage misfortune. Dancing, poetry, baseball and other sports

are encouraged and opponents have called P L Kyodan 'the golf religion'. But daily early morning services are also part of its way of life with a communal breakfast afterwards. Voluntary good works are also sometimes performed.

The organization of P L Kyodan is tightly knit but in many ways traditional. An extensive counselling system is maintained, the therapeutic principles of which are that suffering is a warning from God that there is something wrong in a person's thought, that he is failing in artistic self-expression. Teaching is also undertaken over a wide range of subjects, including traditional Japanese arts.

At the head of the faith are a small elite of Oyasama (parents) who are endowed with a divine gift of diagnosis of personal ills and who can take upon themselves the ills of others. They do not, however, act as ordinary counsellors, whose work involves a large clerical staff. The strong psychotherapeutic emphasis of the movement does not preclude it from maintaining a modern conventional hospital. P L Kyodan promotes extensive propaganda, trains able young men as administrators and recruiting agents and urges all its followers to bring in 20 new believers every month. In the early 1990s the movement was reputed to have more than one million members.

Mandala and Lotus Sutra
Several modern Japanese sects have arisen in the name of Nichiren, the 13th century Buddhist monk who believed himself to be

the national saviour, and who considered that all necessary truth was contained within the Lotus Sutra. The Sutra was held to contain the final teachings of the Buddha, that promised salvation to men by faith and invocation. Nichiren composed a recitation to the Sutra and taught that the mandala, the scroll on which this salutation was written, should be adored. A certain belief in a messiah was also found in the Nichiren teachings of older Buddhist sects.

Reiyuka (the Association of Friends of the Spirit) came into being when a worker in Yokohama who had lost two children began to tend the graves of the temple cemetery. He encouraged others to do likewise and, in 1925, Kakutaro Kubo and his sister-in-law, Kotani Kimi, launched a new movement which attributed contemporary evils to failures in duty to the spirits. The mandala and Sutra were central features of the movement, particularly the transfer of merit to ancestors by reading the Sutra. The home remained the place of worship and an altar and a copy of the mandala were set up by each family of adherents. The movement never developed any intermediary organizations between the home of the believer and headquarters, although periodic conferences are arranged at which individuals are encouraged to express their opinions freely. Perhaps because of this loose structure, and also because of a series of tax scandals in the early 1950s, the movement has been riven by schisms. Despite all these well-reported problems, it still claims between two and three million members.

Hamlyn Group/British Museum

One of the rapidly growing offshoots of Reiyuka is *Rissho Koseikai*, the Society for Righteousness and Friendship. It began in 1938 when Niwano Nikkyo, then 32, and the 47-year-old Mrs Naganuma Myoko combined as organizer and spiritual medium respectively to form a new movement not, initially, very different from Reiyuka.

Subsequently, although continuing to practise two sorts of divination (foretelling the future from a person's name, and by astrological means), Rissho Koseikai came to display a less magical attitude to the still important mandala, regarding it as a liturgical instrument without the intrinsic power imputed to it by other Nichiren sects. Nichiren is not claimed to have been the eternal Buddha and, since her death in 1957, the extreme reverence that had grown up for Mrs Naganuma, once regarded as a living Buddha, has been discouraged.

Repentance, good living, ancestor worship and neighbourliness are demanded. A practical demonstration of neighbourliness is provided by voluntary public service. Central to the sect's success, however, is its development of the counselling system that it inherited from Reiyuka. Each day, small circles gather under a teacher to discuss their personal problems and seek religious solutions. The *hoza* (truth-sitting) is a dramatic departure from Japanese traditional reserve; each sitting is usually drawn from one particular age and sex group. The hoza, the dramatic festivals sponsored by the movement and its well-disciplined organization are responsible for the growth of this

Utensils for the Japanese Tea Company: the serving of tea was elevated by Zen Buddhism into a dignified ritual expressing the beauty to be found in the mundane routine of life. Tea was first brought as a medicinal herb to Japan from China by a priest, Eisai, at the beginning of the 13th century, along with the philosophy of Zen

style of lay Buddhism. With a claimed membership of some five million, it is one of the largest of the new religions.

Aggressive and Intolerant

The most important sect in Japan is *Soka Gakkai* (Value Creation Society) which denies being a religion at all. It claims to be a lay organization that promotes the Nichiren cult *Shoshu*, an extremist cult that emphasizes the mandala's intrinsic power and the mystical oneness of the Buddha, Nichiren and believers. This aggressive movement, which unlike other Nichiren sects denies all other religions, began in 1930 with the publication of the first volumes of *Value Creation* philosophy by Makiguchi Tsunesaburo. He was imprisoned in the Second World War, after which leadership passed to Toda Josei.

Soka Gakkai, in a way not dissimilar to the Jehovah's Witnesses, became the agency of evangelism. Its methods of 'break and subdue' (*shakubuku*) earned the movement a bad reputation, but they achieved results, not least in winning many adherents in Hokkaido, the northern island in which the miners' union, Tanro, had previously held

undisputed sway. Part of its appeal is the clear display of power made by the movement and its methods of proselytizing. It provides, too, a simple folk Buddhism focused on daily worship of the mandala and demands no initial faith.

The movement has evolved an elaborate system of ranks and titles and confers a variety of semi-academic distinctions. It is, in some ways, ruthlessly modern and efficient; in others it maintains the attractions of an ancient cult – clearly an appealing combination to many. The denigration of other religions, the condemnation of political parties as corrupt (and its own support of a Clean Government Party) and the military discipline give an impression of purpose and resolution. In the confusion and scandals of recent decades, it has had great appeal in Japan. Soka Gakkai currently claims 16 million families as adherents, although the true figure may be closer to ten million. (See also SHINTO; ZEN.)

BRYAN WILSON*

FURTHER READING: M.Anesaki. *History of Japanese Religion* (Tuttle, 1963); C.Blacker, *The Catalpa Bow: a Study of Shamanistic Practices in Japan* (Allen & Unwin, 1982); H.B.Earhart, *Religions of Japan* (Harper & Row, 1984); I. Hori, *Folk Religion in Japan* (Univ. of Chicago Press, 1983); K. Nukariya, *The Religion of the Samurai* (Rowman, 1973); H. Neill McFarland, *The Rush Hour of the Gods* (Macmillan, 1967); C.B.Offner and H. van Straelen, *Modern Japanese Religions* (Twayne, 1963); H. Thomson, *The New Religions of Japan* (Greenwood, 1978).

Acknowledging duty only to the one true god, Jehovah, the Witnesses look forward to the early return of Jesus and the establishment of the New World society on earth; to this end, they make use of the media of the competitive business world, proselytizing with pamphlets, recordings, radio and doorstep canvassing

JEHOVAH'S WITNESSES

ONE OF THE MOST RAPIDLY growing Christian sects of the second half of the 20th century has been Jehovah's Witnesses. Distribution of the movement's publications, *The Watchtower* and *Awake!* is done voluntarily by members. By the early 1990s the Witnesses' world membership was put at more than 4,250,000, of whom some 900,000 were in the United States. It was claimed that more than a million new converts had been gained by the movement in the five years to 1992. That year saw the first ever international conference of Witnesses in the former USSR, which met in St Petersburg.

The movement began in 1870 when Charles Taze Russell, a draper's son from Alleghaney, Pittsburgh, became convinced that the Second Coming of Christ was imminent. This idea has recurred often in the United States; in the 1830s thousands had believed William Miller when he calculated that Christ would return in 1843 or 1844. Russell adopted some of Miller's calculations, and in 1875 became himself convinced that Christ had already (but invisibly) returned during the previous year.

He soon came to believe that Christ would be visibly present on earth by 1878. Later he believed that 1878 was the year that the dead had been resurrected in heaven, and he regarded 1914 as the year destined to end the time of the Gentiles, in the great battle of Armageddon foretold in scripture.

Using his considerable personal financial means, he devoted himself to promulgating these ideas. A group of Bible students gathered and Russell became their pastor: the different congregations of Russellites were linked together by a periodical, *Zion's Watch Tower*. In 1884 he formed a legal corporation, Zion's Watch Tower Tract Society, to control the movement's publications. These, over the following years, included his seven-volume work *Studies in the Scriptures*. A system of full-time workers (who later came to be called pioneers) was recruited to distribute the movement's publications.

Never before had adventist ideas been so widely and so quickly diffused as by this organization: by 1914 Russell had followers in all the northern European countries, in South Africa and in many American cities, and his publications were circulating in central African territories. Disappointed expectations over what actually happened in the year 1914 – merely the outbreak of the First World War in Europe, with the United States remaining at first neutral – caused some to withdraw, and after Russell's death in 1916 the entire movement reached a very low point. But for the efficiency of his successor, Judge Joseph Rutherford, it might have faded away altogether.

Deathless Millions

Rutherford inherited a disenchanted rank and file, a revolt in the hierarchy over leadership, schisms among European followers as well as in America, and the suspicion of the United States government that Watch Tower propaganda was subverting the war effort; on this account Rutherford and some of his closest associates were imprisoned in 1918, sentenced to 20 years, but released in 1919, after the end of the war.

Under the slogan 'Millions Now Living Will Never Die', Rutherford launched the movement on a new path, whilst continuing to assert the imminence of the millennium. The year 1874 was superseded by 1914 as the year of Christ's invisible Advent.

Gradually Russell's writings were allowed to go out of print, to be replaced by the many books of Rutherford himself. From 1931, when the name Jehovah's Witnesses was adopted, a mass recruitment policy has been implemented, with door-to-door canvassing, gramophone records and, more recnetly, by advertising and broadcasting.

Throughout the 1930s the central direction of the movement grew: local officials became nominees of district or national authorities that were in turn controlled from Brooklyn, where the movement had

Mass baptism at an International Convention of Jehova's Witnesses in London. Witnesses hope that they will see the time of the battle of Armageddon when Christ will defeat Satan, the United Nations, the Churches and other forces thought to be hostile to Jehovah

its printing and publishing concern and effective headquarters. In the last years of his life Rutherford receded from his central position, and authority in the movement became increasingly anonymous in keeping with its theocratic claims. This trend was continued under the presidency of Nathan Knorr, who succeeded Rutherford in 1943 and Frederick W. Franz who succeeded Knorr after the latter's death in 1977.

The central belief of the Witnesses has remained the imminence of Christ's appearing and the establishment of the New World society on earth. Since 1914, when Christ is held to have established his heavenly kingdom, the movement has not fixed specific dates, although 1918 is regarded as the time when he cleansed the heavenly temple (an analogue with the purging of members disloyal to Rutherford) and 1925 was a year of intense expectation. Informally, there was great hope of 1975 as the time of the battle of Armageddon when Christ and his heavenly hosts will defeat Satan and the armies of the nations, the Churches and the United Nations.

The interim period between 1914 and the establishment of the New World order is held to have been a period in which the last of the anointed class of 144,000, who will reign in heaven with Christ, were being gathered. Some of these are thought still to be alive, and those Witnesses who are certain of this election alone partake of the emblems at the annual memorial supper, whilst others simply attend. From the number who partook in 1966, of the two millions present at the supper throughout the world, it appears that about 10,000 of this class, sometimes collectively referred to as 'God's Woman', then remained alive. This class is the elite of the movement; the differentiation in types of salvation arose under Rutherford and was the theological concomitant of becoming a mass movement. The elect would reign with Christ, whereas other Witnesses, who came to be called Jonadabs, would inherit eternal life on earth. To these must be added a more obscure category of those who had not rejected the truth, who would have a chance to prove themselves during the millennium. Those who failed this test, and those killed at Armageddon, and those who had persecuted Jehovah's Witnesses, would be annihilated.

Prophetic exposition and eschatology (doctrine of the 'last days' and the state to come) constitutes the core of Witness doctrine. Jehovah's principal concern is to vindicate his name, Witnesses are called for this end, and this is the purpose of all history. Jehovah's power is more evident than his love, and man's redemption is only a secondary purpose in his plan. The Trinity is rejected: Jesus in the flesh was not God but a man. His resurrection was spiritual, and it was then that he received immortality. This representation of Christ is analogous to the destiny of the anointed class. As in other adventist movements there is a denial of the immortality of the soul.

Witnesses use their own New World translation of the Bible, which gives renderings that support their teachings. *The Watchtower* is not merely the main vehicle of propaganda, but it is also a vital catechizing instrument. Each week a Watch Tower Study is held in each Kingdom Hall, and a procedure of question and answer ensures that doctrine is thoroughly understood. A public talk is also given weekly, and two other meetings are devoted to methods of evangelization and training of 'publishers'. At a fifth meeting one of the official textbooks is used as a basis of teaching and discussion.

Pioneers and Publishers

Each congregation is presided over by a congregation servant, assisted by five others, and these officials are not locally elected but appointed by 'the Society'. Beyond them, circuit servants and district servants co-ordinate the work of local congregations. Central organization is established through three separate corporations with interlocking directorates who run the publishing concern. Apart from the full-time officials at international, national, district and circuit level, there are also 'pioneers' who, for very modest expenses, devote at least 100 hours a month to selling the movement's literature. Beyond this, every Witness who can is expected to spread the truth, giving his spare time to doorstep canvassing without recompense; all congregation members in fact are known as 'publishers'.

The movement has a dual structure. There is a community of Bible students supposedly held together by nothing but their recognition of the truth, and there is the publishing agency, a human organization working to bring God's word to mankind. In practice the Bible students are organized by the publishing agency, which

Every Jehovah's Witness who can is expected to give his spare time to canvassing from door to door: 'pioneers' devote at least 100 hours a month to selling the movement's literature

Jehovah's Witnesses

collects statistics from every 'publisher' for every hour of his active work for the movement, very much on the model of a large-scale corporation. Divine service is not worshipping but 'publishing.' The organization is not so much concerned with persons as with activity stated in work hours, production figures and sales. The dual structure allows the movement to resolve one of the central paradoxes facing contemporary religious movements: the apparent contradiction between the value-commitment of religious activity, which is essentially extra-rational, and the need for rational organization in the competitive modern world. Distributing literature provides a practical (in contrast to a ritual) activity for members. Continued activity is ensured by the steady flow of titles from the publishing house: old publications are superseded by new periodically, and the existence of a large following ensures a ready market for new books and the possibility of fixing economic prices for them.

At Odds with Government

The movement has frequently been in difficulty with governments in various countries. Witness teaching demands primary loyalty to Jehovah: nation states are sinful entities soon to be swept away, so that Witnesses claim to belong to a different and superior organization. From the mid-1930s Witnesses stopped saluting national flags and in the war years this led to a conflict with the United States government and to widespread public hostility to Witnesses, who eventually obtained exemption from this observance for their children, who would have been expected to salute the American flag at school. In Germany they were banned by Hitler and were put into concentration camps, where they gained a reputation for being able to withstand torture better than most prisoners. The movement was banned in Australia and New Zealand in the Second World War. It has long been banned in Russia, and more recently in Egypt and Malawi.

Witnesses are not pacifists, since they would fight at Christ's command. But they have been conscientious objectors in wars between nations. They sought, but failed to obtain, exemption from military service as ministers of religion in a test case in Scotland. They come into periodic conflict with medical authorities when they refuse blood transfusions on the basis of biblical injunctions (Psalm 16 and 1 Chronicles 11. 17–19). In other matters they accept normal medical treatment. Whilst not intensely ascetic, they follow a rather rigorous code of sex ethics. For moral lapses, as for doctrinal deviations, the offenders are expelled from the fellowship. Dancing, drinking and tobacco are not absolutely prohibited, but the good Witness is too busy and too serious about his evangelizing work to have much time for entertainments and diversions.

BRYAN WILSON

FURTHER READING: For a good general up-to-date account of the movement: Alan Rogerson, *Millions Now Living Will Never Die* (Constable, 1969).

JERUSALEM

JERUSALEM

THE CITY OF JERUSALEM, the capital of King David and his successors and since 1948 the capital of the state of Israel, has been from ancient times a centre of great religious significance. It is mentioned for the first time in ancient Egyptian·texts of the 19th–18th century BC, but archeological excavations have proved it much older. The name of the city means 'Foundation of Shalem (God)' but was later interpreted — as a result of the similarity of sound in the Hebrew word *shalom* meaning peace — as 'City of Peace'.

Jerusalem seems to have been a cult centre from time immemorial. At an early date a hill-fortress, it became a holy city for the Israelites after David had conquered it from the Jebusites at the beginning of the 10th century BC. There David established his capital and brought the central Israelite sanctuary, the 'Ark of the Lord', to Jerusalem. David's son and successor Solomon built a magnificent temple and Jerusalem soon became in Israelite belief the city which 'God had chosen'. This belief was taken for granted by biblical prophets such as Isaiah, and by historians in the books of Samuel, Kings and Chronicles. The Psalms are eloquent witness to the significance of Jerusalem and Zion (one of the hills of Jerusalem, probably the Temple Mount, but used as synonymous with Jerusalem) in Israelite piety and devotion. Jerusalem became the symbol of God's covenant with his people and with the royal house of David; it was regarded as a spiritual capital from which the word of God was to issue forth to all mankind (Isaiah 2.3), as the seat of justice and righteousness (Isaiah 33.5) and as the messianic city of God (Isaiah 66.8) in a redeemed world. The attachment of the Jews to the city, both as an earthly reality and as a symbol of their historical identity and future hopes, is evident both from the ancient Psalms: 'Pray for the peace of Jerusalem!' (Psalm 122.6), 'If I forget you, O Jerusalem, let my right hand wither!' (Psalm 137.5), from the constant evocation of Jerusalem in Jewish liturgy and ritual practice, and from the modern nationalist movement of Zionism.

The spiritual and eschatological significance of 'Jerusalem' became more pronounced during the period of the second Temple built by Herod the Great and after its destruction in 70 AD; and the image of the heavenly Jerusalem complemented that of the earthly city.

The role of Jerusalem in Christian piety and symbolism is determined by two elements. The decisive events of the ministry of Jesus such as the Last Supper, his Passion, Crucifixion and Resurrection, took place in or near Jerusalem and hence Jerusalem, as a city of 'holy places' associated with the life and death of Christ, has always been an object of pilgrimage. To this was added the idea of the earthly Jerusalem as a symbol and terrestrial reflection of the true, ultimate and spiritual Jerusalem in heaven. The latter was symbolically identified with the Church, and a great wealth of images and symbols expressed this identification in poetry and iconography. Occasionally, the idea of Jerusalem fired religious enthusiasm, and together with other social and political factors stimulated powerful religious movements such as the Crusades. Christian spiritual writers (unlike the Jews, for whom the earthly concrete city was always primary in spite of the many additional spiritual meanings) often exhibited an ambivalent attitude to the terrestrial Jerusalem; pilgrimages and the like were seen as a possible temptation to substitute a crudely material conception for what should have been a spiritual symbol for the Kingdom of Heaven.

By the time of the rise of Islam in the 7th century Jerusalem had been established for many centuries as a holy city for both Jews and Christians, and since the founder of Islam had been profoundly influenced by the two earlier religions, Jerusalem very soon came to hold a special place in Moslem tradition. The associations were of course not historical as they had been for Judaism and Christianity but were based on a verse in the Koran (sura 17): 'Praise to Allah who brought his servant at night from the Holy Mosque to the Farthest Mosque.' Whatever the precise original meaning of this verse the earliest Moslem tradition already interpreted it as referring to Mohammed's miraculous journey on a winged steed from Mecca to Jerusalem. During the night of his ascension to heaven to receive his revelation, the prophet was first transported from the 'Holy Mosque' at Mecca to the 'Farthest Mosque' at the site of Solomon's Temple in Jerusalem. Thus Islam absorbed the Judaeo-Christian traditions regarding the sacred character of Jerusalem and the city ranks for Moslems as the third holiest after Mecca and Medina. In fact the Arabic name for Jerusalem is simply *Al-Kuds* ('the Holy One'). In Islam the emphasis is on the prophet's miraculous night journey to the site of the Temple and the Rock; hence the two mosques there are called the 'Dome of the Rock' and the *Al-Aksa* ('the farthest') mosque. In Christianity the emphasis is on the heavenly Jerusalem as a symbol of the Church and man's spiritual home. The earthly Jerusalem, its holy places, Via Dolorosa, the Holy Sepulchre, the Mount of Olives, serve as a reminder of the earthly ministry of Christ. In Judaism, the holiness of Jerusalem derives from the city's character as the centre and concrete symbol of God's covenant with his people, the promise of an ultimate restoration and messianic future. Few cities have acquired so many and so varied religious symbolic significances as Jerusalem.

R. J. ZWI WERBLOWSKY

Jerusalem is a holy city in Judaism, Christianity and Islam, a fact which has frequently contributed to violent conflict *Previous page* Jews at the Wailing Wall, containing stones from the Temple and the traditional site of lamentation for the dispersion of Jewry *Below* The Dome of the Rock, a Mohammedan mosque built on the site of the Temple

Spectrum Colour Library

William Macquitty

Though primarily works of theology, rather than biography, the gospels contain vivid scenes from the life of Jesus which have become inspiring themes of piety and art *Previous page* The infant Jesus in the arms of St Joseph: statue at Mosta in Malta *Right* Two 16th century Bulgarian murals, showing the Nativity scene *(above)* and the flight into Egypt to escape from King Herod *(below) Far right* The baptism of Jesus, with the Holy Spirit descending as a dove: mural at Assinou in Cyprus

Those who have questioned the existence of 'Jesus' have often confused Jesus of Nazareth, who is recorded as having been executed by the Jews, with his theological interpretation, Jesus Christ; the transformation into the Saviour of mankind was largely due to the Apostle Paul

IT WAS ONCE FASHIONABLE in certain circles to deny that Jesus of Nazareth had ever existed. Although this view never became widely established and was rejected by most scholars, it was not wholly wrong. Its chief error lay in confusing 'Jesus of Nazareth' with 'Jesus Christ'. For 'Jesus Christ' generally represents a theological interpretation of the person and career of the historical Jesus of Nazareth, who was crucified by the Romans, outside the walls of Jerusalem, c 30 AD. In other words, it is necessary to distinguish between the historical Jesus and the theological interpretation of him. The task, however, is not easy; but it is vitally necessary, if the origins of Christianity are to be understood.

The historical existence of Jesus of Nazareth must first be established. Generally, the existence of some person from the past is not questioned, unless what is recorded is incredible in terms of ordinary experience. Thus, for example, we do not doubt that Socrates existed and was condemned to death by the Athenians for impiety; but we are sceptical about Osiris whom the Egyptians believed had risen from the dead and had become the ruler of the next world.

Ironically, the best-attested fact about Jesus is that of his death. His execution for sedition, on the orders of Pontius Pilate, the Roman *praefectus* of Judaea, is recorded both by Christian writers and the Roman historian Tacitus, who wrote early in the 2nd century AD. The Christian evidence is especially significant. The execution of Jesus as a rebel against the Roman government of Judaea was an embarrassment to the early Christians. It caused Christianity to be regarded as a politically subversive movement by the Roman authorities, and prompted them to persecute Christians. The gospel writers, therefore, would have never invented such an end for Jesus; in fact, they endeavoured to explain it away.

The Roman execution of Jesus constitutes the strongest evidence of his existence as

It is evident that the Christian gospels contain genuine traditions about Jesus, but, on closer examination, it is clear that they are not accurate historical records of the career of the historical Jesus

a historical person. The subsequent Christian interpretation of his death as a sacrifice to save mankind from perdition must be investigated as a basic factor in the development of Christian theology; but it does not detract from the historicity of the event, which in any case was recorded by Tacitus, an independent witness.

A 'Pernicious Superstition'?

From the certainty of the crucifixion of Jesus by the Romans one must work backwards in an endeavour to reconstruct the course of his life, for our only information about Jesus comes from the New Testament writings, and almost exclusively from the four gospels. Tacitus tells us nothing more than that Pontius Pilate executed Jesus, and that the 'pernicious superstition', as he called Christianity, not only broke out again in Judaea, but spread to Rome. There is a passage about Jesus in the *Jewish Antiquities* of Josephus, the Jewish historian. If the passage were genuine, it would be of great value, because Josephus lived in Judaea shortly after the lifetime of Jesus. However, there is strong reason for suspecting that, as it stands, the passage is a later Christian forgery which replaced the adverse account that Josephus originally wrote.

The Christian gospels appear, at first sight, to be biographies of Jesus, and it is evident that they contain genuine traditions about him. But, on closer examination, it is clear that they are not accurate historical records of the career of the historical Jesus. Instead, they are presentations of someone whom the authors believed was the incarnate Son of God. For example, the earliest gospel, that of St Mark, describes itself as 'the gospel of Jesus Christ, the Son of God'. This fact is of fundamental significance for an evaluation of their testimony since it means that the authors of the gospels were not writing history, but theology. They were using material about the historical Jesus; but they interpreted it to demonstrate that Jesus was the divine saviour of mankind. This estimate of the gospel writers is not intended to convict them of conscious deceit or distortion

Jesus driving the money-lenders out of the Temple, by El Greco: his attack may have been primarily directed at the priestly aristocracy, to whom the economic activities of the Temple were a rich source of income

of their evidence. They were not writing as historians, even though Luke professes to do so (1.1–4); they were writing as convinced Christians about their master, whom they believed was divine, who had risen from the dead, and ascended into heaven, which they located in the sky. They were writing also for fellow Christians, and they drew not upon their own experience of the historical Jesus, but upon traditions which they had inherited about him. Moreover, they all wrote long after the Crucifixion, when the original community of Jesus's disciples and apostles had disappeared in the destruction of Jerusalem in 70 AD. And they wrote for Greek-speaking communities of Christians situated in various places in the Roman Empire, outside Judaea.

The Message of the Gospels

The problem is that a Jew named Jesus of Nazareth, who was executed as a rebel by the Romans about 30 AD, is the subject of four biographical accounts, written some 40 years or more later by followers who believed that he was the Son of God. These accounts were designed to attest his divine origin, to show that he was the Messiah of Israel, that his death was for the redemption of mankind, that he arose from the dead three days after his crucifixion, and that he ascended into heaven, whence he would shortly return with supernatural power and glory to judge the world. Thus, the basic issue is how these extraordinary things about the historical person whom the Romans executed came to be believed during the course of some four decades.

There are two obvious answers. First, that Jesus had told his disciples that he was divine and that his coming death was designed to save mankind, and second, that he did in fact rise from the dead and was seen to ascend into heaven, as the Christian sources relate. But both answers are so fraught with difficulties of various kinds that they cannot be accepted as adequate explanations. For example, no authentic writing by Jesus survives, and we cannot be sure that we have an exact record of his teaching, of what he said and the circumstances in which he said it. Indeed, every recorded saying is essentially obscure, and often conflicts with other sayings. The accounts of his resurrection and ascension are similarly at variance. For example, there is a fundamental

divergence of testimony about the location of these extraordinary events. According to the author of the gospel of Luke and the Acts of the Apostles, the appearances of the risen Jesus took place in and around Jerusalem, and he ascended into heaven from the Mount of Olives; and the disciples were expressly forbidden to leave Jerusalem at this time (Acts 1.4). On the other hand, the gospel of Matthew, with which Mark's gospel appears to concur, locates the appearance of the risen Jesus to his disciples in Galilee, where they had been told to go; and the Ascension apparently took place there (Matthew 28.10,16; 16.7). It is amazing that a difference of opinion about such important events should occur within some 50 years of their happening. And it serves to warn us of the inexact nature or fluidity of the earliest traditions concerning Jesus. There is a similar conflict between the accounts of the birth of Jesus in Matthew and Luke (Matthew 1.18–2.23; Luke 1.26).

The existence of such contradictions about Jesus in the primitive tradition makes one despair of obtaining any reasonably reliable information about him, apart from his crucifixion by the Romans. But the problems already mentioned are not the most serious ones that concern Jesus in the earliest Christian writings. There is another even more basic problem but, paradoxically, although it is so serious, it actually provides the key to a better understanding of the historical Jesus and of the process that led to his divinization.

The Interpretation of Paul

The earliest surviving Christian writings are not the gospels but the Epistles of St Paul (see PAUL). They were written about 20 years before the gospels, and provide evidence of Christian life and thought some 20 years after the Crucifixion. When these epistles are carefully examined they reveal that already an amazing conflict of opinion existed about Jesus. In two separate letters, Paul denounces certain opponents who 'preach another Jesus' and 'another gospel' (Galatians 1.6–9; 2 Corinthians 11.4). Since Paul cannot possibly mean that these opponents were preaching about another person named 'Jesus', his denunciation must signify an interpretation of Jesus different from his own.

This problem is very complicated, and

here a summary statement only can be given of its solution. It would appear that Paul, who had not been an original disciple of Jesus but had been converted by some profound inner experience, became the exponent of a new interpretation of Jesus. Paul believed that this interpretation had been specially revealed to him for the evangelization of the Gentiles. For, although he was a Jew, Paul had a hellenistic background and appreciated the spiritual needs and outlook of contemporary Graeco-Roman society. He was convinced that the interpretation of Jesus presented by the original apostles of Jesus was not adequate to Gentile needs, and that God had therefore given him this new interpretation or 'gospel' (Galatians 1.15–17). Paul's 'gospel' can be reconstructed from his epistles. The main outline is that mankind had become enslaved to the demonic powers that ruled the planets. To save humanity from this fatal condition, God sent into the world a pre-existent divine being, whom Paul called the 'Lord of glory'. Incarnated as Jesus, the demonic powers mistook him for a human being, and crucified him. In so doing, they lost their control of mankind, because the Lord of glory could not be held by his death and rose triumphantly to life (1 Corinthians 2.6–8; Colossians 2.14–15). In his interpretation, Paul paid scant regard to the historical circumstances of Jesus's career; even his crucifixion is ascribed to the demonic powers, with no reference to Pilate and the Jewish authorities.

The 'Other Gospel'

If this was Paul's gospel, what was the other interpretation of Jesus against which he inveighed so strongly? The evidence points unmistakeably to the original apostles and disciples of Jesus, located at Jerusalem, as Paul's opponents and the protagonists of the 'other gospel'. As Jerusalem was destroyed in 70 AD, and the primitive Christian community there and its records lost, this 'other' gospel has to be reconstructed from various indirect sources, including Paul's own writings. However, enough can be learned to know its chief tenets. It appears that the original disciples of Jesus believed him to be the Messiah (*Christos*) of Israel. His death at the hands of the Romans had been a hard blow to their faith; for, according to contemporary Jewish thought,

the Messiah should overthrow Israel's enemies, not be killed by them. However, through visions experienced by certain disciples of Jesus after his crucifixion, it was believed that God had raised him from the dead, in order that he might return again, with supernatural power, to 'restore the kingdom of Israel' (Acts 1.6). His death was explained as a martyrdom for Israel, caused by the nation's failure to accept him as the Messiah. These original Jewish Christians continued to live as devout Jews, worshipping in the Temple. They did not regard their faith in Jesus as constituting a new religion, separate from Judaism; neither did they regard Jesus as divine, because Jewish monotheism precluded any conception of the Messiah as a deity.

Critical analysis of the New Testament writings reveals, therefore, that within two decades of the Crucifixion two different interpretations of Jesus were current within the Church. The original disciples of Jesus proclaimed him as the Messiah of Israel, who had died a martyr's death for his people; but God had raised him up and he would shortly return to complete his messianic role. Paul, in contradiction, taught that Jesus was the incarnation of a divine 'Lord of glory'. His death had been planned by God, in order to save mankind from their fatal enslavement to the demonic rulers of the world.

These evaluations of Jesus were mutually incompatible. As soon as the Jerusalem Christians realized the nature of Paul's gospel, they repudiated both it and him. They sent emissaries among Paul's converts, warning them that Paul was not an apostle and that his teaching was not the original form of the faith. Paul's situation was basically insecure: he could not repudiate the authority of Jesus's own apostles and his own doctrine could easily be rejected as the errors of a late-comer to the faith, who had not shared the original experience of Jesus. Paul's cause suffered defeat, and it is probable that all trace of his teaching would have been lost but for the Jewish revolt against Rome in 66–70 AD when the original Christian community at Jerusalem disappeared during the destruction of the city, and with it its authority and teaching. A rehabilitation of Paul followed, which assured that his interpretation of Jesus as the divine saviour, incarnated and crucified

to save mankind, should prevail and become orthodox Christian doctrine.

Thus, the historical Jesus of Nazareth was transformed into the Saviour God of Christianity. Is it possible to discern behind this transformation something of the original human Jesus? The evidence of the gospels is very puzzling. They all admit that Jesus was executed by the Romans for sedition. This fact would be of superlative importance if Jesus had indeed been guilty of rebellious activity against the Roman government in Judaea for it would mean that, as the Messiah, he had sought to deliver Israel from the oppression of heathen Rome. Such action would not have made him unique; because as Josephus records, many others sought this end and died at the hands of the Romans.

The gospels, however, maintain that Jesus was innocent of sedition, and that the Jewish authorities forced Pilate to execute him on such a charge. Such a miscarriage of justice is feasible; but there is strong reason to think that this gospel presentation of Jesus as innocent of sedition against Rome resulted from consideration of defending Christianity. Critical analysis of the account in Mark of the trial of Jesus, which set the pattern for the other gospels, shows that its author, writing in Rome about 71 AD, sought to explain away the embarrassing fact that Jesus had been condemned as a rebel by transferring the responsibility for the Crucifixion from Pilate to the Jewish leaders. Mark also represents Jesus as ruling that the Jews should pay tribute to Caesar (Mark 12.13–17) and, significantly, he disguises the fact that one of Jesus's apostles was a Zealot, that is, a member of the Jewish 'resistance' against Rome (see ZEALOTS).

Pacifist or Rebel

Looked at carefully, it appears that Pilate condemned Jesus because he thought that he was truly guilty of sedition. And this conclusion is borne out by certain other facts recorded in the gospels. For example, Jesus deliberately planned a triumphal entry into Jerusalem as the Messiah King on his last visit to the city. He checked to see that his disciples were armed before going to Gethsemane (Luke 22.36), and there was armed resistance at his arrest. Such actions are not consistent with a pacifist who endorsed the Roman rule of Judaea, and who wanted

to keep himself aloof from contemporary Judaeo-Roman politics. Instead, they suggest the action of one who believed himself to be the Messiah, divinely charged with the deliverance of Israel from its current subjection to masters, both Jewish and Roman, other than God. And such actions render intelligible his execution by the Romans for sedition.

As far as it is possible to reconstruct the career of Jesus from the problematic evidence of the gospels, it would seem that he succeeded John the Baptist in proclaiming the imminence of the kingdom of God and in seeking to prepare Israel for its coming. The idea of this divine kingdom involved the end of the prevailing world order and consequently the overthrow of the Roman

Mural by Giotto, of the triumphal entry of Jesus into Jerusalem; this is one of the actions of Jesus which suggest that he may have regarded himself as the divinely appointed deliverer of Israel from subjection to rulers other than God. 'And such actions render intelligible his execution by the Romans for sedition'

government. Widely supported in Galilee and popularly regarded as the Messiah, Jesus became increasingly conscious of the opposition of the Jewish authorities, including the priestly aristocracy, from which the high priest was appointed by the Romans. The members of the priestly aristocracy supported Roman rule both in their own interests and because they believed it to be in the best interests of the

nation. Furthermore they derived a considerable income from control of the great Temple at Jerusalem.

It is possible that Jesus finally decided to challenge the Jewish authorities on their own ground, the Temple, and perhaps to seize it and set up a new high priest, who was not a Roman nominee. The Zealots did just this in the revolt of 66 AD. Whether that was his intention or not, Jesus did enter Jerusalem as the Messiah, with his followers, and attacked the economic activities of the Temple, which was a lucrative source of income to the priestly aristocracy. His attack on the Temple seems to have coincided with a Zealot attack on the Romans, which was probably commanded by Barabbas. This apparent coincidence raises the question of Jesus's relations with Zealots. The fact that one of his disciples, Simon, was known as 'the Zealot' indicates that the rest were not; but it also suggests that belief in Zealot principles was not incompatible with adherence to Jesus and that there was probably a close bond of sympathy.

According to the gospels, it would seem that Jesus's attack on the Temple was abortive, but he was too strongly supported to be arrested. The Zealot revolt was suppressed by the Romans with casualties, and Barabbas and others were captured. Jesus stayed on in Jerusalem until the night of the Passover. Realizing that his attempt had failed, he decided to withdraw to Galilee. But his rendezvous in Gethsemane

that night was betrayed by Judas Iscariot, and he was captured after an armed struggle. After interrogation, the Jewish authorities handed him over to Pilate, charged with sedition. It would seem that they accused Jesus as being the leader of the recent revolt, and not Barabbas. Pilate accepted the charge and ordered the Crucifixion of Jesus as the rebel Messiah King of Israel. He also ordered that Jesus should be crucified between two Zealot prisoners, whom he evidently regarded as Jesus's followers.

The story of the empty tomb (Mark 16) appears to be a later explanation of the disciples' conviction that they had seen Jesus alive again after his death. However, although they believed that he had risen from the dead, Jesus was not seen

by any non-believer nor did he resume his former life. Instead, it was claimed that he had ascended to heaven, whence he would soon return to complete his messianic mission. His Jewish disciples devoted themselves to proclaiming him as the Messiah to their compatriots; and it was left to Paul to transform Jesus into the Saviour God of mankind.
(See also CHRISTIANITY.)

S. G. F. BRANDON

FURTHER READING: S.G.F. Brandon, *Jesus and the Zealots* (Scribner, 1968); J. Bell, *Roots of Jesus* (Doubleday, 1983); D. Duling, *Jesus Christ through History* (Harcourt Brace Jovanovich, 1979); S. Ogden, *The Point of Christology* (Harper & Row, 1982).

Ashmolean Museum

The bishop's ring, gold with an amethyst, is worn on the third finger of the right hand. In the occult tradition, the amethyst is 'the jewel of the high priest, of one who is not confused, distracted or overwhelmed by the intense fascination of external phenomena.' In this sense it protects the wearer from drunkenness, which is its old traditional role. It is also used in magic to gain political power

sense; it was its peculiar occult property, that gave it a place among sacred gems.

The scheme of classifying the various stones and their properties involved the planets, whose influences were believed to be very strong in certain stones. Consequently, they were considered to be their vehicles or transmitters.

Quartz is one example. It is particularly associated with the moon, and is an important constituent of the earth's crust. It has been compared with the reproductive system because, just as gold is concealed in quartz, so is the sex factor contained within the human organism. Quartz is also supposed to possess the remarkable property of rendering opaque bodies invisible. Apollonius of Tyana, the famous 1st century mystic (see APOLLONIUS), used it for this purpose when Caesar Domitian suddenly summoned him from a great distance. The sage made himself invisible, materialized before Domitian, and subsequently dematerialized again, reappearing shortly afterwards near the distant Mt Vesuvius.

In modern times, a Viennese scientist named Pribill attempted to demonstrate this property of quartz. He claimed that the secret lay in the way in which the stone had been cut for magical purposes since time immemorial, maintaining that it was cut to a certain angle and placed in the mouth after exposure to tropical sunlight. The magician then intoned a secret incantation which, combined with the occult properties of the sun-impregnated quartz, gradually caused his body to disappear.

The Crystal Window

The moon is also associated with rock crystal, which stimulates the faculty of clairvoyance. This stone is also used in healing; the affected part is immersed in water charged with the psychic energies

From the regal diamond to the humble coral jewels and semi-precious stones have been valued not only for their rarity and beauty but for their place in occult symbolism; their traditional associations with the planets accord them mysterious powers for good and evil

JEWELS

KETHER, THE SUPREME Crown of the topmost sefiroth of the cabalistic Tree of Life — studded with gems of elemental brilliance, glistering fire, shining water, sparkling air, and richly glowing earth — is the archetype of all earthly crowns that have adorned prophets, priests and kings throughout

the ages. In former times, jewels were often selected for their symbolic value: the diamond for unyielding durability, the pearl for purity, the flaming ruby for the administration of justice, the topaz for nobility and regal splendour; all have formed, at sometime, an essential part of royal diadems.

Behind these more obvious attributions lay a complex scheme of occult correspondence elaborated by priests, magicians, wizards and sages. The entire mineral kingdom was involved, and even stones that were not, strictly speaking, precious stones became endowed by tradition with celestial values that exalted them to the rank of veritable jewels. Yet it was not merely the symbolic value that mattered, nor the intrinsic worth of a stone in a commercial

Magical Use of Gems

If thou wilt know whether thy wife is chaste or no.
Take the stone which is called Magnes, in English, the lodestone, it is of sad blue colour, and it is found in the sea of India, sometimes in parts of Almanie, in the province which is called East France. Lay this stone under the head of a wife, and if she be chaste, she will embrace her husband, if she be not chaste, she will fall anon forth of the bed . . .

If thou wilt provoke sorrow, fear, terrible fantasies, and debate.
Take the stone which is called Onyx, which is of black colour. And the kind is best which is full of white veins. And it comes from India, unto Arabia, and it be hanged upon the neck, or finger, it stirs up anon sorrow or heaviness in a man, and terrors, and also debate, and this has been proved by men of late time.

If thou wilt overcome thy enemies.
Take the stone which is called Adamas, in English speech, a Diamond, and it is of shining colour, and very hard, in so much that it can not be broken, but by the blood of a goat, and it grows in Arabia, or in Cyprus. And if it be bound to the left side, it is good against enemies, madness, wild beasts, venomous beasts, and cruel men, and against chiding and brawling, and against venom, and invasion of fantasies . . .

If thou would make any man's wit sharp and quick, and augment his riches, and also prophesy things to come.
Take the stone which is called Smaragdus, in English speech, an Emerald. And it is very clear, shining through, and plain, but it that is yellow is better. It is taken out of the nests of grypes or griffons, it does both comfort and sane, and being borne, it makes a man to understand well, and gives to him a good memory, augments the riches of him that bears it, and if any man shall hold it under his tongue, he shall prophesy anon.

The Boke of Secrets of Albertus Magnus, of the vertues of herbs, stones and certayne beasts

---

which the crystal is thought to contain.

The best documented case of crystallomancy, or divination by the crystal, is that of the Elizabethan magicians Dr John Dee and Edward Kelley (see DEE). The crystal, or the shewstone as they called it, served as a window revealing other realms of existence. The classical scholar, Meric Casaubon, described their occult experiments, and the process by which they summoned angels to appear forms the substance of one of his treatises. This process was known as scrying. Kelley was the scryer or seer, and Dr Dee recorded the visions which his collaborator received. A complex system of magic derives from the work of these magicians which involves a weird and unearthly language called Enochian, communicated by the angels.

The pearl and the moonstone are other gems connected with the moon, the moonstone being a direct image of its namesake, while the pearl represents the purity and virginity traditionally associated with that solitary planet.

The pearl, the typical stone of the sea, is attributed to the moon owing to its influence over sea tides and women, whose monthly cycle corresponds to the lunar cycle. Its iridescent qualities link the pearl to astral visions in contrast to visions of brilliant light, which characterize solar or spiritual experiences exemplified by the topaz and diamond. This is why pearls are frequently worn during ceremonial invocations of lunar forces which involve astral activity. Another moon jewel is amber, whose positive electrical characteristics link it with animal magnetism and the voluptuousness of sensual love. It is worn while casting enchantments and is said to render its wearers, especially women, irresistibly attractive.

To Mercury are assigned chiefly the opal, the agate, and to a lesser extent, alexandrite, tourmaline and Iceland spar (a colourless, transparent stone). The opal has the power of luring its possessor into strange and unknown realms, probably because Mercury, in one of his forms, is the guide of souls that have quitted earth and wander in the kingdom of the dead.

The subtle emanations of the agate avert or offer protection against violent storms, due to the close connection between Mercury and the element of air. Thus any air movement, from breeze to tempest, falls naturally within his province. The agate is also potent against the sting of scorpions, because Mercury's activities include miracles of healing.

Tourmaline absorbs light and conducts electricity, hence its affinity with Mercury whose nature typifies the electrical phenomena of transmission. Because they polarize light alexandrite and Iceland spar are classed as Mercurial stones.

Venusian influences are concentrated in the emerald and the turquoise. In ancient Egypt the emerald stood for resurrection; it was used in the construction of talismans and amulets which symbolized the periodic return of the spirit of man (see EMERALD). The Eye of Horus which was often depicted in emerald was symbolic of reproduction and of the door to the womb through which the spirit entered to take on flesh for its reappearance on earth. The emerald was worn to achieve a favourable reincarnation; in later ages it was believed to ensure perpetual fertility.

Both the emerald and the turquoise were used in rites for inciting love and passion. Both these stones typify the transmission of vital force from one organism to another.

Venus is associated with the element of water, and therefore with the aquamarine and the beryl, both of which represent water in the mineral kingdom. Paracelsus (see PARACELSUS) claimed that a person's familiar spirit could be invoked in visible form in a mirror of beryl. Its power of facilitating intercourse with familiar spirits caused it to be worn by people wanting to know the inmost secrets of others.

Power and Radiance

The topaz, yellow diamond, cat's eye and chrysolite are particularly attributed to the Sun and, in the case of the cat's eye, to the Sun's associated sign, Leo. The glorious gold of the topaz symbolizes the Sun in the mineral kingdom. This planet, whose symbol in the animal kingdom is the lion, typifies courage, royalty and leadership, and the topaz makes its bearer fearless and wise. It is also a remedy against lunacy, because it concentrates the solar rays and neutralizes the baleful effects of the moon. The topaz also gives power over wild beasts, which, interpreted in terms of the human organism, implies the conquest of man's lower nature and its transformation into the nobility, symbolized by the king of the beasts, the lion.

The yellow diamond is attributed to the Sun for similar reasons, while the chrysolite, as its Greek name signifies, is a golden stone and also a vehicle of solar energy. It bestows the power of acquiring wealth, as do all solar stones.

If radiance is the special attribute of the Sun, fiery energy characterizes Mars. The stone ascribed to this characteristic of Nature is the ruby, which represents the spirit of violence and destruction. This stone is also associated with blood, the special vehicle of energy. Robert Fludd, the 17th century mystic and philosopher (see FLUDD), likened the ruby to the red earth, or flesh, of which Adam was formed.

There are, however, more sinister stones connected with Mars, one of which is the snake-stone, another the greenish turquoise. To both these gems are attributed certain occult powers pertaining to corruption and putrefaction; the snake-stone because of its connection with Scorpio, the zodiacal sign associated with Mars; the greenish turquoise because of its association with Venus, and its tendency to deteriorate into green. This not only destroys its value but suggests the outer allurement and inner corruption of Venusian attraction. These stones are connected with the infernal rites of necromancy, and the putrefying substance associated with alchemy.

To Jupiter, the father of the gods, were assigned the amethyst, the sapphire and the lapis lazuli. The deep blue of the lapis lazuli symbolizes the highest form of Jupiter, whose 'pure' colour is the uncompromising blue of heaven. In earliest times, before he became father of the gods, Jupiter had a feminine as well as a masculine aspect; and lapis lazuli is the Stone of Laz, the Arabian goddess of love. The sexual organ of Ishtar, the Assyrian Venus, was sometimes carved in this stone.

The violet amethyst is the stone traditionally associated with episcopal rank. It is the jewel of the high priest, of one who is not confused, distracted or overwhelmed by the intense fascination of external phenomena. In this sense the amethyst preserves its wearer from drunkenness. In some legends of the Holy Grail, the sacred vessel is said to have been fashioned of pure amethyst. This jewel is also employed in magical rites to achieve political power and other types of ascendancy over the masses. In its highest aspect, however, it was believed to confer the Vision of Love, whereby Jupiter, represented by the wise ruler, governed the universe.

Jewels of Darkness

Like lapis lazuli, the sapphire also had its feminine symbolism, and in one of the ancient Indian Tantric texts the goddess Lalita is described as 'the Sapphire Devi (goddess) whose slender waist, bending beneath the burden of the ripe fruit of her breasts, swells into jewelled hips heavy with the promise of infinite maternities'. According to the 19th century occultist,

Madame Blavatsky, the Buddhists ascribed to the sapphire 'a sacred magical power, which every student of psychological mesmerism will understand, for its polished and deep-blue surface produces extraordinary somnambulic phenomena'.

The star-sapphire, the onyx, the black diamond and the chalcedony are attributed to Saturn, the oldest of the gods. The star-sapphire symbolizes a void of darkness with a starry light at the heart which represents Saturn who, as the earliest, was also the sole light.

The dull and often black onyx is attributed to Saturn on account of the gloomy and leaden nature of that planet. It is used by sorcerers in works which are connected with malediction and death.

The black diamond is connected with the idea of nothingness, the starting point, the mystical void or chaos out of which all things emerged. It also typifies the pupil of the eye, and the Hebrew cabalists assigned to it the letter *Ayin*, which means an eye. The black diamond is therefore a symbol of Sight in Darkness, and of the Unseen Seer. Magicians seeking information, while remaining unseen, employed the Evil Eye; evil because feared; feared because unseen, although known to be present. The black diamond, with that curious reversal characteristic of many ancient symbols, from being an emblem of the Evil Eye, came to be regarded as a charm against it.

Chalcedony, a kind of onyx, is ascribed to Saturn because it is said to drive away

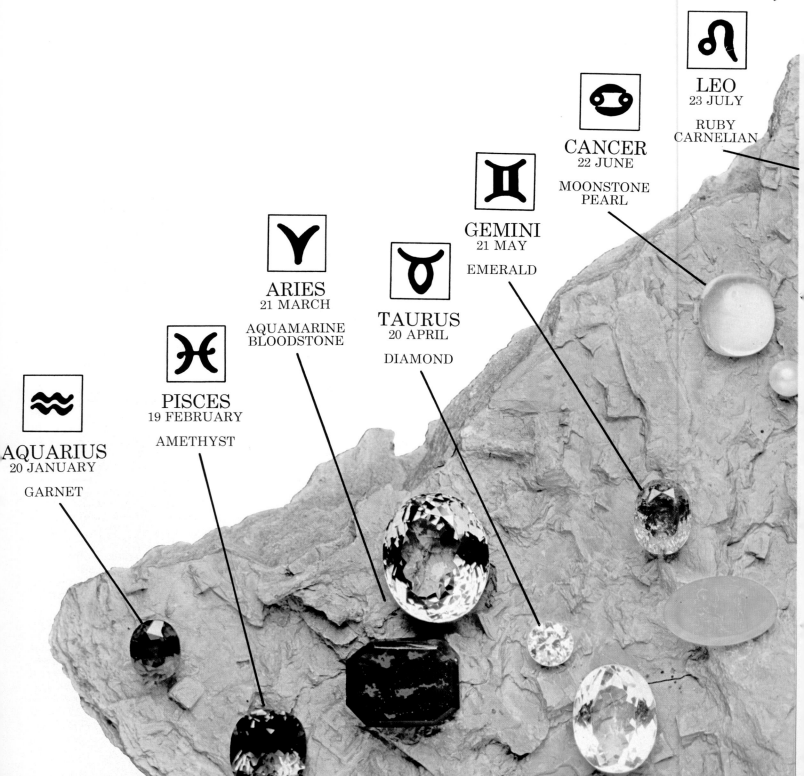

LEO
23 JULY

RUBY
CARNELIAN

CANCER
22 JUNE

MOONSTONE
PEARL

GEMINI
21 MAY

EMERALD

ARIES
21 MARCH

AQUAMARINE
BLOODSTONE

TAURUS
20 APRIL

DIAMOND

PISCES
19 FEBRUARY

AMETHYST

AQUARIUS
20 JANUARY

GARNET

sadness; and Saturn is the epitome of melancholy and dark dread. A person who wears this stone is believed to be protected from the depressing influences symbolized by this planet.

To the ultimate God is ascribed the white diamond, the essence of brilliance. This jewel is a symbol of the True Will, of spiritual energy in its purest form.

In Tantric Buddhism the diamond is likened to the *vajra*, or thunderbolt, symbolic of the Adamantine Consciousness which sustains and underlies existence. It is always coupled with the lotus, the feminine aspect of Consciousness, which acts as the objectifying agency of manifestation. The celebrated Tibetan prayer *om mani padme hum* (O, the jewel in the lotus), refers to the

J. M. Pulsford/Institute of Geological Sciences

diamond vajra in union with its vehicle of manifestation. It is force manifesting as form; will manifesting as idea; the self manifesting as the world.

Disastrous Diamonds

In geometry, the diamond is constructed from a vesica, a pointed oval, which is formed by two intersecting circles. The vesica, like the lotus containing the vajra, also contains a diamond. The vesica was known under the name of the Evil Eye, and the talisman used to avert its baleful powers was the phallus. Thus both Eastern and Western systems of symbolism, associate the diamond with the emblem of male creative energy.

The legends surrounding such historic

stones as the Regent Diamond, the Great Mogul, the Orloff Diamond, the Moon of the Mountains, the Koh-i-Noor and the Hope Diamond illustrate a totally different aspect of the diamond. The last of these has occult interest. It is said to have been stolen from an Indian temple and was sold to Louis XIV in 1668. The man who sold it was struck by various misfortunes, during which he lost all his money. He set sail for India again to make a second fortune but died during the journey. This diamond next appeared adorning the Marquise de Montespan, the beautiful and infamous mistress of Louis XIV who was involved with a group of magicians headed by the obscene Abbé Guibourg. He performed a series of Black Masses at her instance, in order that she

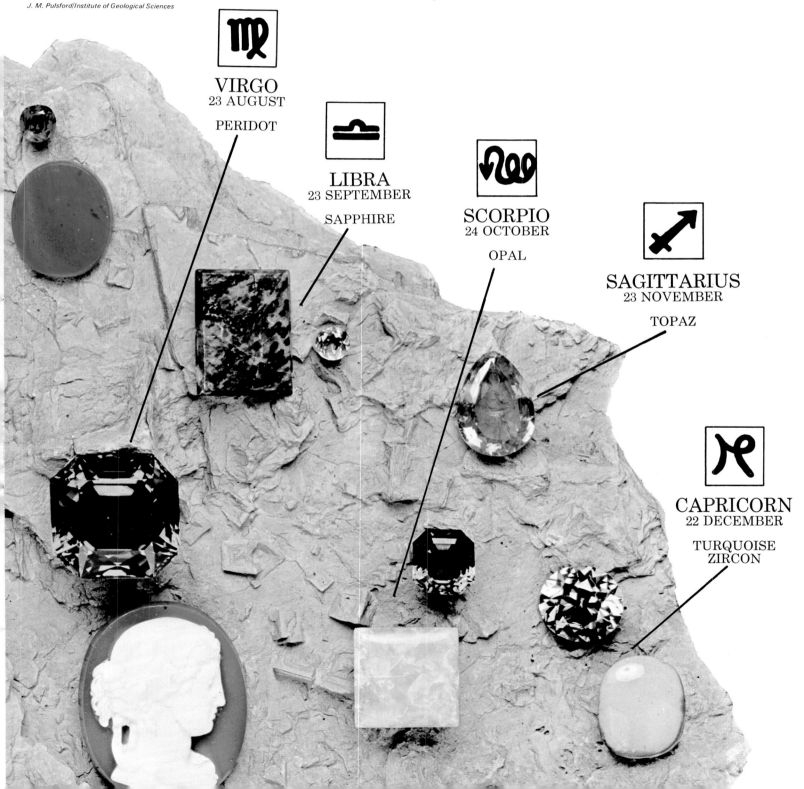

VIRGO
23 AUGUST

PERIDOT

LIBRA
23 SEPTEMBER

SAPPHIRE

SCORPIO
24 OCTOBER

OPAL

SAGITTARIUS
23 NOVEMBER

TOPAZ

CAPRICORN
22 DECEMBER

TURQUOISE
ZIRCON

might obtain supreme power and bind the king's affections to herself alone. During the ritual, Guibourg slashed an infant's throat, the blood being consecrated over the naked body of the living altar, the Marquise herself. It was said that her sole ornament during the rite was the diamond. It was charged by the blood of repeated murders, committed to the accompaniment of diabolical profanations and blasphemies. But the evil sorceries recoiled upon the Marquise, for instead of advancing her cause in the royal household, she experienced an unobtrusive fall from favour (see BLACK MASS).

A century later the same diamond is said to have been in the possession of Marie Antoinette, and again it brought disaster for the 'Diamond Necklace Affair' was one of the incidents that led up to the French Revolution. Marie Antoinette lent the diamond to the Princesse de Lamballe. Shortly afterwards, fate overtook the Princess and she was butchered by the mob, parts of her body being displayed under the windows of the Temple where Louis XVI and his family were imprisoned.

Various other misfortunes attended successive owners of this malignant stone. It is said to have been bought for £18,000 by the London banker, Henry Thomas Hope, after whom the stone was named. In due course his descendant, Lord Francis Hope, came into possession of it, and he lost his fortune shortly afterwards. The trail of disasters continued – suicide, fatal accident, bankruptcy, disgrace – covering in all a period of two hundred years.

The Philosophers' Stone

The alchemists believed the diamond to have attained the pinnacle of beauty and perfection, equal only to that of gold among metals and the Sun among planets. Among the symbols of the alchemists was the Shameer, the strange diamond wrested from the beak of a cock, with which Moses is said to have cut the precious stones for the ephod, a Jewish priestly vestment, and which opened for King Solomon the ultimate gates of wisdom.

But of all precious stones, the star ruby is undoubtedly the most magical. It represents the creative energy of the Sun, or creator star, and symbolizes the star of magic, the pentagram. This star has been used from earliest times to conjure and control angels,

---

The Purity of the Pearl

The idea of pearly purity is inseparably linked with the name Margaret, derived from the Persian *Murwari* (pearl, or child of light) . . . The use of the word as a proper name among the early Christians was doubtless suggested by the sweet simplicity and loveliness of the pearl, and by the beautiful symbolical references to this gem in the Scriptures; and the meaning of the name has been strengthened by the pure lives and the good deeds of the many beautiful Margarets in all lands, including the virgin martyr, St Margaret of Antioch . . . who, before the fifth century, was the embodiment of feminine innocence and faith overcoming evil, and also is often represented wearing a string of pearls.

G. F. Kunz and C. H. Stevenson
The Book of the Pearl

---

demons, elementals and occult entities of all kinds.

The elusive yet far-famed Philosophers' Stone which the adept Trautmansdorf claimed to have discovered was bean-shaped and of reddish hue, emitting flashes of light when in total darkness. It is interesting to compare this with an Indian Brahmin's account of the Pentarbe, a magic stone that was exhibited before Apollonius of Tyana: 'In the night-time it glowed like fire, for it is red and emits rays; and if you look at it, it smites your eyes with a thousand gleams. And this light within it is a spirit of mysterious power, for it absorbs to itself everything in its neighbourhood.'

The Eastern version of the Philosophers' Stone seems to have been the fabled Chintamani, or wishing-gem which has the power to grant all desires. It is said to have belonged to Brahma, the creative aspect of the Hindu Triad. A *Tantra* describes the Supreme Goddess, united with her lord in a room of Chintamani stone, surrounded by a grove of heavenly trees on the island of gems, set in the ocean of ambrosia.

Of no less interest are the toadstones and corals of witchcraft: the Kaustubha jewel of Hinduism and the lightning stones of the ancient Mexicans.

Sir Walter Scott described his family's most curious possession as 'a toadstone . . . a celebrated amulet. It was sovereign for protecting new-born children and their

---

mothers from the power of fairies, and has been repeatedly borrowed from my mother, on account of this virtue.'

The toadstone was any stone that resembled in shape or colour the toad or frog. But the most treasured kind was supposed to be found in the head of a living toad. In *As You Like It* Shakespeare speaks of 'the toad, ugly and venomous', as wearing 'a precious jewel in his head'. This stone was held to be an infallible remedy against curses and witchcraft.

The coral was believed to have similar powers. Paracelsus claimed that the wearing of red corals was a remedy against melancholy. Red corals transmit the solar influence; brown corals, on the contrary, transmit lunar vibrations. The red variety wards off evil spirits while the brown attracts them and helps them to manifest.

In Hinduism, the Kaustubha was a jewel obtained at the churning of the ocean, after Indra, the king of the gods, had been cursed by Shiva for slighting the sage Durvasas. It was a wish-granting gem worn by Krishna and Vishnu.

Lightning stones, sometimes known as thunderbolts, were created when the god of fire, in the form of lightning, flashed into sand, fusing and converting it into vitreous serpentine tubes. The ancient Mexicans revered them as the phallus of the fire god, and used them in their rituals of fertility.

During the course of centuries the tradition of the secret significance of jewels and precious stones became obscured and debased. The ascriptions of various stones to individuals, according to their date of birth, were calculated according to planetary influences operating through the Zodiac. And to the twelve zodiacal signs were allotted the stones with which tradition has familiarized us. In this way, the tradition has been passed down and become merged in the lore concerning the lucky stones and charms of modern astrology.

(See also ALCHEMY; EMERALD; JADE; PEARL; PHILOSOPHERS' STONE.)

KENNETH GRANT

FURTHER READING: G.F. Kunz, *The Magic of Jewels and Charms* (Lippincott, Philadelphia, 1915); W. Crow, *Precious Stones*, rev. ed. (Aquarian Press, 1980); Aleister Crowley, *Liber 777* (Neptune Press, rev edn, 1955); M. Uyldert, *The Magic of Precious Stones* (Turnstone Press, 1981).

Founded by James Jezreel, the New and Latter House of Israel preached exclusive salvation to its believers. But schism followed Jezreel's death and the massive half-built temple, a testimony to the prophet's power, fell into ruin

J. J. JEZREEL

THE NEW AND LATTER House of Israel, also known as the Jezreels or Jezreelites, were a minor religious sect of the 19th century. Until 1960 the terraced houses of Upper Gillingham in Kent were overshadowed by their headquarters, a great ruined hulk of a building. Its sides were adorned with

huge plaques of carved trumpets and scrolls and local legend had it that the tower was built by the Jezreelites to reach to heaven, but the money ran out before that desirable end could be achieved. Since the followers of this sect made it a point never to cut their hair or shave, it was popularly believed by schoolboys that the Jezreelites expected God to return to earth and pull them up to heaven by their hair.

The truth is in a sense even more unlikely than the local stories. The massive tower was, begun by the founder, James Jershom Jezreel, and should have served as a central preaching home for his sect. Jezreel's origins remain mysterious; he is known at one time to have served as a

private in the army. He arrived in Gillingham in 1875 as James White but after getting in touch with a small religious group who believed themselves to be the elect of God, he announced himself as the messenger of the Lord and took his new name, a move which provided him with a fine apocalyptic set of initials. Jezreel's views were set down in 'the Flying Roll' which he claimed was divinely inspired and which distinguished his followers as the 144,000 (mentioned in Revelations 7.4) whom God had specially marked for salvation. It was in essence the same message preached by the 18th century prophetess Joanna Southcott (see SOUTHCOTT); and a similar exclusivity lives on in the teachings of the Jehovah's Witnesses

and of the British Israelites. Jezreel acknowledged his debt to Joanna Southcott and called himself the Sixth Trumpeter — one of a succession of people who had presented the new revelation.

He soon gathered around him a group of faithful followers and was able to move into Woodlands — a large house in Gillingham. There, he opened a school which taught a very narrow curriculum largely based upon Jezreel's own writings. He was not unaware of the importance of music and singing and this became a central part of the services which he held. In its daily conduct the sect had all the characteristics of the Protestant underworld. Like the aged retainer in Emily Bronte's *Wuthering Heights*, they 'ransacked the Bible, pulling all the promises to themselves and flinging all the curses on others.' At the same time exclusive and eclectic, the New and Latter House of Israel clung to the belief that they and they alone were chosen by God.

The school and the centre at Woodlands drew the movement together in Gillingham, and converts in other places sold up their belongings and came to join the community. They deposited their worldly wealth in the treasury and many began to run the businesses which Jezreel started to set up in connection with the society. These included printing shops to produce the tracts and copies of the Flying Roll, and general stores and cobblers to serve the Jezreelites and any others who would use them. The organization was never very large but it attracted a number of wealthy people who

An artist's impression of Jezreel's tower, which was intended to serve as the head-quarters of the Jezreelite movement at Gillingham in Kent; according to local legend, the tower was planned to reach heaven

put their entire fortunes at the disposal of Jezreel. Soon he conceived of a great temple which would serve as the focal point for his new religious community.

The Reign of Queen Esther

Land was bought high above the Medway River and, after the builder had modified the original plans, the work was under way. Below were to have been the printing presses while above it was intended to provide a great preaching deck where the prophet could address the faithful. In 1885 the foundations had been laid and building began when disaster struck — Jezreel himself, the successor of Joanna Southcott, the Prophet of God, died and the sect was thrown into disarray. Many followers were unable to believe that God's own prophet could have died and the leadership was very much in doubt until Jezreel's widow, now named Queen Esther, by sheer persistence and imperious self-will gained control.

In contrast to Jezreel, Queen Esther was singularly lacking in tact and organizational ability, she was autocratic and proud and soon complaints of her rule became widespread. People who had given all their money to the movement demanded it back, and some claimed to have been left in

appalling circumstances by the Mother of Israel as the new leader styled herself. The society was threatened with schism and the threat became a reality when one faction seceded and moved to London. Work on the temple was held up when the builders demanded their money, and finally stopped when the money was not forthcoming.

The local press was loud in its denunciation of the Jezreelites and it was in the midst of a decidedly hostile community that Esther herself died in 1888. Serious dissension broke out among the remaining followers of Jezreel and the movement split into warring groups, just as the various sects claiming descent from Joanna Southcott had split earlier. There was a short revival of fortunes when an American calling himself Prince Michael arrived to claim leadership, but his endeavours to re-establish the New and Latter House of Israel met with no lasting success.

The London secessionists carried on and up to the late 1950's bearded speakers at Hyde Park Corner were still telling of the wonders of the Flying Roll. They disclaimed any connection with the Gillingham believers who lingered on, their temple uncompleted and derelict; in 1960 the edifice was destroyed. Although the New and Latter House of Israel has ceased to exist, buses still stop at 'the Jezreels', copies of the Flying Roll can still be bought, and James Jershom Jezreel is still reckoned as the Sixth Trumpeter by the present followers of Joanna Southcott, the Panacea Society of Bedford.

J. S. GUMMER

Jihad

An Arabic word meaning a 'striving', used specifically in Islam to denote a holy war or religious crusade against unbelievers; Mohammed resorted to arms to suppress his opponents in Mecca and later Moslem rulers often proclaimed jihads: those who died fighting in such a war became martyrs and were assured of eternal bliss with Allah: in a broader sense jihad means the struggle against one's lower nature.
See ISLAM; WAR.

Sonia Halliday

JINN

JINN IS A better spelling for the common English 'genie'. According to the Koran, Jinn were created of scorching heat or of a smokeless flame, and by popular report inhabited the earth long before Adam. It was believed that they lived underground or in Mt Qaf, which is said in Arabic mythology to encircle the earth.

Jinn are frequently mentioned in the Koran. Seemingly, pagans had treated them as semi-divine, for sura 6.100 says they worshipped them alongside God and sura 37.158 that they believed in a relationship between God and the jinn. But in general, the jinn are treated as a race parallel, though inferior in honour, to man. Solomon is said to have commanded troops of them (sura 27.17; 34.11), his power over them being popularly believed to have lain in a ring inscribed with God's greatest name.

Jinn are mortal, are believed to propagate their species and to be long-lived. God created men and jinn to serve him but many jinn are unbelievers and will go to hell. The first part of sura 72 tells of some jinn who heard Mohammed reciting the Koran and became believers, and sura 46.28–31 tells of jinn hearing the Koran, summoning their people to belief, and warning them God cannot be frustrated.

Pagans, says the Koran, accused prophets, such as Noah, Moses and Mohammed of being jinn-possessed, 'majnun' (a word which is now used generally to mean mad). Such accusations were strenuously denied. In the same way, when Mohammed was called a poet, this was refuted – not on the score of poetry being held disreputable, but because Arabs believed poets were inspired by jinn. Mohammed insisted that his inspiration came from God.

Jinn are generally thought of as having a group existence, with no separate identity, but there are classes which do have an individuality. Among these is the *ifreet*, mentioned once in the Koran (sura 27.34), as offering to bring Solomon the Queen of Sheba's throne. They are dreaded for their maliciousness. Another class is the *ghul* (from which the English word ghoul is derived), said to be ugly but to be able to change its form. It lurks in desert places, lights fires to mislead travellers, and entices them to their destruction. According to tradition, Mohammed denied the existence of the ghoul, but this has not made people abandon the belief.

There is some doubt about Iblees (from Greek *diabolos,* devil), chief of the devils (in Arabic, *shayatin,* plural of *shaytan,* Satan). He is called one of the jinn (sura 18.51), and Iblees says God created him of fire (sura 7.11), which connects him with the jinn; but elsewhere he is a rebellious angel cast out of heaven because he refused to join the other angels in obeying God's command to do obeisance to Adam. The Koran speaks both of devils and jinn listening outside heaven and being driven away by a bright flame, and it is uncertain whether devil is another name for jinn, or whether they both attempt to learn heaven's secrets.

Tradition often mentions jinn. It says everyone has a partner, one from the jinn and one from the angels; the former is disposed to lead one astray, though Mohammed's jinn had accepted Islam. A tradition tells of an ifreet of the jinn unsuccessfully trying to interrupt Mohammed's prayers. Another says that on the first night of Ramadan the devils and rebellious jinn are chained. One says house snakes must not be killed, for they are resident jinn; but another says one should tell the snake to go away. If it remains after a third telling it is to be killed, for it is an infidel. Warning is given to bring children inside in the evening, for jinn are about and may seize them.

An Ifreet

The caravan . . . came at last, at the fall of a certain night, to a column of black stone to which a strange being was chained, one half of whose body was visible and the other half deeply hidden in the ground. The upper half seemed to be that of some monstrous birth imprisoned there by infernal powers. It was as black and large as the trunk of an old and naked palm-tree; it had two great black wings and four hands, of which two were like the taloned feet of lions. A shaggy covering of rude onager-tail hairs moved savagely upon the terrible head, while under the roofs of the sockets flamed two red eyes, and a third shone immovably green like that of a tiger or a panther, between the twin horns of the bull-like brow.
The Thousand and One Nights
(trans by Powys Mathers)

Right A 19th century illustration from *Sindbad the Sailor* showing an ifreet – a malicious type of jinn – being burned out of the sky

Jinn are believed to live in trees, wells, marshes, uninhabited and even inhabited houses, and to frequent lonely roads, market places, cemeteries, privies and drains. A pillar of sand rushing across the desert is a jinn driving along, and so is a waterspout. Inter-marriage between humans and jinn is possible, but the human partner may suffer.

Fortunately there are various methods of protection from the dangers of the jinn. If one climbs a date palm the jinn can be effectively frightened by singing, so that the work can proceed without incident. Loud sounds, music, and the shrill cries of women at weddings scare them away.

Jinn fear iron and steel, so some people wear a steel ring, and others put daggers or knives in places where protection is sought. Salt is another means of protection, for jinn abhor it.

Koranic and other sacred words are the most effective protection. Written charms, bearing verses from the Koran, names of God, magic squares, a group of magical signs called the seven seals, are commonly tied on children and animals and are also worn by adults. They protect the wearer from the machinations of the jinn who, in addition to producing calamities, are notorious for causing diseases. The last sura of the Koran includes a petition for protection from the jinn.

Some modern Moslems have tried to explain away the jinn, even suggesting they were microbes. Mohammed Ali, in his commentary on the Koran, has various explanations. At times he seems to feel they were devils invisible to men, but elsewhere he suggests they were strong men, slaves employed by Solomon, or Jews who heard the Koran recited. However, the common people's belief in a race of jinn who can harm or sometimes help, is more in keeping with the original meaning.

JAMES ROBSON

FURTHER READING: E. Westermarck, *Ritual and Belief in Morocco* (Universal Books, 1968); A. S. Tritton, *Islam, Beliefs and Practices* (Hutchinson: Hillary House, 1966); T. P. Hughes, *A Dictionary of Islam* (International Publications Service, 1976).

British Museum/John Freeman

Did Joan of Arc's voices really come from God? Posterity, like her own time, has been curiously ambivalent in its attitude to the Maid of Orleans; at various times and in different quarters, she has been seen as a great warrior patriot, a deluded hysteric, a Devil-inspired witch and a stained-glass-window saint

JOAN OF ARC

THERE ARE FEW people nowadays who would dispute the spiritual stature of Joan of Arc, one of the most remarkable women who has ever lived, although over five centuries after her death there is still no common agreement as to the exact nature and source of her inspiration. The opinion of the judges at her trial in 1431, however, which led to the stake, was totally at variance with this assessment. They held that her visions were worthless, denied her the gift of prophecy, accused her of sorcery and above all censured the heretical pride which had induced her to believe that she was answerable only to God, and not to God's ministers on earth, which her judges represented.

A similar contradiction of views has persisted down the intervening centuries; defended in her own century by Thomas Basin, historian and Bishop of Lisieux, in Shakespeare's *Henry VI* Joan was represented as 'a sorceress condemned to burn', in fact, a witch (a view which was also put forward in recent times by Margaret Murray in her *Witch-Cult in Western Europe*). In the 16th century the Jesuit Father Guillaume Postel, himself known to practice magic and alchemy, defended her. In France Voltaire took the view that she was an unhappy wretch, given to hallucinations; and not long after Joan had begun to achieve the status of a national heroine, the celebrated writer Anatole France echoed this view of her as a deluded unfortunate in a biography published in 1908. Immediately, the Scottish writer Andrew Lang replied with his own biography, *The Maid of France*, maintaining that it was Anatole France himself who was deluded. In Bernard Shaw's eyes, Joan was a Protestant who insisted on the validity of her own personal vision, contrary to the view of Paul Claudel and Charles Péguy, the eminent Roman Catholic poets, who revered her as a mystic and a saint.

Voices of the Saints

The historical truth behind all these opinions is hard to establish. It has been suggested that she was the illegitimate daughter of Louis d'Orleans and Queen Isabeau, widow of Charles VI, and therefore half-sister of the Dauphin, Charles VII. Although this claim fails to stand up to close examination, it is strange, nevertheless, that the Dauphin gave her a coat of arms – an azure shield, a silver sword with a gold pommel, supporting a gold crown and flanked by two fleurs-de-lis in gold – a tremendous honour for an uneducated peasant girl. Despite this, it seems much more likely that she was the daughter of prosperous peasants from the village of Domrémy in Lorraine, close to the border of the kingdom of France, which at this time covered the region of Paris and was being sorely harrassed by the English.

The meteoric rise to fame of this illiterate country girl, her astonishing career, her miracles and her eventual martyrdom all stem from her belief in her power to deliver France from the English, a power which she was convinced had been divinely conferred on her for this purpose. As a little girl, she would often have been told how the kingdom of France had been lost by a wicked woman (Queen Isabeau, who had defected to the side of France's enemies), and that a virgin would restore it. There was another story that at the beginning of the 15th century a soothsayer named Marie d'Avignon had gone to the King and told him that the country was about to be ravaged by war, but that a maid would come who would lead France to victory. Since Joan was probably familiar with both these legends, she would not have thought it strange when 'voices', which she later identified as those of St Gabriel, St Michael, St Marguerite and St Catherine, began speaking to her one day when she was about 13 years old. Under a 'fairies' tree' close to her home, she made a vow to remain a virgin and to live a pure and godly life. At first the voices told her to go to the land of France, but later, when the news of the siege of Orleans reached Domrémy, they instructed her to rescue the city.

Despite her spirituality and growing reputation as a young visionary fallen from heaven, Joan was very much aware of practical realities, and her skill in dealing with unforeseen problems was considerable. In 1429 she asked the officer in command of her area, Robert de Baudricourt, to provide her with a horse and escort to enable her to go and see the Dauphin. After insisting that she should first be exorcized by a local priest, de Baudricourt agreed to her request. Furnished with an introduction to the Dauphin, Joan set off across occupied France to Chinon. Difficulties seemed to vanish before her; she made her way past road blocks, ambushes and sentries. When she arrived at Chinon, Charles hid himself among his courtiers, but she recognized him immediately, went up to him and whispered in his ear certain facts which were known only to him. Joan assured Charles, who had been thinking of relinquishing his throne, that he would be victorious and would reign with power and honour. She made four predictions: that she would deliver Orleans, if she were taken there with the troops; that Charles would be crowned at Rheims with Joan herself at his side; that Paris would return to French control, and that the Duke of Orleans would come back to France.

God's Field Commander

The court at Chinon was immediately mistrustful of this strange young girl who said she consorted with saints and angels, and who announced that she was sent by God; they suspected that she might be using diabolic powers. Joan had to undergo a lengthy ecclesiastical examination at Poitiers, in which she conducted herself well and impressed the clerics favourably. Later, with Charles, she declared that she would fight and that she was able to command through the grace of St Michael. Charles was convinced. Joan was sent to Tours and provided with armour and troops. She requested that a sword be brought to her from behind the altar of the church of St Catherine-de-Fierboys. On her standard, to which she was entitled by her military rank, was painted the King of Heaven holding an orb, together with the words 'Jesus Maria'. Thus equipped, she set out to join the army at Blois for the relief of Orleans.

At first, her military campaign was successful. Orleans was relieved, the English put to flight, and town after town in the Loire fell before her. On 17 July 1429 Charles was duly crowned at Rheims, as she had predicted. But victory was shortlived; on 23 May of the following year, outside the walls of Compiègne, she was taken prisoner and handed over to John of Luxembourg, the Burgundian commander, who eventually sold her to the English. Held captive in the castle of the Luxembourgs at Beaurevoir she again heard 'voices'; and obsessed with the idea of going to the help of the people of Compiègne, she leapt from the tower, suffering minor injuries. A second attempt to escape was similarly unsuccessful. Joan was then moved to Rouen, the English military centre, and imprisoned in the castle.

Her trial, on the charges of sorcery and heresy, began early in 1431. The English, for political reasons, were determined that Joan should be convicted, in the hope

Mansell Collection

Three images of St Joan *Left* An idealized portrait of Joan as the saintly patriot *Right* Joan brought to trial as a heretic, weak against the combined might of Crown and Church: illustration from the Armagnac manuscripts *Following page* An incarnation of purity and truth, Joan leads the French troops into battle. She believed her bravery to be a gift from God, who had sent her to deliver France from the English: 19th century painting by Frank Craig

Was Joan a Witch?

This intriguing theory of Joan's death has been rejected by most scholars

The witch-cult being a survival of an ancient religion, many of the beliefs and rites of these early religions are to be found in it. Of these the principal are: the voluntary substitute, the temporary transference of power to the substitute, and the self-devotion to death. As times changed and the ceremonies could no longer be performed openly, the sacrifices took on other forms . . . when the time came for the God or his substitute to be sacrificed, recourse was had to methods which hid the real meaning of the ceremony; and the sacrifice of the incarnate deity, though taking place in public, was consummated at the hands of the public executioner . . .

Read in the light of this theory much of the mystery which surrounds the fate of Joan of Arc is explained. She was put to death as a witch, and the conduct of her associates during her military career, as well as the evidence at her trial, bear out the fact that she belonged to the ancient religion, not to the Christian . . .

The belief that Joan was God Incarnate will account, as nothing else can, for the extraordinary supineness of the French, who never lifted a finger to ransom or rescue Joan from the hands of either the Burgundians or the English. As God himself or his voluntary substitute she was doomed to suffer as the sacrifice for the people, and no one of those people could attempt to save her . . .

An intensive study of this period might reveal the witch organisation at the royal Court and possibly even the Grand-master to whom Joan owed allegiance, the 'God' who sent her. Giac, the King's favourite, was executed as a witch, and Joan's *beau duc*, the Duke d'Alençon, was also of the fraternity.

Margaret Murray *The Witch-Cult in Western Europe*

that this would discredit Charles and so improve their failing fortunes. Joan was handed over to Pierre Cauchon, a dispossessed anglophile Bishop who had applied for the office of judge in the hope of personal preferment; to this end he selected a tribunal likely to favour and achieve a conviction.

Trial and Judgement

The lynchpin of Joan's trial was to resolve whether it was God or the Devil who guided her. The theologians of the Church, the clerics and masters of the University of Paris were agreed that Joan had used witchcraft. It was claimed that the judges had proof that she was a 'magician, a heretic, a schismatic'. It was alleged that her 'voices' were the result of mandrake, a plant containing a narcotic juice which causes delirium and to which many magical properties were ascribed, including the power of speech; it was said that Joan had kept a root of this plant in her bodice. Her judges insisted that her apparitions were in fact infernal spirits, that her voices were satanic interventions, that her premonitions were witchcraft, and that her battles were diabolic crimes.

The indictment held that she was 'superstitious, a soothsayer, an idolator, an invoker of devils, a blasphemer against God and his saints'. It enumerated her 'detestable and wicked crimes and sins' as fruits of her 'proud spirit'. The Inquisition refused to believe that the saints had visited her. Charles VII's coronation had been 'a work of hell', because she had invoked evil spirits. It was further maintained that she was 'perfidious, cruel, tainted with human blood'. The University of Paris, whose opinion had been sought, affirmed that Joan was 'a woman of Belial, Satan and Behemoth'. On these grounds the accused was found guilty of heresy, and liable to the extreme penalty unless she submitted. Confused and appalled at her imminent fate, Joan recanted and was taken back to prison. Abjuring her recantation, she was handed over to the secular arm and on 30 May 1431 was burned as a relapsed heretic.

Seen to Exhale a Dove

After the fire had consumed her, there were some who doubted whether she had actually suffered this fate, so the executioner was ordered to separate the ashes and show the people that her remains really were there, as it was thought that her witchcraft had caused her to disappear, just at the crucial moment. The believers wept and crossed themselves; they thought that they had burned a saint, and it was murmured that as she breathed her final breath, she was seen to exhale a dove, the symbol of the Holy Ghost. The executioner cut open her pathetic remains, and destroyed what was left of her entrails. He was ordered to throw the heart and the ashes into the Loire lest any miracle-working relics should remain.

At Joan's trial, the most highly esteemed judges, jurists, prelates and the Dominican Inquisitor had affirmed her diabolism, her heretical and schismatic condition; only Jean Gerson, Master of the University, had defended her in the first place and declared her innocence when the clerics united against her. Some years later, however, in 1456, other equally eminent judges with similar assurance proclaimed the iniquity of her first trial, asserted her orthodoxy and admirable merits, and annulled the judgement of 1431. Nearly five centuries later, in 1909, Joan was beatified and in 1920, canonized by the Roman Catholic Church. On the latter occasion, one saw the curious spectacle of her being acclaimed at the same time by the Royalists and by the Communists, who saw her as a daughter of the revolutionary people, by the anti-clerical faction who saw her as an opponent of the priests, by the militant atheists and by the occultists. More recently still — and perhaps still more curious — Joan of Arc, whose effigy with its sword and banner may be seen in many cathedrals, was described by the eminent Jesuit, Cardinal Danielou, as 'a model of lay saintliness'.

Thus the Church, which had first sent her to her death and centuries later canonized her, has now placed her on the fringe of its holy community and regards her as a laywoman, as if she were not recognized among its saints.

F. RIBADEAU DUMAS

FURTHER READING: W.P. Barrett, *The Trial of Joan of Arc* (Gotham House, 1932). See also Frances Gie, *Joan of Arc* (Harper and Row, 1981); J. Michelet, *Joan of Arc* (Univ. of Michigan Press, 1957); R. Pernoud, *Joan of Arc* (Stein and Day, 1969); M. Warner, *Joan of Arc: the Image of Female Heroism*.

How can innocent suffering be reconciled with the image of a just God? This is the central theme of the book of Job

JOB

PROBABLY THE MOST significant book in the Hebrew Bible, the book of Job expresses in dramatic form a great crisis that had gradually built up in Hebrew religion, and it represents a noble but unsuccessful attempt to solve that crisis.

Ancient Hebrew religion was essentially ethnic in character. It centred on the relation between God, Yahweh (see YAH-WEH) and his chosen people, Israel. In this relationship, the individual counted only in so far as he promoted or hindered the nation's service to its god. He had no ultimate significance; when he died, his shade descended into the gloomy depths of Sheol, beyond the care or interest of Yahweh. The only hope was that his pious service to Yahweh would be rewarded by a long and prosperous life, and that his children would succeed him within the holy community of Israel.

Hebrew religion in its early form, therefore, held no promise of a happy life after death. Many Israelites found consolation in the mortuary cults of Canaan, which presupposed that the dead lived on in their tombs; but such practices were fiercely condemned by the Yahwist prophets. In time, however, a sense of individuality began to emerge, and it coincided with a significant development in the conception of Yahweh. The prophets increasingly emphasized both Yahweh's omnipotence and his moral character. This changing conception inevitably raised a difficult problem about the fate of the individual and Yahweh's attitude to him. Experience often showed how specious was the Yahwist doctrine of man; for frequently it was not the pious but the wicked who lived long and prosperously. How was this fate to be reconciled with the idea of Yahweh as a just god? For there was no hope of restitution in the grim pit of Sheol. This problem was felt most keenly by those who wished to believe in the justice of Yahweh, but could not close their minds to the facts of experience. Such a one was the anonymous author of the book of Job who sought to answer this challenge to his faith in Yahweh.

Satan Challenges Job

The book of Job contains a multitude of literary problems for which no certain solution has been found. Scholars date the book between 700 and 200 BC. They are generally agreed that the prose prologue and epilogue were originally distinct from the main poetical dialogue, and that the speech of Elihu (Job 32–37) was a later interpolation. Of Job himself nothing is otherwise known although there are a few brief references to him in the Bible.

The prologue (Job 1–2) sets the scene for the ensuing drama. It starts by representing Job as a rich sheikh, dwelling in the land of Uz (possibly the neighbourhood of Edom or the Hauran, east of the Dead Sea). He is described as 'blameless and upright, one that feared God, and turned away from evil'. The scene then changes to the court of Yahweh, where the 'Sons of God' assemble, and among them comes Satan. At this stage in Hebrew thought Satan was not yet the Devil, but a cynical observer of mankind. When Yahweh praises the rectitude of Job, Satan answers that Job fears God because God has blessed him with success and happiness. And he goes on to suggest that if misfortune befell Job, he would renounce God. The challenge is accepted, and God allows Satan to afflict Job.

In the subsequent series of personal disasters Job loses all his wealth and his children are killed. But his faith in God is not shaken. Satan, however, is not impressed, and suggests that Job's integrity would not stand up to the test of physical suffering. Yahweh again allows Satan to try the unfortunate Job. He is tormented by boils; in his misery 'he took a potsherd with which to scrape himself, and sat among the ashes'. His wife exhorts him to renounce God and die; but he remains steadfast in his allegiance. Then Job's so-called 'comforters', Eliphaz, Bildad and Zophar, visit him. They do not come to comfort him, but to endeavour to explain Job's misfortune in terms of the traditional Yahwist view of life. With their arrival the prologue ends. The stage is now

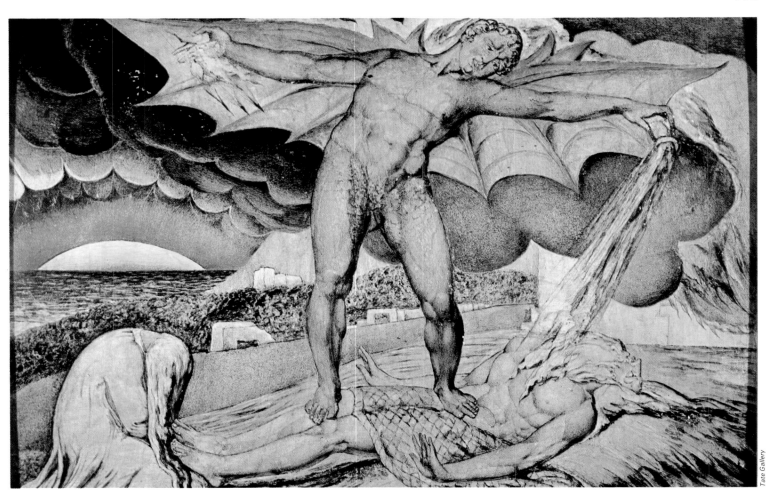

set for the series of dialogues in which Job and his 'comforters' debate the cause of his unhappy lot.

Job's problem is that of reconciling innocent suffering with belief in a just and omnipotent God. The poignancy of Job's dilemma lies in his acceptance of the orthodox Yahwist creed that man did not survive death. This belief is presented with vivid imagery (Job 14.7–12):

> For there is hope of a tree,
>   if it be cut down, that it will sprout again . . .
> But man dies, and is laid low;
> Man breathes his last, and where is he?
> As waters fail from a lake,
> And a river wastes away and dries up,
> So man lies down and rises not again,
> Till the heavens are no more he will not awake,
>   Or be roused out of his sleep.

The theme of the 'comforters' is that misfortune is the inevitable penalty of misdoings (4.7–9):

> Think now, who that was innocent ever perished?
> Or where were the upright cut off?
> As I have seen, those who plough iniquity,
>   and sow trouble reap the same.
> By the breath of God they perish,
>   and by the blast of his anger they are consumed.

But Job knows that he has not merited such punishment, and he rejects their shallow philosophy. As the dialogue proceeds, Job turns more to interrogating

Challenging his faith, Satan smites Job with boils: from the series illustrating the book of Job by William Blake

God than answering his 'comforters'. In the depth of his despair, he implores the Almighty to cease from tormenting him. But he cannot leave the problem of the seeming injustice of God, and finally he calls on God to justify himself.

God's answer is to overwhelm Job by a parade of his cosmic activity, so that Job's personal problem is dwarfed into insignificance, and he is made to abhor himself in

The Splendour of God

Then the Lord answered Job out of the whirlwind:
Gird up your loins like a man;
I will question you, and you declare to me.
Will you even put me in the wrong?
Will you condemn me that you may be justified?
Have you an arm like God,
  and can you thunder with a voice like his?
Deck yourself with majesty and dignity;
  clothe yourself with glory and splendour.
Pour forth the overflowings of your anger,
  and look on every one that is proud, and abase him.
Look on every one that is proud, and bring him low;
  and tread down the wicked where they stand.
Hide them all in the dust together;
  bind their faces in the world below.
Then will I also acknowledge to you,
  that your own right hand can give you victory.
Job, chapter 40

dust and ashes (chapters 38–41). This was the only solution that the author could offer for the problem of innocent suffering. In the prose epilogue that follows, an even more unsatisfactory ending is offered. God rebukes Eliphaz and his friends, and endows Job with greater prosperity than he had before, thus endorsing the orthodox view that God rewards the just with material blessing (Job 41.7–17).

The book of Job, or at least the poetical part of it, is thus a noble failure. Its author had agonized over the problem of innocent suffering, but had failed to find a really adequate moral answer. The tension was only eased finally in the 2nd century BC, when Hebrew religion accepted belief in a resurrection of the dead and a post-mortem judgement (see JUDGEMENT OF THE DEAD).

An ancient Mesopotamian writing that is sometimes called 'The Babylonian Job' contains a long complaint from a just man overwhelmed by undeserved misfortune. But the purpose of the writing seems rather to be that of commemorating the ultimate saving intervention of the god Marduk than of discussing the problem of innocent suffering in relation to the gods.

S. G. F. BRANDON

FURTHER READING: R.H. Pfeiffer, *Introduction to the Old Testament* (Harper and Row, rev. ed., 1948); J. Hastings ed., *Dictionary of the Bible* (Scribner, rev. ed., 1963); L. Besserman, *The Legend of Job in the Middle Ages* (Harvard Univ. Press, 1979); R. Gordis, *The Book of God and Man* (Univ. of Chicago Press, 1966).

The teaching of St John of the Cross, contained in his beautiful mystical poems and commentaries, reveals how the soul becomes purified in its development towards a perfect union with God

JOHN OF THE CROSS

THIS GREAT SPANISH mystic was the third son of Gonzalo de Yepes, a Castilian silk-merchant. When Gonzalo died, less than three years after John was born, the family fell into great poverty and the mother and the eldest child, Francisco had to work to support them. John himself, as he grew up, was apprenticed to various trades but was able to attend the Jesuit grammar school at Medina. At the age of 21 he entered the Carmelite monastery in the same town, taking the name of John of St Matthias. He then went to study at the University of Salamanca and in 1567, at the age of 25, he was ordained priest, after which he returned to Salamanca for a final year of study. He had already formed a wish to enter into a stricter way of life and had contemplated joining the austere Carthusian Order, when a meeting with Teresa of Avila brought a realization of his true vocation. Teresa had already begun her great work of Carmelite reform and had been instructed to found two monasteries for Carmelite friars who wished to practise the primitive rule (see TERESA OF AVILA).

John met Teresa immediately after his ordination and when he had finished his studies, along with two others he entered the reformed house at Duruelo, and changed his name to that of John of the Cross. For some years all went well, but in 1575 a violent reaction set in against the whole movement for reform and John was imprisoned at Toledo by a Carmelite community of the mitigated rule, who were opposed to reform. He was placed in a small, badly-lit cell, where he was inadequately fed and harshly treated in an attempt to persuade him to give up his adherence to the reform. His spirit remained unbroken and after some eight or nine months he escaped from Toledo to southern Spain. For the remaining 13 years of his life he acted as confessor and spiritual adviser to many nuns of the reform, in addition to holding various administrative positions in the Order. He died in 1591, at the age of 49.

Journey of the Soul

Apart from his letters of spiritual advice, John's systematic treatment of mystical theology is contained in a number of poems, which he subsequently explained in a series of commentaries. *The Spiritual Canticle* is a long dialogue between the soul, the Bride, and her Beloved, clearly inspired by the Song of Solomon in the Old Testament. The greater part of this poem was composed during his imprisonment in Toledo, the commentary having been written in 1584 and later revised. The Bride complains of her Lover's absence and tells of her longing for him. He is all in all to her, yet he eludes her. But this is the testing, purifying process, to prepare her for the raptures of final union.

Ascent of Mount Carmel is a study of the process by which the soul reaches the heights of mystical contemplation. It is cast in the form of a commentary on a poem, *The Dark Night* (composed between 1579–81), though there is another commentary on the same poem, written apparently at much the same time as *The Ascent*. A later poem, *Living Flame of Love*, was composed at some date between 1582–85, with a subsequent commentary. It is universally recognized that John's poetry is of the highest quality, although his prose style is of a lower level of inspiration.

Two other works should also be mentioned: John's remarkable drawing of Christ crucified, the result of a vision, and his sketch-plan of the Ascent of Mount Carmel, which summarizes his teaching on the subject of spiritual and mystical progress.

The basis of the teaching of John of the Cross, drawn largely from his own experience, is that the human person is, in St Augustine's words, 'made for God' and can only be fulfilled, perfected, become fully itself 'in God'. He describes the process by

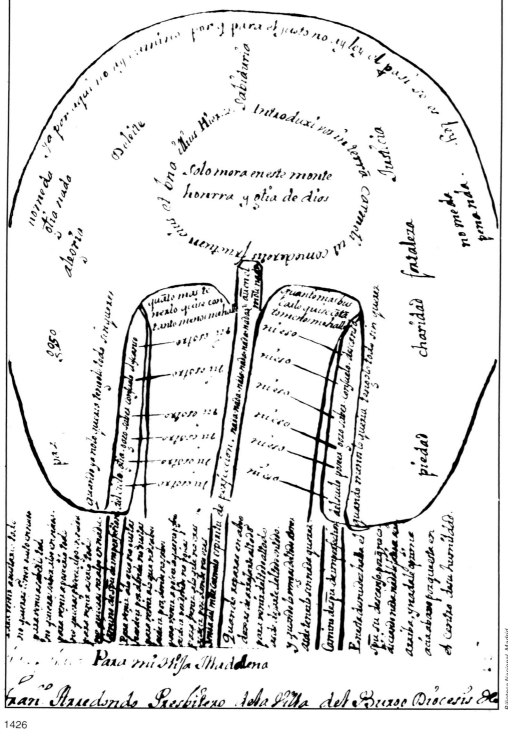

Left St John's sketch-plan of the Ascent of Mount Carmel: a summary of his teaching, it depicts the process by which the soul reaches the heights of mystical contemplation *Right* An inspired re-creation of a familiar theme: the Crucifixion by Salvador Dali, from a drawing of a vision by St John; below the cross is a seascape reminiscent of the Sea of Galilee

which this absorption into God is achieved and the state of the soul when thus absorbed. John's teaching is addressed primarily to the enclosed, 'contemplative' religious, though it has its value for all Christians. Whilst he sketches out an ideal, typical journey of the soul towards God, he is the first to insist that no two souls are alike and that each man's way of coming to God will be peculiar to him and will not necessarily be helpful to another. Yet there is little doubt that what John has to say has been, and will be, of practical value for all who are seriously interested in the mystical way.

Night of the Senses

The soul moves towards God in two stages, which are really complementary aspects of one conditioning. That conditioning is the stripping away of all the obstacles that come between the creature and its Creator. The obstacles may be divided into what may roughly be called moral and what may be described as psychological. The moral obstacles are the desires which spring from selfishness or any form of self-regarding feelings. These must be purged away in the 'night of the senses'. All stirring of desire, even for innocent pleasure, must be 'mortified', put to death, annihilated. This purification is the work of normal asceticism, the ordinary acts of self-denial, self-discipline, the refusal of all enjoyment, the training of the will to an actual preference for the harder, more distasteful, more painful. Thus, he says: 'Strive not after that which is most easy, but after that which is most difficult . . . not after that which is most pleasant, but after that which is most unpleasant. . . Strive not to desire anything but rather nothing.'

'The night of sense is common and the lot of many; these are the beginners. The night of the spirit is the portion of the very few. The night of sense is of ordinary occurrence. Recollected persons enter the dark night sooner than others after they have begun their spiritual course. In general there lapses no great length of time after they have begun, before they enter the night of sense, and most of them do enter it, for they suffer aridities' (a feeling of distaste for prayer and that sense of the absence of God, which are the special suffering of those whose lives are, by dedication, God-centred and prayer-centred).

'During the aridities of the night of sense, God is drawing the soul out of the way of sense into that of spirit, from meditation to contemplation . . . God is leading them by the way of contemplation, which knows no imagination or reasoning . . . All they have to do is to keep their souls unembarrassed and at rest from all thoughts and all knowledge, contenting themselves with directing their attention simply and calmly towards God. . .'

The second stage of this purifying process is the 'Night of the Soul' or 'the Spirit', a night more terrible still, in which the soul, passive under the influence of God, finds memory, imagination, intellect, and will itself emptied of everything that is familiar and normal. This is because the normal objects of

memory and imagination, of intellect and will are necessarily finite and therefore, compared with the infinity that is God, can only betray and falsify the ultimate truth. If the powers of the soul are to be made fit for the vision of God they must be stretched beyond their normal capacity. So long as they are concerned with what is less than the pure being of the Infinite, they will be unable to rise above their own limitations. Nor can the soul achieve this purification by any effort of its own. God takes charge and does the work in and for the very centre and core of its being.

A Positive Purgation

All this sounds, and could be interpreted as being, so negative and destructive as to be totally inhuman, Yet, in principle, there is no difference between the demands of John of the Cross and the obligation that the poet John Milton felt himself to be under, '. . . to scorn delights and live laborious days'. For the doctrine, however starkly and forbiddingly stated, is essentially positive and constructive. The purgation is, and must be seen to be, no more than a means to an end, an end that is one of total fulfilment, perfection, sheer bliss. Certainly it should not be interpreted as suggesting that any created reality is in itself tainted, corrupt, sinful. Not only would this be contrary to the whole Christian belief in the creative activity of God and in the Incarnation which implies the involvement of God in his own creation; it is also contrary to John's own attitude. His poetry is filled with a sense of the beauty of creation, which would be impossible in a man who had stripped himself of all appreciation of natural reality:

Of flowers and emeralds fine
Gathered when dawn's dews gleam,
Gay garlands we shall twine,
Fragrant with your love's tender breath,
Bound with one hair of mine.

John's doctrine is essentially one of balance. In God is found the fullness of all perfection, of beauty, of happiness, of wisdom. To arrive at union with that source of all that is worth while it will be necessary to pass through a preparatory stage in which experiences of everyday life seem to disappear. But the more completely the soul gives itself up to this process of purification, the more rapidly and completely will it find again all that it had thought lost, all that and so much more. Yet, if the surrender is not total, if the ascetic is in effect giving up *in order to* profit more completely, this is no true purgation. It is simply an act of selfishness. So the surrender must be absolute with no thought of recompense.

Again, as is the way of mystical writers, the final union of the soul with God is pictured in language drawn from the analogy of human love-making:

O, burning, burning sweet!
O wound, O welcome blow!
O gentle hand, O touch that soothes and thrills,
Filling with life complete,
Cancelling all I owe:
Love's sword revives even as it kills.

By contrast, John's prose commentary, couched in the language of scholastic metaphysics, loses something of this passion. 'The end I have in view is the divine Embracing, the union of the soul with the divine substance. In this loving, obscure knowledge God unites himself with the soul eminently and divinely.

'This knowledge consists in a certain contact of the soul with the Divinity, and it is God himself who is then felt and tasted . . . This touch of knowledge and of sweetness is so deep and profound that it penetrates into the inmost substance of the soul . . . The soul prays to see the Face of God, which is the essential communication of his divinity to the soul, without any intervening medium, by a certain knowledge thereof in the Divinity. This is something beyond sense and divested of accidents, inasmuch as it is the contact of pure substances, that is of the soul and of the Divinity . . .'

Although much of John's teaching is concerned with the process of purification, and he insists on the need for self-denial, the 'self' here is not the true personality, but represents all those tendencies and limitations in our nature which impede our true self-development. In the end, our happiness is seen to lie in the perfection of love, which transforms, as only love can, through union with the beloved. 'At the end of life it is on love that we shall be judged.'

THOMAS CORBISHLEY

FURTHER READING: K. Kavanaugh, trans., *The Collected Works of St. John of the Cross* (ICS Publications, 1979); R.P. Hardy, *The Search for Nothing* (Crossroad, 1982).

Giraudon/Bibliothèque de Moulin

The book of Jonah is important not only because of its descriptions of the adventures of Jonah, but because it carries a warning from God against Jewish religious exclusiveness

JONAH

IN POPULAR THOUGHT Jonah is inevitably linked with the 'whale' that swallowed and regurgitated him. It is unfortunate that attention is concentrated so excessively on this intriguing incident, for it means that the real significance of Jonah's story is missed.

According to a brief reference in 2 Kings 14.25, Jonah, the son of Amittai, was a native of Gath-hepher and renowned as a prophet; he seems to have lived in the 8th century BC. The book of Jonah, which records his adventures, was written much later and probably dates between 400 and 200 BC. Its author is unknown.

The book of Jonah can be classified

For Christians, the story of Jonah has come to be linked with the Resurrection, for Christ likened Jonah's experience in the belly of the whale to his own three days 'in the heart of the earth' *Left* **Illustration from the 12th century** *Bible de Souvigny* **showing Jonah being cast from the boat into the jaws of the whale, to abate the storm** *Right* **Jonah disappears into the body of the whale; detail from a mural by Giotto in the Scrovegni Chapel, Padua**

as a *midrash*, a Jewish moral tale, destined to correct the Jewish disposition to believe that God was concerned only with the Jews, and not with the Gentiles also. Jonah typifies Jewish exclusiveness, and his story is intended to show how God sought to persuade him to take a wider view of human needs and divine providence.

The story opens with Yahweh (see YAHWEH) commanding Jonah: 'Arise, go to Nineveh, that great city, and cry against it; for their wickedness has come up before me.' Jonah tries to avoid the mission, but not from fear as it later transpires. He takes a ship from Joppa to Tarshish, which was probably a Phoenician port in the western Mediterranean; its remoteness from Palestine indicates Jonah's desire to get as far

away as possible from the God of Israel. But Yahweh was not to be thus circumvented. He sends a storm that almost wrecks the ship. And the sailors said: 'Come, let us cast lots, that we may know on whose account this evil has come upon us.' The lot falls on Jonah. Realizing he is the cause of impending disaster, Jonah tells the Phoenician crew: 'Take me up and throw me into the sea; then the sea will quiet down for you; . . . it is because of me that this great tempest has come upon you.' When they do so, Yahweh 'appointed a great fish to swallow up Jonah; and Jonah was in the belly of the fish three days and three nights'. It should be noted, incidentally, that the Hebrew *dagh gadhol* means 'great fish', not necessarily a whale; it is in the

reference to the story in the gospel of Matthew (12.40) that the English translation presents the monster as a 'whale'.

At Yahweh's instruction, the great fish 'vomited out Jonah upon the dry land'. Having learned his lesson, Jonah proceeds to Nineveh and proclaims Yahweh's message. What Jonah had originally feared then happens. The Ninevites repent and Yahweh forgives them. To Jonah this was intolerable, for the Ninevites were the pre-eminent enemies of his people. In his anger, he reproves Yahweh for not punishing the hateful nation. He has to be taught a further lesson. It is very hot, and Yahweh causes a gourd to grow up miraculously and shade Jonah. But as Jonah is rejoicing in the shade, Yahweh destroys the gourd, and as Jonah faints

Scala

Jonah

After three days and three nights in the belly of the whale, Jonah is thrown up onto dry land: 19th century German print

Ted Binet

under the hot wind, the divine lesson is finally driven home. Jonah is reproved by Yahweh for lamenting the destruction of the gourd, while desiring that Nineveh and its inhabitants should all perish.

The historical significance of the book of Jonah thus lies in its being a Jewish protest against the racial exclusivism of the Jews. But in Christianity it acquired another significance: 'the sign of Jonah' became a prototype of the Resurrection of Jesus. Jesus is recorded to have said: 'For as Jonah was three days and three nights in the belly of the whale, so will the Son of man be three days and three nights in the heart of the earth (Matthew 12.40). The symbolism caught the imagination of the early Christians, and depictions of Jonah being cast to the sea monster (shown as a kind of dragon) and resting under the shade of the gourd often appear in the iconography of the catacombs and the sculptured sarcophagi of the 4th and 5th centuries. The use of 'Jonah' as a synonym for one who brings or attracts misfortune derives from the predicament in which the Phoenician sailors found themselves.

FURTHER READING: L.H. Brockington in *Peake's Commentary on the Bible* (Nelson, 2nd ed., 1962); M. DeHaan, *Jonah, Fact or Fiction* (Zondervan, 1957); P. Fairbairn, *Jonah* (Baker, 1980); B. Vawter, *Job and Jonah:* (Paulist Press, 1983).

Joseph of Arimathea

In the Bible the rich Jew who took Christ's body from the cross for burial; in the Middle Ages he became the subject of many legends concerning the Holy Grail which he caused to be made and in which he caught the blood of the crucified Christ: according to one account he brought the precious relic to Glastonbury in Britain, the site in the ancient Isle of Avalon, where, in obedience to a vision, he built a chapel.

See GLASTONBURY; GRAIL.

Biblioteca Nazionale Centrale, Florence

Joss-stick

A fragrant tinder mixed with clay; burnt as an offering in Chinese rituals because the aromatic smell is thought to be pleasing to the gods and possibly odious to evil spirits: the word joss, meaning a Chinese idol, was coined by 16th century Portuguese sailors in the East Indies, and derives from the Latin *deus* meaning god.

See PERFUME.

Camera Press, London

Journey

Symbol of man's attempt to gain salvation, spiritual perfection, paradise; examples include Christian's journey in *Pilgrim's Progress*, and the quest of the Grail; a method of attaining holiness or wisdom is often called a path, road or way; in the religion of Isis human life was a voyage across the sea of the sinful world; similarly a pilgrimage is an expedition to a holy place for spiritual merit.

See PATHS; PILGRIMAGE.

JUDAISM

It is as inconceivable to have Judaism without the Jewish people, as it is to have Christianity without Jesus

The progenitor of all subsequent monotheistic religions, Judaism is based on the belief that there is only one God. Unlike other faiths, Judaism is centred not on a prophet or saviour but on the idea of a chosen people

A SIGNFICANT FACTOR in the understanding of Judaism is that it centres around a people, rather than an individual. Important though Moses or Abraham or Isaiah are for Judaism it is quite possible to imagine the Jewish faith without any of these. But it is as inconceivable to have Judaism without the Jewish people as it is to have Christianity without Jesus, Buddhism without the Buddha or Islam without Mohammed.

In 1992, it was estimated that there were about 18 million Jews throughout the world,

of whom some 7 million were in the United States, about 3,500,000 in Israel, and the remainder distributed over the rest of the world. Some of these have no religious belief whatsoever, but the majority do subscribe to the faith known as Judaism, though with many differing emphases in matters of both belief and observance.

One large division (an ethnic rather than a doctrinal one) is between Oriental Jews, together with those whose ancestors came from Spain and Portugal, and Jews from other parts of Europe. The former are known as Sefardim (from the Hebrew name for Spain, Sefarad) or Sephardim, and the latter as Ashkenazim (from the Hebrew name for Germany, Ashkenaz, from which many came). The differences between these

Previous page The idea of the Jews as the chosen people has been partly responsible for the persecution and hostility they have encountered: *Mohammed ordering the execution of Jews*, from a 16th century Turkish manuscript *Above* In accordance with Levitical law, every Jewish male must be circumcised on the eighth day after his birth. Originally a rite of initiation, it is now practised mainly for health reasons: *Circumcision of the Children of Israel*, by the 18th century Venetian painter G. B. Tiepolo. *Above right* Satirical drawing of the Jews of Norwich which appeared in the Jews' Roll, a list of tax payments in Henry III's reign. Antisemitic feeling ran high in medieval Europe, and in England Jews were afforded protection only on payment of exorbitant taxes

Mary Evans Picture Library

two groupings are in minor liturgical rites, customs and popular foods.

Another division is between Zionists, who see the main future for Jews in the State of Israel and who tend to look upon the Jews as a nation, like the English or the French, and the non-Zionists, who see Judaism purely as a religion, and in non-nationalistic terms. This does not rule out the existence of many religious Zionists and there are even a few anti-Zionists. Still another significant division is between Orthodoxy and Reform; the main difference between these two groups concerns the nature of revelation and the permanent binding character of the ceremonial law.

The Crown of the Torah

The Jewish place of worship is the synagogue, from a Greek word meaning simply 'place of assembly'. Some Reform synagogues are called 'temples', chiefly because Reform Jews, unlike the Orthodox, do not believe that the Temple in Jerusalem will be rebuilt in the days of the Messiah and animal sacrifices again offered there, so that the synagogue has now taken the place of the ancient Temple. In the modern synagogue the rabbi and the cantor – the reader of the prayers to music – officiate at the services, but there is nothing in Jewish teaching to prevent any Jew from officiating at any service, including the marriage service. The rabbi is not a priest. The word rabbi means 'teacher' or 'master' and his chief function is to be an expounder of the Jewish religion. There is, in fact, no priesthood nowadays in Judaism except for vestigial remains of a very peripheral order. Jews claiming descent from the Temple priesthood, who frequently have the name Cohen (from the old Hebrew name for priest) recite the priestly blessing 'May the Lord bless you and keep you' in Orthodox synagogues on the great occasions of the year, but otherwise very little is left in present-day Judaism of the hereditary priesthood.

In fact, until the 14th century there were no professional rabbis, Jewish teachers earning their living by practising such crafts as that of physician, while teaching Judaism without fees in their spare time. The rabbis of an earlier period were drawn from every walk of life. Some of them were businessmen, others smiths or cobblers. The sole qualification was proficiency in the

Torah. This word, meaning 'teaching', refers in the first instance to the Pentateuch, the Five Books of Moses, but then, by extension, to the whole range of Jewish teaching.

There is to be observed in Jewish history a definite substitution of an aristocracy of learning for the older aristocracy of the priesthood. This received its most dramatic expression in two sayings dating from as early as the 2nd century: that only the son of a king can be a prince and only the son of a priest can be a priest, but the crown of the Torah lies in a corner and anyone capable of so doing can don it; and that a bastard learned in the Torah takes precedence over an ignorant High Priest. Love of learning and respect for things of the mind has been a distinguishing feature of Judaism, so that a non-believing Jew like Freud could still feel himself strongly attached to Judaism for this reason.

The Thirteen Principles

The most obvious way of describing a religion is to state the beliefs it expects from its adherents. There are, however, notorious difficulties when one tries to describe Judaism in this way. There has never been in Judaism any proper machinery for the formulation of dogmas, no synod or body of representative Jewish teachers to decide authoritatively and categorically what it is that a Jew must believe in order to be a Jew. This has resulted in a very wide range of diverse views among Jewish theologians.

It would be wrong to conclude, as many 19th century scholars were in the habit of doing, that Judaism has no dogmas, that a Jew can believe what he likes and still remain an adherent of Judaism. This is clearly an absurd position to adopt: as Solomon Schechter (d.1915) pointed out, it would make the central idea of Judaism the dogma of having no dogma. What does emerge from a study of the classical sources of Judaism – the Bible, the Talmudic literature produced in Palestine and Babylon during the first five centuries AD, and the medieval Jewish writings – is a kind of consensus of opinion among believers as to the distinguishing features of Jewish belief but with much room for individual interpretation and the possibilities of strong but legitimate differences in some matters.

With these reservations, the 13 principles of the Jewish faith can be examined as for-

mulated by the greatest Jew of the Middle Ages, Moses Maimonides (1135-1204). These are the nearest thing to a Jewish catechism. They have been printed in many prayer books and are recited daily by the pious. But many modern Jews do not accept them without considerable qualifications and there are other beliefs, such as that of the divine election of Israel, for example, which are not included among the 13 but which many Jews would consider to be basic. Maimonides's principles are: belief in the existence of God; in his unity; his incorporeality; his eternity; that God alone is to be worshipped; belief in the prophets; that Moses is the greatest of the prophets; that the Torah is from heaven, that it is unchanging; belief that God knows the deeds of men; that he rewards the good and punishes the wicked; belief in the coming of the Messiah; and in the resurrection of the dead.

The first five principles have to do with the nature of God. Maimonides's choice of principles was chiefly in response to the particular challenges of his day and the second, third and fifth principles are fairly obviously directed against Christianity. In the Middle Ages and later there were to be found Jewish teachers of note who were prepared to acknowledge that the Christian doctrine is not tritheism and that Christianity is not 'idolatry'. But Jews have been unanimous in declaring the doctrine of the Trinity, and especially the doctrine of the Incarnation, in which Jesus of Nazareth is the Second Person in the Trinity, to be a breach of pure monotheism and therefore incompatible with Jewish belief. The Jewish declaration of faith is the *Shema*, 'Hear, O Israel; the Lord our God, the Lord is One' (Deuteronomy 6.4). The Jewish child is taught to recite the verse as soon as he can speak. The devout Jew recites it daily in the morning and at night. The dying repeat it as life's last affirmation.

Beyond Time and Space

There has been a wide spectrum of belief regarding the nature of God, from the negative theologians who wax eloquent in declaring how little one can say of God as he is in himself (some of these observe that one cannot, strictly speaking, say that God exists, since 'existence' is a term too heavily laden with human associations) to the Jew of simple faith who is not bothered at all by the problem of anthropomorphism. Even the belief that God can, if he so chooses, assume a bodily form (as in the legend, when he appeared on the altar in the Temple to consume the sacrifices in the form of a lion of fire) is not, according to some theologians, sufficient to cause those who hold it to be excluded from Judaism. Maimonides does, indeed, declare such persons to be heretics and his third principle states this emphatically but some of Maimonides's critics, while themselves rejecting any belief in God's corporeality, feel that the anthropomorphisms in Scripture encourage this belief so that, although the sophisticated understood these in a nonliteral sense, the more naive believers cannot be condemned for holding opinions which, for them, have the full sanction of holywrit.

God is beyond time and space (the fourth principle) and the universe is subordinate to him. He is both transcendent and immanent. He is apart from the world and yet involved in it. Judaism rejects both deism, which denies God's immanence in the universe, and pantheism, which denies his transcendence and identifies God with the universe.

Prayer and worship are to be offered to God alone (the fifth principle). Even prayer to God through an intermediary is forbidden. In the hasidic movement (see HASIDISM), which arose in the 18th century, one does, however, find the idea of prayer through an intermediary, the hasidic saint or master. This was one of the reasons why the movement in its early stages met such vehement opposition from the rabbis. But the prayers are never offered to the holy man. It is rather that he prays on behalf of others who present their petitions to him; the hasidic movement believed that the prayers of the holy teacher can accomplish that which sinful men are incapable of achieving by themselves.

The sixth to the ninth principles (belief in the prophets of whom Moses is the greatest, and in the heavenly origin and unchanging character of the Torah) are concerned with revelation. The seventh and ninth principles have been particularly stressed by Maimonides as a response to Christian and Islamic claims that a greater prophet than Moses had arisen and that Judaism, though once valid, had been superseded. Until modern times, with very few exceptions, Jewish teachers held that the books of the Hebrew Bible (the 'Old Testament') were divinely revealed to man. The Torah was seen as twofold: firstly the written Torah, or the Pentateuch and the other books of the Bible, and secondly, the oral Torah or the teachings held to have been conveyed by God to Moses by word of mouth, together with those elaborations now found in the rabbinic works produced during the first five centuries AD, the most important of which is the Talmud. There are two Talmuds; the Palestinian edited around the year 400, and the more authoritative Babylonian edited around the year 500.

Orthodoxy and Reform

Orthodoxy holds fast to the position that the present text of the Pentateuch is the word of God, infallible, sublime, created before the world came into being. Both the written and the oral Torah are from God in a direct sense with the corollary that the precepts of the Torah in their rabbinic interpretation are eternally binding upon Jews and immutable. In the Orthodox view all biblical criticism, whether 'higher' or 'lower' (that is, literary criticism and textual criticism) is heresy because it expresses doubts as to the present text and because it sees the Pentateuch itself as a composite work produced at different intervals and with contradictions between the Codes of Law in it.

Reform Judaism, on the other hand, accepts the new picture of the Pentateuch and the rest of the Bible which has emerged, as the result of modern historical investigation and criticism. Reform holds to the view that a radical re-interpretation of what revelation means is now called for and abandons the idea of an immutable law.

A compromise position between Orthodoxy and Reform is represented chiefly in the United States by Conservative Judaism, to which the precepts are binding not because they were given by God, in the direct sense in which Orthodoxy understands it, but because God is seen, as it were, as being in the process as a whole. The real source of authority is the tradition of the Jewish community of believers, just as the Church in Catholicism is for Roman Catholic Christians.

To illustrate the differences, an example can be given from the dietary laws, such as abstinence from eating pork and shell-fish. Orthodoxy insists on the observance of the laws as God-given ordinances. Reform leaves such observances to the individual conscience but holds in any event that it is the moral, rather than the ceremonial, law which is permanently binding. Conservative Judaism believes that the binding character of these laws derives not so much from any kind of direct divine communication but because the laws have evolved through the historical experience of the Jewish people. They are therefore part of the divine-human encounter in human history and can serve in the present, as they have done in the past, in furthering the ideal of holiness in daily living. With regard to the ethical law there is unanimity among all sections of Jewry that this has binding force for all time.

The tenth and eleventh principles (that God knows the deeds of men and rewards or punishes them accordingly) are accepted in outline by all religious Jews, although there is considerable difference of opinion as to the exact nature of divine Providence and as to how reward and punishment are to be understood. Does the doctrine mean that God rewards directly in life those who keep his laws and punishes those who do not, or that virtue brings its own reward and vice its own punishment? Does it mean that there is reward and punishment in the afterlife and if it does, what is the nature of heaven and hell? Is there a hell at all and, if there is, is it a place or a state of remoteness from God? Is punishment in hell eternal or only for a period? On these questions there are still differing answers among Jews.

The Beginning of Redemption

The twelfth principle refers to the belief frequently mentioned in the Bible that the day will come when this world will perfected, when war and hatred will be banished from the earth, when the Kingdom of God will be established and all men will recognize him as their Maker. The Orthodox belief is in a personal Messiah (a word meaning 'the anointed one', in reference to the practice of anointing kings with oil), a human being of great renown but in no way divine, who will be a descendant of King David and who will be sent by God for this purpose.

Non-Orthodox opinion since the last century has tended to place all the stress on a dawning of the messianic age and to

The annual feast of the Passover celebrates the Exodus from Egypt when God rescued the enslaved Jews from Egyptian bondage. Today on Passover Eve, Jews eat bitter herbs, to remind them of slavery, and drink wine, in celebration of their freedom: 13th century Haggadah illustrations of the plagues of Egypt

Palphot

Keystone

'A bastard learned in the Torah takes precedence over an ignorant High Priest'. Torah means 'teaching' and refers in the first instance to the Five Books of Moses (the first five books of the Bible) but by extension to the whole range of Jewish teaching *Above* At a children's village in Israel the class learns to read from the Torah *Left* In the synagogue part of the Torah is read each week

reject the doctrine of a personal Messiah as savouring too much of the magical. The basic idea is that God will eventually intervene in human affairs so as to bring about the perfect society envisaged.

In the 19th century many Jews tended to interpret the doctrine in purely naturalistic terms, that better education and social reforms in the Western world would themselves bring about the millennium. The horrors of the 20th century have made such a belief in automatic human progress towards the desired goal look improbable, even ludicrous, although this theory is by no means dead. It has been related by many to the events which led up to the establishment of the State of Israel. The facts of the holocaust in Europe, in which 6 million Jews died, and the setting up of the State of Israel have both encouraged religious Jews to see the new state as having messianic dimensions. A number of religious Jews today tend to look upon Israel as 'the beginning of redemption', believing that the first steps have been taken towards the realization of the age-old messianic vision. At the same time, they believe that the world still

Judaism does not believe that salvation is only possible for Jews but that the righteous of all people have a share in the world to come

needs redemption and that the full realization of the perfect society under God for all mankind, is still awaited. It will only be achieved when God himself intervenes. It should be noted that messianic beliefs concern events here on earth. Whatever the Jewish views on the afterlife, Judaism believes that God will not permanently abandon this world to chaos, and that one day humanity here on earth will achieve complete redemption.

Immortality of the Soul
The last principle, relating to the resurrection of the dead, has also been variously interpreted. Originally, the doctrine of the reurrection referred to the dead rising from their graves and living again here on earth. It was closely connected with messianic hopes. After the advent of the Messiah, the resurrection would take place on earth. As its name implies, the doctrine means that death really is death and resurrection a new birth of the body. In the course of time, however, the doctrine of the immortality of the soul entered Judaism. There may be traces here and there in the Bible of the doctrine that the soul lives on after death but these are few and vague. When the two doctrines – of the resurrection and the immortality of the soul – were fused, as eventually happened, the official view became that when a person dies his soul lives on in another realm until the resurrection, when it is reunited with the body on earth.

Reform Judaism, and for that matter even some Orthodox interpreters, prefer to think, as Maimonides seems to have done, of the doctrine of the immortality of the soul as the really significant part of this principle. Many modern Jewish thinkers accept this with the proviso that it does not refer to the mere survival of a nebulous 'soul' but to the continuing existence of the total human personality which, it is claimed, is really what is implied in the doctrine of the resurrection. It must also be appreciated that Judaism is not a religion of salvation, in other words, Judaism sees this life as good in itself, and not only as a means of acquiring eternal life. Life would be worth living even if this world were all humans can hope to have. The paradox inherent in Judaism, as a religion that is both this-worldly and other-worldly, was finely expressed by the 2nd century teacher who

said: 'Better one hour of good deeds and repentance in this world than the whole life of the world to come; but better one hour of spiritual bliss in the world to come than all the life of this world.'

Judaism is a people-centred religion but it is not an exclusive religion. Converts are accepted, although they are required to show evidence of sincerity. Moreover, Judaism does not believe that salvation is only possible for Jews but that the righteous of all peoples have a share in the world to come. The idea that the religion depends on the people of Israel is frequently expressed, in the Biblical phrase, by saying that God has chosen Israel. This notion presents difficulties of its own and is liable to misinterpretation. There is nothing racialist about the doctrine that Israel has been chosen to serve God and all humanity. The convert to Judaism, of whatever colour of skin and of whatever background, becomes a full member of the Jewish community.

Tensions inevitably exist between the universalism taught by Judaism – God as the Father of all mankind – and the particularism inseparable from the idea of divine election. But the majority of religious Jews prefer to live with the tensions, trying to further the richness of the idea of Israel as God's covenant people without losing sight of the fact that, as Judaism itself repeatedly stresses, God loves all men.

That this is no idle dream can be seen from the contribution Judaism has made in the past to civilization. Judaism's daughter religions, Christianity and Islam, have received many of their most significant beliefs and institutions from Judaism: the doctrine of the one God, the patterns of worship in church and mosque, the reading of the Scriptures, the teachings of the prophets. The stories of the book of Genesis, for instance, with their strong moral sense have been a powerful aid in the moral education of children of Jewish and other faiths. Movements for social reform and freedom have found inspiration in the Old Testament passion for justice and the narrative of the deliverance from Egyptian bondage. Words like *Hallelujah* and *Amen* have become part of the vocabulary of worship for millions. The rhythm and concreteness of Hebrew prose and its powerful idioms have influenced, through biblical translation, all European languages.

Festivals and Rites
Jewish practices are of two kinds, the ceremonial and the ethical. On the ceremonial side, there are colourful rituals both in the home and the synagogue. The sabbath and festivals are celebrated with joy. These always begin at nightfall and end at nightfall. On the eve of the sabbath, two candles are lit as a symbol of peace in the home and of increased spiritual light. The master of the house recites a benediction over a cup of wine in which he praises God for creating the world and giving his people sabbath rest. Tuneful table hymns are sung during the meal, the whole family joining in. The sabbath is a day of rest and of spiritual refreshment.

Orthodoxy adheres strictly to the laws prohibiting all kinds of creative activity on the sabbath in acknowledgement of God as Creator and giver of life's blessings. Some Orthodox Jews refrain even from turning on electric lights on the sabbath. Orthodox Jews do not ride on the sabbath, do not write, engage in business, smoke or carry anything in the street. Reform Judaism has relaxed many of these laws but has not lost sight of the ideal of the sabbath as a day devoted to spiritual pursuits.

During the sabbath service in the synagogue, a scroll of the Pentateuch is taken from its place in the Ark at the eastern end of the synagogue and carried in procession around the building while the congregation stands. The scroll must be written by hand and there are detailed rules which the scribe must observe while carrying out his sacred task. It is adorned with silver ornaments, especially bells which tinkle while it is being paraded. A portion is read from it each week; this portion is divided up and members of the congregation are given in turn the honour of reading from the scroll (or, since many cannot read the Hebrew nowadays, of having it read for them).

In this way the whole of the Pentateuch is read each year. The reading of the complete scroll is concluded in the autumn of the year. On this occasion no sooner is the reading complete than it begins again. The persons given the great honour of reading the last portion and the first of the new cycle are called respectively: 'Bridegroom of the Torah' and 'Bridegroom of Genesis'. These two invite the rest of the congregation to festivities to mark the event.

When asked if a Jew might hunt animals for sport, an 18th century rabbi replied that he could not imagine a Jew wishing to do so

The Jewish calendar is rich in festivals. The three pilgrim festivals (so called because in Temple times people would go up to Jerusalem, then in joyous pilgrimage to the Temple) are the Passover in the spring, Pentecost seven weeks later, and Tabernacles in the autumn. Passover is in celebration of the Exodus from Egypt, when God led the enslaved people out of Egyptian bondage; in their haste to depart, they had no time to bake their bread properly, so that they were obliged to eat unleavened bread. On Passover eve, in a delightful home ceremony, the family partake of unleavened cakes and they eat bitter herbs as a reminder of the bitterness of slavery, and they drink wine, in joy at their new-found freedom. At this meal the *Haggadah* (literally 'the telling') is recited. This is a dramatic presentation of the Exodus, culled from biblical and other sources, in the course of which the youngest child present asks four questions regarding the unusual ceremonies he sees around him; his father and the rest of the company reply. Pious Jews refrain from eating any leavened bread during the whole eight days' duration of the festival.

Pentecost is a celebration of the giving of the Torah, that is, of the revelation on Mt Sinai, as told in the book of Exodus. During the synagogue service of the day the portion from Exodus, describing this tremendous event and containing the Ten Commandments, is read from the scroll. Tabernacles celebrates the dwelling of the Israelites in 'booths' in the wilderness after they had gone out of Egypt. Many Jews build a booth in their gardens, the roof of which is open to the sky, in which they eat all their meals for the seven days of the festival. On this festival a palm branch and other plants are taken in the hand during the recitation of Psalms in the synagogue in thanksgiving for God's bounty.

Historically considered, the three pilgrim festivals were originally agricultural feasts pure and simple, but the genius of Judaism transformed them into festivals celebrating historical events. Some Jewish thinkers today see this as part of a long process in which religion was gradually freed from subservience to particular places. Unlike many pagan gods, the true God is not bound to single spots on the earth's surface and he manifests himself through human history.

The Day of Atonement

The New Year festival in the autumn is a solemn occasion, the major portion of the day being spent in prayer. In the home on the eve of the festival an apple is dipped in honey and eaten at the festive meal, while prayers are offered to God to grant a sweet and good year. The central feature of the synagogue service on this day is the blowing of the ram's horn, the oldest musical instrument known to man. Many ideas have been read into this ceremony, the best-known of which is that the piercing sound of the horn affords a shrill warning to man to awake himself to his duties and responsibilities in the year ahead. Another explanation is that trumpets are blown at the coronation of a king and at the beginning of the New Year, so God is hailed as king of the universe.

On the tenth day after the New Year festival there falls the great fast of Yom Kippur, the Day of Atonement. Devout Jews fast for 24 hours, partaking of no food or drink whatsoever and spending the better part of the day in prayer. The Day of Atonement is a day of pardon. Jews confess their sins and throw themselves on the divine mercy. But solemn though the day is, it is in a way a joyous occasion, because on it man is reconciled to his God and to his fellows. The name 'Black Fast', which is sometime given to it by non-Jews, is a misnomer. In fact, the readers of the services and many members of the congregation dress in long white robes, which symbolize purity and divine compassion.

Obligations of the Faithful

Two minor feasts are Purim (literally 'lots'), celebrating the deliverance of Jewry from the machinations of Haman as recounted in the book of Esther, and Hanukkah (literally 'dedication') celebrating the deliverance of the people in the days of Antiochus and the re-dedication of the altar, as told in the books of the Maccabees. On Purim the book of Esther is read amid general jollification. On each of the eight days of Hanukkah candles are kindled in the Menorah (candelabrum), one on the first day, two on the second and so on (see CANDLE). Legend has it that when the soldiers of Antiochus IV profaned the Temple, there was only one small jar of pure oil uncontaminated. This was used for kindling the Temple Menorah and, although there was only sufficient for one night, it burned miraculously for eight days. The miracle of oil became symbolic of the victory of the spirit which is the main theme of the Hanukkah festival.

The most vivid description of what Judaism demands of its adherents is found in the book of Deuteronomy (6.4-9):

Hear O Israel: The Lord our God is One Lord; and you shall love the Lord your God with all your heart, and with all your soul, and with all your might. And these words, which I command you this day, shall be upon your heart; and you shall teach them diligently to your children, and shall talk of them when you sit in your house, and when you walk by the way, and when you lie down, and when you rise. And you shall bind them as a sign upon your hand, and they shall be as frontlets between your eyes. And you shall write them upon the posts of your house, and on your gates.

The passage is repeated in slightly different words in Deuteronomy 11. At an early period in Jewish history the last verses were taken literally, so that to this day the devout Jew has these two inscribed on parchment and fixed in a little case (the *mezuzah*, 'doorpost') at the door of his house, reminding himself of God's law whenever he enters and leaves his house. Similarly, the passages, together with two others inscribed on parchment, are placed into little boxes known as *tefillin*, meaning 'attachments' or 'phylacteries'. They are affixed with leather straps to the left arm, opposite the heart, and to the head and worn during prayer; they symbolize the Jew's dedication of mind, heart and hand to God's service.

Ritual observances, important though they are in the scheme of Judaism, are far from being the main features of the Jewish faith. At the heart of Judaism is an ethical affirmation. This is that man can imitate God by practising justice, righteousness and holiness and by showing compassion. This is how to be God-like. It is for this reason that those biblical passages which voice passionate concern for the downtrodden and which speak in urgent terms of the pursuit of justice, have always been favourite Jewish texts; such as those enjoining concern for the poor and needy, for the hired servant and for the stranger; the spirit of neighbourliness, and just, upright dealings. There are innumerable examples of this demand for sound ethical conduct.

Telaviv Museum/A.P.A.G.P. Paris

The rabbis, the post-biblical teachers, elaborated on these precepts, discussing in great detail, for example, the question of fair prices and fair and unfair competition in business; of the laws against over-charging and having false weights and measures; of the prohibition on misleading others and the need for a community to take adequate care of its poor and needy; of regulations between employers and employees, parents and children. Even animals have their rights and should be treated with kindness. A distinguished 18th century rabbi, when asked if it was permitted for a Jew to hunt animals for sport, replied that he could not imagine a Jew wishing to do any such thing.

Jewish ethical teaching is not confined to laws and deeds alone. There has grown over the centuries a vast moralistic literature produced by Jewish teachers and studied by Jews regularly, inculcating the formation of good character traits and the rejection of vicious tendencies. Hatred of one's neighbour, sloth, pride, lust, anger, spite, envy and jealousy, are to be fought against, while compassion, benevolence, the love of learning and of one's fellow-men are to be pursued.

In the words of an 11th century Jewish moralist, Judaism knows of 'duties of the limbs' but even more important are the 'duties of the heart'. In a passage of the Talmud it says that there are three distinguishing marks of the Jewish people: they are compassionate, they are bashful, and they are benevolent. It is the heart of man

Jew with the Torah, a painting by Chagall; the persons having the honour of reading the last and first portions of the Pentateuch each year are called respectively 'Bridegroom of the Torah' and 'Bridegroom of Genesis'

that God wants.

The conflict in man's soul between his higher and lower nature is described by the Talmudic rabbis as a conflict between the 'evil inclination' and the 'good inclination'. By the evil inclination they mean man's ambitions and his bodily instincts. These, though called 'evil' because they can lead to such, are essential to life and provide it with its driving power.

With some exceptions, Judaism is not an ascetic faith but it maintains strongly the need for self-control. Its ideal is neither life's denial nor its exploitation but its sanc-tification. In a rabbinic homily the Torah, the law of God, is compared to a plaster on a wound. While the healing plaster is on the wound, the wounded man can eat and drink safely and freely and the wound will not fester.

As Judaism sees it, humans should not try to live as hermits or recluses. They should live in society and be of constant help to their fellows; they should marry and have children, they should enjoy life as a precious gift from God, but they should always be aware of the call to higher things and see themselves, in the marvellous imagery of Jacob's dream in Genesis, as a ladder with its feet firmly planted on earth but with its head reaching to the heavens.

Across the World

Over the centuries Jews have spread across virtually the whole surface of the globe, but immigration to Israel since 1948 has reduced the numbers in some countries to almost nothing. By the end of the 1980s only handfuls of Jews could still be found in Pakistan, Malaysia, Burma, Indonesia and Nicaragua, for example, and there was doubt as to whether any Jews remained in Communist China. Judaism has had a long history in China, where the first synagogue was built in 1163 in Kaifeng, for Jews who had come from Persia and India along the Silk Road. By the 1940s there were 30,000 Jews in China, concentrated mainly in Shanghai, but most of them left the country after the Communist takeover in 1949.

India has a long and interesting Jewish history. The Bene Israel, the largest group of Indian Jews, claim descent from a shipload of emigrants fleeing from Palestine in the 2nd century AD, whose vessel was wrecked on the Indian coast south of Bombay. They settled down in the country and their descendants gradually mingled their own customs with those of their Indian neighbours. Under the British there were also flourishing colonies of Jews of Middle Eastern origin in Bombay and Calcutta. The Cochin Jews of the Malabar coast traced their ancestry to immigrants who arrived before the 10th century, but most of them have now moved to Israel.

A particularly fascinating group are the Falasha, the so-called black Jews of Ethiopia. According to legend, they are

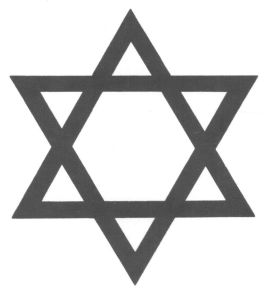

descended from the Jewish retinue of Menilik, the son of King Solomon and the Queen of Sheba (see ETHIOPIA). The Falasha are really African by race, but Jewish by religion; their Judaism is of an extremely antique kind. Contact between them and the rest of the Jewish world was broken for centuries and was not restored until 1867.

The Falasha experienced growing hostility from the Ethiopian government in the years following the Second World War; after 1974 they were so fiercely persecuted by the new Communist regime that many of them fled to misery and starvation in refugee camps in the Sudan. In 1984-85 a secret rescue programme named Operation Moses airlifted some 7000 of them to safety in Israel and others were rescued later in the

The Star of David (in Hebrew 'Shield of David', *Magen David*) as a symbol of Jewry was adopted as the emblem of the Zionist organization in 1897 and is now part of the flag of the State of Israel

decade. Another group of 'black Jews' are the Lemba in South Africa, who are apparently descended from Falasha who moved south.

This short survey of the Jewish faith can be fittingly concluded with a Talmudic tale about the great teacher Hillel who lived over 2000 years ago. A prospective convert to Judaism came to Hillel and asked the sage to teach him the whole Torah while he stood on one leg. Hillel replied: 'That which is hateful unto thee do not do unto thy neighbour. This is the whole of the Torah. The rest is commentary. Go and learn!'
(See also ANGELS; BAPTISM; DANIEL; DEAD SEA SCROLLS; ELECTION; EZEKIEL; FIRST MAN; GOLEM; JERUSALEM; PROPHECY; YAHWEH; ZEALOTS.)

L. JACOBS*

FURTHER READING: Leo Baeck, *This People Israel: The Meaning of Jewish Existence* (W.H. Allen, 1965) is an explanation of the Reform position. R.Charing, *The Jewish World* (Time-Life, 1983); H.Essrig, *Judaism* (Barron, 1984); E. Kedourie, ed., *The Jewish World* (Abrams, 1979); L.Jacobs, *Principles of the Jewish Faith* (Vallentine Mitchell); S. Schechter, *Studies in Judaism* (Meridian Books, N.Y., 1958).

JUDAS

THE MOST FAMOUS traitor of history, Judas Iscariot has naturally not fared well in subsequent remembrance. In the lowest circle of Dante's hell, the Devil as 'Emperor of all the realms of woe', encased to his chest in ice, chews three arch-sinners in his three monstrous mouths. One mouth gnaws on the head of Judas, and in the other two are mangled the bodies of Brutus and Cassius, the treacherous assassins of Julius Caesar. At one point in the story of St Brendan's voyage (see BRENDAN), the saint sees the unhappy Judas sitting naked on a rock, buffeted by the waves. He explains that he is allowed out of hell to squat forlornly on this rock on Sundays and Christian feast days. There were other stories that when Christ harrowed hell and released the souls of the dead, Judas, Cain and Herod were left behind there.

The meaning of 'Iscariot' is uncertain. It may simply indicate the village from which Judas came (*Ish Kerioth*, 'man of Kerioth'). Or it may be derived from Latin *Sicarius* ('assassin'), which would mean that Judas was one of the fanatical Jewish patriots called Zealots (see JESUS; ZEALOTS). In that case, it may be that Judas's real motive in betraying Jesus was his bitter disappointment at the latter's failure to take political action.

The gospels, however, imply that Judas acted as he did out of sheer greed. Mark

(chapter 14) says that Judas went to the chief priests and agreed to betray Jesus to them for money. At the Last Supper, Jesus predicted that one of the disciples would betray him, and each of them said sorrowfully, 'Is it I?' Jesus said, 'It is one of the twelve. . .' Later, knowing that Jesus was in the garden of Gethsemane, Judas led there a party with swords and clubs, sent by the chief priests, and identified Jesus by kissing him and calling him 'Master'.

The gospel of Matthew (chapter 26) adds that the amount of money involved was 30 pieces of silver. When Jesus predicted the

12th century carving from Old Sarum showing Judas in the mouth of hell

Michael Holford

betrayal, Judas said, 'Is it I, Master?' and Jesus answered, 'You have said so.' Luke (chapter 22) says that Satan entered into Judas to cause his treachery, and makes it clear that the point of the betrayal was to give away Jesus's whereabouts at night so that he could be arrested quietly withoout creating a disturbance among the crowd assembled in Jerusalem for the Passover.

The traitor's kiss took a strong hold on the imagination of later generations, and so did the scene at the Last Supper. In medieval representations of it, Jesus and the rest of the disciples are frequently shown sitting at one side of the table with the traitor alone at the other. On the table there is often a plate containing a fish, and this fish and the seat of Judas have a role in the Grail legends (see GRAIL).

There are two very different accounts of what happened to Judas afterwards. One (Matthew, chapter 27) is that when he saw that Jesus was condemned, Judas repented of what he had done and tried to return the money to the authorities, but they took no notice. So he threw the pieces of silver down in the Temple, 'and he went and hanged himself.' But Acts (chapter 1) says that he used the money to buy a field, 'and falling headlong he burst open in the middle and all his bowels gushed out.'

Later it was generally accepted that Judas had hanged himself on a tree, and various different trees were associated with the deed. One of them, *Cercis siliquastrum*, is called the Judas-tree.